"THE GATES UNBARRED":
A HISTORY OF UNIVERSITY EXTENSION
AT HARVARD, 1910–2009

"The Gates Unbarred"

A History of University Extension at Harvard, 1910–2009

Michael Shinagel

Harvard University Extension School monograph
Printed by Puritan Press, Hollis, New Hampshire, 2009
Distributed by Harvard University Press, Cambridge, Massachusetts

Shinagel, Michael 1934—
The Gates Unbarred: A History of University Extension
at Harvard, 1910-2009 /
by Michael Shinagel—1st ed.
p. cm.
Includes 20 halftones, bibliographical references, and index.
1. Education.   2. History of United States Education.
3. History of Continuing Higher Education.
4. History of Harvard University.   5. Lowell Institute of Boston

ISBN 978-0-674-05135-5

Typeset at Puritan Press, Hollis, New Hampshire

Distributed by Harvard University Press
Cambridge and London

For Marjorie Lee North,

Ever true North on my life's compass.

Con amore.

M.S.

CONTENTS

IMAGE CREDITS

ACKNOWLEDGMENTS

I am grateful to the following colleagues for their assistance, both direct and indirect, in the preparation of this volume: John F. Adams, Patricia Bellanca, George Buckley, Nora Cameron, Linda A. Cross, Raymond F. Comeau, Andrew Engelward, Leonard Evenchik, William Fixsen, L. Dodge Fernald, Delia Gerraughty, Lilith Haynes, Leslie Helmuth, Mary Higgins, Wayne Ishikawa, Catalina Laserna, Mark Lax, Henry H. Leitner, Susan McGee, Peter O'Malley, Owen Peterson, Jeffry Pike, Christopher Queen, Sue Weaver Schopf, Suzanne Spreadbury, and Carol Stuckey.

Two Harvard Extension students, John Matthew Axten and Patrick Schneiter, ably assisted me in archival research at Harvard. Barbara Meloni, public services archivist, and her staff at the Harvard University Archives were especially helpful in making available photographs, correspondence, and newspaper clippings related to the early years of University Extension.

I also acknowledge the support and cooperation of John Lowell and William Lowell of the Lowell Institute. John Lowell granted me access to the Lowell Institute archive at the Boston Athenaeum, particularly the trustee annual reports. Almyra M. LaBerge, legal secretary to William Lowell, also was very helpful.

Finally, I express my special thanks for the patience and professionalism of Linda Newberry in typing the many versions of this manuscript to its final form, and to my erstwhile Harvard English Department colleague, Seamus Heaney, for his memorable "Villanelle for an Anniversary" and his blessing that I include it in this history.

MICHAEL SHINAGEL

Harvard After Dark

At the time I was writing this history in 2008, University Extension at Harvard had been in continuous operation for nearly a century, during which time it had provided collegiate and graduate instruction to an estimated half-million women and men in its academic programs. But since it operated in the evening, it was often overlooked or totally ignored by the chroniclers, official and unofficial, of Harvard University.

For example, when I consulted Samuel Eliot Morison's official history of 1936, *Three Centuries of Harvard*, I found no mention of University Extension or the Commission on Extension Courses in his chapter "The Lowell Administration," even though President Lowell established both entities in his first year, 1909-10. Similarly, in 1948 Lowell's official biographer, Henry A. Yeomans, to whom he left his papers, produced a 550-page opus titled *Abbott Lawrence Lowell* that discussed in detail Lowell's great educational reforms: the undergraduate concentration and distribution system, the tutorial system, the reading period (self-education), the undergraduate House system, and the Society of Fellows, but, surprisingly, there was no mention or discussion of Lowell's major role in the creation of the Commission on Extension Courses in Greater Boston or the establishment of University Extension at Harvard under the deanship of James Hardy Ropes in 1910. Even the lengthy memorial minute written after his death in 1943 by a blue-ribbon committee, consisting of Alfred North Whitehead, Julian L. Coolidge, Henry A. Yeomans, Archibald T. Davison, Harold H. Burbank, and A. Chester Hanford, chairman, for the records of the Faculty of Arts and Sciences neglected to mention his role as the founder of University Extension.[1]

More recent historians of Harvard, such as Richard Norton Smith (*The Harvard Century*, 1986), John T. Bethell (*Harvard Observed*, 1998), and Morton and Phyllis Keller (*Making Harvard Modern*, 2001), all neglect the role of University Extension in the history of Harvard in the twentieth century. Upon reflection, this neglect of University Extension seems neither benign nor malign; it was just that this academic program was nontraditional and it operated at night.

I originally intended to title this centennial history *Harvard After Dark*, both to acknowledge the nocturnal nature of the academic program and to suggest the obscure reputation that had kept it in the dark all these many years. As I spent time researching the Lowell Institute papers in the archives at the Boston Athenaeum and the University Extension archives at Harvard, I became impressed by the historic educational role played by University Extension both at the University and on the national stage. As I hope will become clear in the pages that follow, University Extension has served as a community resource to the city of Boston since its founding in 1910, and in this respect it was very much an extension of the original vision of John Lowell, Jr., when he established through his will the Lowell Institute in 1835.

A. Lawrence Lowell, in his dual role as the trustee of the Lowell Institute and the newly elected president of Harvard, created the Commission on Extension Courses as his first major educational initiative, an historic achievement that regrettably his biographers and the historians of Harvard in the twentieth century have not acknowledged properly. I hope that this oversight will be corrected by this history.

In the early years of University Extension, the number of courses offered and the number of degrees awarded were modest, but the quality of the faculty and the reputation of the academic programs were never compromised from the outset.

With the post-World War II directorship of Reginald H. Phelps, University Extension became a much more proactive academic program of the University, establishing a pioneering role in such major educational innovations as radio and television collegiate instruction, kinescopes developed for the US Navy, both the nuclear submarine and the surface fleet, and outreach to the community during the social unrest of the late 1960s (particularly Cambridge and Roxbury). After many years of stasis, University Extension grew in size with many more courses and many more graduates, while maintaining the outstanding academic quality of the faculty involved.

During the last three decades University Extension School, under my direction, has maintained the momentum of growth of courses and of graduates, notably through the introduction of graduate degrees in both the liberal arts fields and the professional fields, such as biotechnology, museum studies, journalism, environmental management, educational technologies, among others. The development of a first-class distance education program and the introduction of daytime Harvard College courses offered online to Extension students locally, nationally, and internationally have resulted in more educational innovations and more international student enrollments. When University Extension was founded, the students were all local from Greater Boston. Today our students number more than 14,000 women and men annually, and they represent more than 120 countries. The visions of John Lowell, Jr. and of A. Lawrence Lowell have broadened into an international academic program at Harvard recognized as among the best in the United States in quality and reputation.

Although it was tempting to title this centennial history with my original idea of *Harvard After Dark*, after consultation I was persuaded by my senior Harvard Extension School colleagues not to focus on the obscurity associated with this remarkable academic program, but to highlight instead the century of access to Harvard and to evening instruction in Harvard Yard for so many women and men over the years. The current title derives from the celebratory poem "Villanelle for an Anniversary," composed by Seamus Heaney on the occasion of Harvard University's sesquitricentennial in 1986, which aptly and memorably summed up the nocturnal Harvard Yard experience of Harvard Extension School students and faculty for a century:

VILLANELLE FOR AN ANNIVERSARY

A spirit moved. John Harvard walked the yard.
The atom lay unsplit, the west unwon.
The books stood open and the gates unbarred.

The maps dreamt on like moondust. Nothing stirred.
The future was a verb in hibernation.
A spirit moved, John Harvard walked the yard.

Before the classic style, before the clapboard,
All through the small hours of an origin,
The books stood open and the gates unbarred.

Night passage of a migratory bird.
Wingbeat. Gownflap. Like a homing pigeon,
A spirit moved, John Harvard walked the yard.

Was that his soul (look!) sped to its reward
By grace or works? A shooting star? An omen?
The books stood open and the gates unbarred.

Begin again where frost and tests were hard.
Find yourself or founder. Here. Imagine
A spirit moves, John Harvard walks the yard,
The books stand open and the gates unbarred.

"The Gates Unbarred" is the distinctive feature of the open enrollment and ready access to Harvard that has characterized University Extension. The history that follows tells the full story of what it has meant to the University, the Boston community, the nation, and now the world to provide a Harvard education, in part or in whole, to hundreds of thousands of women and men who availed themselves of this access to Harvard Yard in the evening, where "the books stand open and the gates unbarred."[2]

After finally completing the research and the writing of this centennial history of University Extension, I feel a little like Samuel Johnson, who wrote at the conclusion of his "Preface to *A Dictionary of the English Language*" in 1755: "In this work, when it shall be found that much is omitted, let it not be forgotten that much likewise is performed."

"THE GATES UNBARRED":
A HISTORY OF UNIVERSITY EXTENSION
AT HARVARD, 1910–2009

JOHN LOWELL, JR. (1799–1836)

The founder of the Lowell Institute.
Portrait by Charles Gabriel Gleyre, painted in Egypt
at the time of the execution of the will endowing the Institute.

CHAPTER I

Genesis

The Benefactor, John Lowell, Jr.

In the beginning there was John Lowell, Jr. The eldest son of Francis Cabot Lowell and Hannah Jackson, John Lowell was throughout his short life always known as John Jr. He wrote: "I was born in Boston the 11th of May, 1799, at an immature birth, my mother having brought me into the world three months before the completion of the usual time, the consequence of which was a feeble constitution in my earliest years."[1]

His poor health inclined him toward a melancholic temperament, and his years as an undergraduate at Harvard were so unhappy that after two years he left in 1815 to follow the sea as his calling. In the next two years he sailed to India twice to fulfill a childhood fascination with books of travel and seafaring. He was an avid reader and book collector all his life. By the time he was twenty his health had improved, and he used his father's inheritance to become a merchant, eventually amassing a fortune in the textile industry as a manufacturer of cotton cloth. At the age of twenty-five he fell in love with Georgina M. Amory, his cousin by marriage, and they married on April 6, 1825. The ensuing five years were a happy time for Lowell as his wife presented him with two daughters and his business prospered. But his happiness was short-lived because in November 1830 his wife died of scarlet fever, and within two years his two daughters, aged five and two years, also succumbed to the disease.

To recover from his loss, Lowell sold his properties and transferred his business enterprises to his cousin John Amory Lowell prior to sailing from New York in 1833 for an extended trip around the world. During his trip he kept a journal and also maintained a correspondence with his cousin. In Rome he hired a Swiss artist, Charles Gabriel Gleyre, age twenty-eight, to accompany him on his travels for the sum of $500 a year plus expenses, and to record by his sketches and watercolors the exotic people and places they saw. Some 200 drawings and canvases from the Lowell world tour are still in the possession of the family, including a striking portrait of John Lowell, Jr. resplendent in Arab costume. In 1840 Gleyre settled in Paris and eventually had Renoir and Monet among his pupils.

In the early decades of the nineteenth century Boston was a center of the Lyceum movement, a precursor of what we now know as adult education. John Lowell, Jr. was a founding member of the Boston Society for the Diffusion of Useful Knowledge in 1830 with Daniel Webster serving as its first president. When Lowell set off on his world tour in 1833, he drafted a will stipulating that in the event of his death, one half of his estate be awarded to the Boston Society to promote their lectures for the general public.

On April 1, 1835, debilitated by a lingering fever and disease, John Lowell, Jr., with a sense of his mortality, sat on the ruins of a palace on the banks of the Nile River in Luxor, Egypt, in the magnificent valley of the pharaohs, to write at length to his cousin, John Amory Lowell, his revised will for what would become the endowment for the Lowell Institute of Boston.

He stipulated in his detailed will that half of his wealth be put in trust so that the income be used for "the maintenance and support of Public Lectures to be delivered in said Boston upon philosophy, natural history, and the arts and sciences . . . for the promotion of the moral and intellectual and physical instruction or education of the citizens of the said city of Boston. . . . It is also provided that the said trustee or trustees shall appoint the persons by whom and the subjects on which the said lectures shall be delivered."

Lowell then proceeded to give "directions on the subject of said lectures" by specifying the moral and religious subjects he thought most appropriate, such as "lectures to be given on natural religion showing its conformity to that of our Savior"; "lectures to be delivered on the historical and internal evidences in favor of Christianity"; and avoiding "all disputed points of faith and ceremony" by directing the lecturers "to the moral doctrines of the Gospel."

Lowell next turned to lectures aimed at enhancing "the intelligence and information" of his native New Englanders by authorizing "courses of

Lectures to be established on physics and chemistry with their application to the arts, also on botany, zoology, geology and mineralogy, connected with their particular utility to man." And if additional funds should be available, "the trustee may appoint courses of lectures to be delivered on the literature and eloquence of our language and even on those of foreign nations if he sees fit." He also granted the trustee discretionary powers "from time to time [to] establish lectures on any subject that in his opinion the wants and taste of the age may demand, and he may abolish those already established replacing them by others that he thinks more useful."

"On the appointment and duties of lectures," Lowell proposed that "a lecturer may be taken on trial, but no one shall be appointed for a longer term than four years." Each lecturer would "deliver two courses of lectures on the subject for which he is appointed; one popular to be delivered three times a week, at an hour convenient to the public between the beginning of November and that of May; the other more abstruse, erudite and particular, to be delivered more frequently and at such times as may suit the convenience of those whose wish it is thoroughly to understand and examine the subject of the lecturer." Prior to being assigned as a lecturer, the professor is to receive from the trustee "an instrument in writing stating his compensation and the duties required of him." The trustee also had the authority to suggest that the lecturer "receive from each scholar [or student], who can afford it not exceeding the value of two bushels of wheat for the course of six months, but for the abstruse course only and not for the popular." Clearly, Lowell in drafting his final will was influenced by his membership in the Boston Society for the Diffusion of Useful Knowledge five years earlier, and he wanted the public lecture courses to be free for those of meager means and of minimal expense ("the value of two bushels of wheat") to those who could afford it for the "abstruse" or "erudite" longer courses.

Finally, "on the appointment and duties of the trustee," he was concerned that there be an established line of succession, so that "each trustee shall appoint his own successor within a week after his accession to his office," and "in selecting a successor the trustee shall always choose in preference to all others, some male descendant of my Grandfather John Lowell." The income of the trust would provide the trustee with a "reasonable sum" as compensation "to be paid annually" as approved "by the trustees of the Boston Athenaeum," and the trustee would keep a complete record of lecturers, subjects taught, salaries paid, and other activities connected with the trust and deliver it on the first day of January to the trustees of the Boston Athenaeum.

What was truly remarkable about John Lowell, Jr.'s final will was the clarity of his vision in establishing the trust with half of his estate and the detailed blueprint he drew for the lecturers, the subjects of the lectures, the role of the trustee, and the dedication to promoting "the prosperity of [his] native land, New England" through public education. Although in ill health and depressed, he could sit in the Palace of Luxor and envision how his benefactions would have an enduring effect on the life of Boston. Toward the end of his will he wrote: "The trustee shall require of every person attending the lectures to be neatly dressed and of an orderly behavior. The popular courses always, and the others when practicable are designed for females as well as males." In an age when women were denied educational opportunities, John Lowell, Jr., on the banks of the Nile River in 1835, made certain that they were included in his prescient vision of adult education in the city of Boston.

After drafting his historic last will and testament, and mailing it off to his cousin John Amory Lowell, John Lowell, Jr. would have less than a year to live. His travels eventually took him to India, but he was fatally ill when his British steamer landed in Bombay on February 10, 1836. He died within three weeks of reaching shore on March 4, but news of his death did not reach the Lowell family in Boston until July. He died just two months shy of his thirty-seventh birthday, yet his letter establishing a lecture series in perpetuity for the citizens of Boston assured him a measure of immortality.[2]

According to John Lowell, Jr.'s eulogist, Edward Everett, in a speech delivered at the official inauguration of the Lowell Institute at the Odeon on December 31, 1839, the munificent sum of $250,000 "generously set apart by him for this purpose ... is, with the exception of the bequest of the late Mr. Girard of Philadelphia, the largest, if I mistake not, which has ever been appropriated in this country, by a private individual, for the endowment of any literary institution."[3]

CHAPTER II

The Lowell Institute of Boston

John Amory Lowell, the First Trustee

John Lowell, Jr. was called "a young Bostonian intended by nature for a statesman, whom the caprice of fortune had made a merchant." The same could have been said, perhaps even more so, of John Amory Lowell, his cousin, his closest friend, and his designee as the first trustee of the Lowell Institute.[1]

John Amory Lowell distinguished himself at an early age. He entered Harvard College in 1811, at the age of thirteen, and spent his freshman year rooming in the home of President Kirkland, with Edward Everett, an eminent scholar and orator, as his tutor. Eventually Everett would become governor of Massachusetts and president of Harvard (1846-49). Lowell's sophomore roommate was John P. Bigelow, who was destined to become mayor of Boston.

After graduation Lowell entered the world of business, becoming director of the Suffolk Bank by the age of twenty-three and marrying his first cousin, Susan Cabot Lowell, in 1822. In his meteoric career he established his reputation as a prominent banker, treasurer of several major cotton mills, a member of the Harvard Corporation, and the trustee of the newly founded Lowell Institute.

After settling the estate of John Lowell, Jr., the new trustee had a capital fund of $250,000, the interest from which produced an annual budget for the Lowell Institute of some $18,000, which was a considerable sum at the time, for the purpose of arranging lecture series by eminent scholars. To launch the Lowell Institute lectures he acquired access to the Odeon, a hall that accommodated 2,000 people with excellent acoustics. And on the evening of December 31, 1839, Lowell's former Harvard tutor, Edward Everett, addressed the audience with a moving memoir of John Lowell, Jr., an inaugural lecture he repeated on the evening of January 2, 1840.

In its first full year of operation the Lowell Institute sponsored three lecture series: Professor Benjamin Silliman of Yale College on geology, Reverend John G. Palfrey on "Evidences of Christianity," and Thomas Nuttal of the Philadelphia Academy of Natural Sciences on botany. Silliman gave twenty-one lectures, Palfrey eight, and Nuttal eighteen. The level of public interest in these initial lecture series can be appreciated by the following description of Professor Silliman's popularity as a science teacher:

> So great was his popularity, that on the giving out of tickets for his second course, on chemistry, the following season, the eager crowd filled adjacent streets and crushed in the windows of the "Old Corner Book Store," the place of distribution, so that provision for this had to be made elsewhere. To such a degree did the enthusiasm of the public reach at that time in its desire to attend these lectures, that it was found necessary to open books in advance to serve the names of subscribers, the number of tickets being distributed by lot. Sometimes the number of applicants for a single course was eight to ten thousand.

The lectures were presented at the Odeon until 1846, when they migrated to the Tremont Temple, then to Marlboro Chapel, and eventually to Huntington Hall at the Massachusetts Institute of Technology.[2]

Toward the end of the nineteenth century, the Lowell Institute had established a remarkable record of providing educational opportunities for an eager public in Greater Boston: more than 430 lecture series or 4,400 free lectures on science, religion, literature, and art by the leading authorities in these fields. The list of lecturers reads like a *Who's Who*, with names like Charles Lyell in geology, Henry Adams and Jared Sparks in American history, Asa Gray in botany, Mark Hopkins in religion, Louis Agassiz in the sciences, Cornelius C. Felton in classical civilization, William Dean Howells and James Russell Lowell in literature, Oliver Wendell Holmes in medicine, William James in psychology, Oliver Wendell Holmes, Jr., and A. Lawrence Lowell in government.

When Harriette Knight Smith was preparing her *History of the Lowell Institute* at the end of the nineteenth century, she asked Dr. Oliver Wendell Holmes, shortly before his death, "How do you estimate the influence which the Lowell Institute has had upon the intellectual life of the country?" He replied, "When you have said every enthusiastic thing that you may, you will not have half filled the measure of its importance to Boston—New England—the country at large." He concluded, "No nobler or more helpful institution exists in America than Boston's Lowell Institute."[3]

John Amory Lowell died November 13, 1881, but before his death he received many honors for his distinguished career, including an honorary Doctor of Laws degree from Harvard University, election to the American Academy of Arts and Sciences, presidency of the Boston Athenaeum, and major roles in the administration of the Museum of Fine Arts and the Massachusetts Historical Society. But the service that was closest to his heart, and that he discharged with dedication and determination, was his historic role as the first trustee of the Lowell Institute for forty-two eventful and productive years.

Augustus Lowell became trustee of the Lowell Institute upon his father's death. He had attended Boston Latin School and Harvard College but was an indifferent student. He did excel, however, in business, directing banks and heading cotton textile companies to create a family fortune far in excess of his father's. Unlike his father and several generations of Lowells before him, Augustus did not become a member of the Harvard Corporation; he became a member of the MIT Corporation in 1873 and served faithfully in that capacity for nearly twenty-five years.

As the second trustee of the Lowell Institute, Augustus Lowell continued the practice established by his father of selecting the ablest Lowell lecturers he could find. He was not constrained by family modesty, however, to invite his two sons to deliver series of lectures: Percival Lowell, an astronomer and the eldest, in 1894 gave six lectures in a series titled "Japanese Occultism," and in 1895 another series, "The Planet Mars." Abbott Lawrence Lowell, a lecturer in the department of government at Harvard, gave a course of lectures titled "The Governments of Central Europe." In choosing his successor, Augustus sensed that Percival would be too involved in his scientific work to serve effectively as trustee, and he accordingly decided that his second son, a lawyer and an academic, would be the more appropriate choice, a decision he set down in writing as early as 1881.

Augustus Lowell served ably as the second trustee for nineteen years, acting as a transitional figure between John Amory Lowell and A. Lawrence Lowell. His great success lay in the world of business where he was able to amass a vast fortune estimated at seven times the worth of his father's. He had five children, two sons and three daughters. He impressed upon his sons a Brahmin sense of noblesse oblige. They were independently wealthy, he informed them, and therefore they "must work at something that is worthwhile, and do it very hard," as Lawrence Lowell later recalled. Augustus Lowell's youngest daughter, Amy, was to achieve national recognition as a poet and critic, matching the eminence of her two brothers. Augustus Lowell's success as a paterfamilias complemented his success in business. The early success of MIT owed much to the vision, money, and administrative acumen of Augustus Lowell as well.[4]

PRESIDENT A. LAWRENCE LOWELL

President of Harvard University, 1909–1933
Trustee of the Lowell Institute, 1900–1943

CHAPTER III

Pro Bono Publico

President A. Lawrence Lowell and the Creation of the Commission on Extension Courses

In 1900 Augustus Lowell died and his son Lawrence succeeded him as the third trustee of the Lowell Institute at the age of forty-four. He had graduated from Harvard College and Harvard Law School before embarking on his legal practice, but eventually he shifted his interest to the study of government and began writing books on the subject: *Essays on Government* (1889), and *Governments and Parties of Continental Europe* (1896). His writings attracted the attention of President Charles W. Eliot of Harvard, and in 1900 he extended to Lowell an appointment as professor of the science of government. Lowell abandoned his law career and devoted himself to his academic career, teaching Government 1 to hundreds of Harvard students and writing *The Government of England*, which established his reputation as a scholar.

In 1897, prior to his appointment as professor of government and as trustee of the Lowell Institute, A. Lawrence Lowell had assumed his father's seat as a trustee of the Massachusetts Institute of Technology. In 1900, therefore, he was in the unique position of having first-hand knowledge of both Harvard and MIT for his new assignment as head of the Lowell Institute. The endowment of the Lowell Institute now exceeded $1,000,000 and generated an annual income of more than $50,000. In his dual role as trustee of MIT and of the Lowell Institute, he had reviewed and reorganized the free courses he sponsored into a coherent two-year curriculum at the School for Industrial Foremen at MIT, and when participants complained that the word "foremen" was too restrictive, he changed the name to the Lowell Institute School "under the auspices of MIT." He also sponsored elementary courses at the YMCA, courses on divinity at

King's Chapel, and other courses around Boston. He was an active innova-
tor, consolidator, and administrator in his new role as trustee.[1]

Well before he became president of Harvard, Lowell's annual reports
on behalf of the Lowell Institute reveal his evolving vision for "University
Extension." In his annual report for 1906-07 he stated:

> I am also planning to give, in co-operation with Harvard
> University, a number of systematic courses on subjects of liber-
> al education.... the plans for these are not complete, and it
> may not be possible to begin next year; but if they do succeed
> they will open a new avenue of usefulness of the kind intended
> by John Lowell, Jr., whose plan was really what is now known
> as University Extension.[2]

This plan so intrigued Lowell that he succeeded in implementing it
on schedule. His annual report for the following year, in 1907-08, revealed
that he managed to persuade some Harvard senior faculty colleagues to
teach their regular courses again in the evening for the Lowell Institute:

> The plan of conducting, in cooperation with Harvard
> University, a somewhat new kind of University Extension, was
> put into operation last year. The plan consists of giving as far as
> possible to the public, without charge, some of the general
> courses given at Harvard, especially those open to freshmen.
> During the past year the general course in History, known as
> History I in the college, was given this way; and a course in
> English Literature and Composition corresponding in part to
> different courses in college was given the same way. In both of
> them there were two lectures a week. The class being divided
> into sections which met an instructor for a third hour each
> week. All the persons who applied for the Literature courses
> could not be admitted because the largest lecture hall in the
> Medical School can seat only three hundred persons.
>
> The experiment will be an interesting one, although it may
> be too early as yet to predict its value to the community.

Lowell's "experiment" was received with unprecedented enthusiasm by the
community, for the collegiate courses sponsored by the Lowell Institute in

cooperation with Harvard University were attracting record enrollments, as Lowell noted in his annual report.

Much of the popularity of the Lowell Institute collegiate courses was owing to a combination of the outstanding quality of the Harvard faculty members and the inherent interest in their subject matter. In his annual report for 1908-09, Lowell listed the following faculty, topics, and enrollments for the collegiate courses offered:

> Charles T. Copeland's course in *English Literature and Composition* registered 790. 150 received certificates.
>
> Josiah Royce's course *General Problems in Philosophy* registered 300. 58 received certificates.
>
> A. Lawrence Lowell's course *Modern Constitutional Government* registered 152. 33 received certificates.
>
> George Palmer's *History of Ancient Philosophy* course registered 372. 89 received certificates.

According to the account of one student, described as "a well known president of a representative women's club" in Boston, that was printed in the *Boston Evening Transcript* on June 15, 1910, we have a first-hand report on the diverse and highly motivated students eager to learn from Professor George Herbert Palmer of the Harvard philosophy department:

> At the stroke of eight every lecture evening notebooks were spread and until nine o'clock not a glance wandered to the clock nor was there any sign of wavering interest. The students were all voluntary seekers of knowledge who elected philosophy as an aid in constructive thinking. Young and old, black and white, artisans and teachers, men and women—who had questioned the meaning of life, and the universe, were eager to compare their thoughts with the questioners of all time. It was an audience to challenge any professor's attention and respect, as it did that of Professor Palmer.[3]

The appeal of teaching such a mixed, mature, and motivated student population was obviously instrumental in attracting leading members of the

Harvard faculty, first to the collegiate courses and soon after to the regular courses offered by the Commission on Extension Courses.

Impressive as Palmer was in teaching ancient philosophy, and as solid as Royce and Lowell himself were in teaching moral philosophy and government, respectively, the star platform performer clearly was Copeland, who in time would become the legendary "Copey of Harvard." In 1905 he began teaching English 12 in Harvard College and soon it became the most famous writing course in the country, boasting among its students such eminent writers as T.S. Eliot, Robert Benchley, Walter Lippmann, Conrad Aiken, John Dos Passos, Brooks Atkinson, and John Reed. On January 17, 1927, he appeared on the cover of *Time* magazine and became a national figure whose reputation rested solely on his prowess as a teacher and public reader. His classes in University Extension—and at Harvard Summer School, as at Harvard College—were invariably among the most heavily subscribed and the most memorable for students of all ages. Copey loved a large and appreciative audience, which helped to explain why he regularly taught Extension courses at Harvard. He retired from Harvard in 1932 as the Boylston Professor of Rhetoric and Oratory.[4] All the lectures for the collegiate courses were held in Boston to make them readily available to the public and to abide by the terms of the will of the founder. Lowell was sensitive about his "being both trustee and lecturer," and to preclude any potential conflict of interest, he explained in his annual report: "I thought it better not to pay myself anything for conducting the course."

On October 26, 1908, President Eliot of Harvard submitted his resignation, and it was agreed that it take effect on May 9, 1909, to commemorate the fortieth anniversary of his election to the office. The choice of a successor to Eliot proved an easy matter, as A. Lawrence Lowell was elected by the Harvard Corporation on January 13, 1909, and confirmed by the Board of Overseers. Lowell's interest in education stemmed from his duties as trustee of the Lowell Institute on the one hand, and from his commitment to Harvard as a professor of the science of government and as an appointed member of academic committees on the other. In being called to the presidency of Harvard he was in a position of leadership to effect his plans for educational reform.

When A. Lawrence Lowell became president of Harvard University in May 1909, he was fifty-two years old and for nearly a decade had managed the affairs of the Lowell Institute. He resolved to retain his role of trustee, but he wisely delegated the task of overseeing the endowment of the Lowell Institute to Augustus P. Loring, as he recorded in his report of July 1909 to the Boston Athenaeum. In his dual role he could use the resources of the Lowell Institute and of Harvard University to envision an expanded role for popular and adult education for the citizens of Boston.

As his early annual reports as president of Harvard reveal, his first major undertaking, before embarking on the ambitious program for reforming undergraduate education at Harvard College, was to put into effect his already formulated scheme from the Lowell Institute for a program of University Extension. In his first annual report as president for the academic year 1908-09, he considered it noteworthy to write: "As the various directions in which the University extends its instruction to persons not enrolled among its regular students have not, apart from the Summer School, fallen within the province of any single department in the University, it may be well to refer to them here. They are, in fact, more numerous than is commonly supposed." Lowell then proceeded to describe the range and variety of these educational efforts at Harvard, notably "the Lowell Institute Collegiate Courses [which] mark an interesting experiment, that of substantially repeating for the benefit of the public courses given to students in college, under conditions which require the same amount of work and the same examinations."

The public demand and potential for "popular education" had impressed Lowell both in his role as trustee of the Lowell Institute and in his personal experience the preceding year in teaching the collegiate course *Modern Constitutional Government* to more than 150 adult men and women. He now sought to set forth in his annual report the sort of systematic instruction that was essential to meet the needs of the adult community:

> The time when the public can gain a great deal from mere lectures is passing away, and it would seem to be important that any popular education at the present day should be systematic—as carefully organized and as thoroughly tested as instruc-

tion given in the University itself. What is needed now is not
so much stimulation of popular interest in intellectual affairs, as
well-ordered instruction, with a rigorous training of the mind;
and the experiment of these Collegiate Courses would appear
to show that there are many people in our community, who
have not been to college, but who have the desire and the apti-
tude to profit by so much of a college education as, amid the
work of earning their living, they are able to obtain.

It would seem to be the duty of every institution of learning
in this country to use its resources for the benefit of the surrounding community, so far as that can be done without
impairing its more immediate work; but in doing this the institutions in the neighborhood ought by cooperation to avoid
waste of effort. If all the universities and colleges in the vicinity of Boston would combine on a common plan to provide systematic popular education the aggregate amount of instruction
offered might be very large without over-burdening any one of
them. Since the time covered by this report a conference looking to that end has held several meetings, and is preparing plans
for systematic cooperation of a most useful kind.

The *pro bono publico* spirit of "popular education" articulated by Lowell
above indicated that he believed part of his mission as an educator was to
make available the resources of Harvard for the benefit of Boston, just as
the Lowell Institute, founded by his ancestor, had been doing for more
than seventy years.[5]

As President Lowell settled into his new office and his new role of
leadership, he continued to conduct the affairs of the Lowell Institute. But
as his annual reports for both institutions in 1909-10 clearly show, the
symbiosis of the two posts in furthering his designs for University
Extension was ideal. In his annual report for the Lowell Institute he noted
that the collegiate courses, "conducted in co-operation with Harvard
University," included Charles Townsend Copeland's *Lives, Characters, and
Times of Men of Letters, English and American*; Arthur Bushnell Hart's
Constitutional and Political History of the United States, 1789-1895; and
Charles J. Bullock's *Public Finance*. But the popularity of the collegiate

courses only convinced Lowell that a more comprehensive and systematic scheme would do the work required, and he accordingly arranged for meetings with the heads of the other major institutions of higher education in Greater Boston to create a consortium.

In his Lowell Institute report he recorded that "a plan was agreed upon whereby Harvard University, Boston University, Boston College, Massachusetts Institute of Technology, Simmons College, Tufts College, Wellesley College, and the Museum of Fine Arts should offer courses under the control of a joint committee that should provide a program each year, affording large opportunities for popular education without excessive burden on any one of the institutions. The Collegiate Courses, hitherto given by the Lowell Institute ... are incorporated in the plan." This consortium, Lowell explained, has "established a combined system of University Extension on a considerable scale, while the standard is maintained by the fact that the courses must be approved by the joint committee, and count towards a university degree. For this purpose Harvard, Tufts, and Wellesley have agreed to give a new degree of Associate in Arts, which will require no entrance examination, and no college residence, but of which the requirements will be substantially equivalent to the bachelor's degree.... This provision will put a college degree within the reach of school teachers to whom it opens a chance of promotion in their profession, and to everyone who attends the courses it means an inducement to follow a more systematic plan of study." Whereas the Lowell Institute had for years only provided series of lectures for the public on assorted topics, now it had aligned itself with Boston's foremost institutions to provide courses leading to a college degree that was "substantially equivalent" to a bachelor's degree from Harvard or Tufts or Wellesley. Lowell saw this "new plan" as a conscious attempt to "carry out more completely than ever the idea of John Lowell, Jr."

The authorities of Harvard University, Tufts College, the Massachusetts Institute of Technology, Boston College, Boston University, the Museum of Fine Arts, Wellesley College, and Simmons College had now completed their plans for University Extension courses in Boston for the year 1910-11. The courses the consortium proposed to give were designed to benefit students who could not attend college and corresponded as closely as possible with courses regularly given in the various institutions involved. They were conducted in the same manner and those taking a course were required to do the same amount of work required of a regular college student. One great advantage of these courses was that they were to be given by regular professors and instructors of the various institutions interested and no instructors were employed who were not thoroughly competent teachers. This work included the Lowell Institute collegiate courses and many of the Boston University courses for teachers.

In his second annual report as president (1909-10), Lowell regarded the developments in University Extension of sufficient significance to the Harvard community that he devoted a considerable portion of his text to that topic and readers were referred to a report of "the new Dean for University Extension," which became a regular feature of annual reports from that year forward. Unlike his annual report for 1909-10 for the Lowell Institute, President Lowell seized this occasion to distinguish between the traditional curriculum at Harvard, which offered many regular courses of instruction for undergraduates and graduate students, and the nontraditional curriculum of popular education, which was perforce more limited because "there are no highly advanced students in specialized fields," and since Extension students "are almost always hard at work" and not in residence, "they can take only one or two courses at a time." Therefore, it was important to the Extension curriculum that courses not necessarily be numerous, "but that they should be of the best quality and should change a good deal from year to year."

Lowell consistently stressed the need for quality in Extension courses and thought this could best be guaranteed if each of the leading institutions in Greater Boston was persuaded to join in a common effort to provide such instruction. The formation of a "permanent Commission on Extension Courses," with representatives from these institutions under the administrative control of Harvard, was the solution Lowell sought and succeeded in creating in January 1910. "The Commission arranges with instructors in these institutions for courses which are equivalent to, and usually identical with, courses offered to their own students, and which are followed by examinations of the same character and standard." These courses, according to Lowell, were to be supported in part by low tuition fees paid by the students and in part by subventions from the Lowell Institute and from the Boston Chamber of Commerce.[6]

At a meeting of the Harvard Board of Overseers on February 23, 1910, a plan establishing the Department of University Extension under the authority of the Faculty of Arts and Sciences was officially approved.

To ensure the success of this venture, President Lowell appointed James Hardy Ropes '89, Hollis Professor of Divinity, as the first dean of University Extension, and created an administrative board for University Extension with the new dean as its chairman. As Lowell observed, "the existence of a Dean and Administrative Board lends dignity and stability to the work, and promotes permanence and the maintenance of a high standard both for the winter courses and the Summer School." Dean Ropes would assume administrative control over University Extension, the Summer School, and Special Students at Harvard.

Lowell realized that the Extension courses fell under the purview of the Faculty of Arts and Sciences, and since these courses could be counted toward a Harvard or Radcliffe degree, he felt he needed to distinguish between the regular Harvard and Radcliffe Bachelor of Arts and the new Extension degree of Associate in Arts, the only difference being the absence of a residence requirement or an entrance examination. He wanted the new degree to be of comparable quality:

> The new degree will be obtained chiefly by school teachers and is of interest mainly to them. It is of consequence for them, because in some of the large cities study that counts towards a college degree is demanded for any promotion, and the attainment of such a degree is a prerequisite for teaching in high schools. Now the degree of Associate of Arts, which suffices for admission to our Graduate School, has been accepted by the School Board of Boston for both of these purposes, and hence fulfills the objects that the teachers have in view. No doubt the degree will be attained from Harvard by few men, and probably not by many women from Radcliffe, but that is no measure of its importance, and still less of the value of the extension courses to the great numbers of people who take less than seventeen of them. The very fact that they count for a degree lays

on the Faculty a responsibility, and furnishes to the public a guarantee, that their standard shall be maintained.

The impetus for an Extension degree comparable to a college degree came from Boston school teachers who, after years of valuable teaching experience, found themselves unable to complete such a degree in their spare time. A committee of twelve teachers, led by Miss Florence E. Leadbetter of Roxbury High School, was appointed by the superintendent of the Boston School Committee in November 1907 to investigate opportunities for collegiate courses and a college degree that would be accessible to teachers from Boston and environs. In time Miss Leadbetter and her colleagues sought the assistance of A. Lawrence Lowell and the Lowell Institute, but it was not until Lowell became president of Harvard that the school teachers had renewed hope for a college degree through Extension courses. The remarks by President Lowell in his annual report for 1909-10 on the new degree were addressed as much to Miss Leadbetter and her committee of school teachers as they were to members of the Harvard community. For he did sympathize with their dilemma and, when the opportunity presented itself, he championed their cause. It was in part due to his intercession that the school board of Boston accepted the new degree as qualification for teaching in high school.

The progress of the new program was monitored closely by Harvard, the Lowell Institute, and the Boston press. By the end of the first semester, the following statistics were assembled: the Commission offered eleven courses and enrolled 606 students (400 women, 206 men); the average age of the men was thirty-five years, of the women thirty-six years. About one-third of the students were school teachers, one-third were students or "at home," and one-third represented such occupations as clerks, stenographers, and bookkeepers. The most popular course was Copeland's *English Literature of the Nineteenth Century* with 254 enrolled. By the end of the year, the Commission had sponsored 16 courses, enrolled 863 students, and cited 395 certificates of completion. President Lowell's vision of University Extension at Harvard and under the auspices of the Commission on Extension Courses in Boston had become an established enterprise.

In his annual report to the Boston Athenaeum in 1911, he reinterpreted the will of John Lowell, Jr. to conform to his own vision:

> John Lowell, Jr. was ahead of his day. His conception was what would now be called University Extension, and it may be that his ideas were in part derived from, or informed by the College de France. He intended the lecturers to teach throughout the year, giving one popular and one advanced course.... But he failed to perceive that University Extension can hardly be successful without a connection with a large institution of higher learning; and in fact it had been found from the outset impossible to offer the advanced instruction he directed without some connection of that kind.

The effect of the newly established Commission on Extension Courses in the Harvard and Boston communities was reflected in the press. In March, 1910, the *Harvard Bulletin* applauded this cooperative venture in university extension as "of great importance," concluding that the "association ... of the various colleges and universities in this vicinity shows that they are rivals only in the sense that each is trying to do all it can for the benefit of the public."

The next few years saw a gradual increase in the number of courses offered from the original sixteen in 1910-11 to twenty in 1912-13 and twenty-four in 1915-16. Although each member institution in the Commission was represented by its faculty, Harvard contributed by far the most instructors each year, with names like Copeland, Greenough, and Osterhout being complemented in these early years by George Pierce Baker in dramatic literature, George Howard Parker in zoology, and Josiah Royce in philosophy. In the year 1912-13, for example, nearly half the courses were taught by Harvard faculty, as more than a thousand students enrolled.

The *pro bono publico* purpose of the Commission on Extension Courses enabled it to add member institutions if they could help further its educational aims. In 1913-14 Dean Ropes recorded in his annual report the addition of the school committee of the City of Boston as a member of the Commission and noted that "several courses have been planned for 1914-15 in consultation with the School Committee in order to meet the

special needs of Boston teachers." As promised, the following year's program did indeed offer *The Supervision of Teaching in Elementary Schools* by
two Harvard professors (Moore and Holmes) at "Boston schools convenient for the majority in each section." In 1915-16 the Massachusetts Board
of Education was added as a member of the Commission. And as the
course program grew to meet the educational needs of its assorted con-
stituents, so did the enrollments, which by the seventh year of operation
exceeded 1,500.

Although Lowell as president of Harvard could rely on Dean Ropes
for running University Extension at Harvard and chairing the
Commission on Extension Courses, as trustee of the Lowell Institute he
also had to keep himself personally informed on the progress of the programs. Happily, he enjoyed a warm rapport with Ropes, and the two men
maintained an easy and open line of communication that enabled Lowell
to record in his annual reports for the Lowell Institute developments in
University Extension. As trustee, Lowell saw that the general public lectures for the community that were so central to the mission of the Lowell
Institute in its earlier years now no longer attracted the large audiences
that popular courses in University Extension did. He therefore decided as
trustee to shift his support to the Commission on Extension Courses with
the hope "that the share of pecuniary aid the Lowell Institute can give
these extension courses will be even larger in the future." In fact, Lowell
in his annual report for 1911-12 felt that the Lowell Institute could afford
sufficient funds "to give these courses without charge; but Dean Ropes is
rather of the opinion that the charge is an advantage, as not being large
enough to discourage anyone or to be really felt a burden, while keeping
out persons who do not intend to take the courses seriously."[7]

President Lowell was known to be the prime mover behind University
Extension, and it was to him that inquiries were addressed from around
the country. He corresponded with members of school boards, officers of
national extension organizations, and fellow university presidents. For
example, he responded to the "broad question" posed by President Frank
L. McVey of the University of North Dakota on October 4, 1916, "Has
University Extension justified itself?" with this assessment: "I suppose, as
in everything in the world, there is extension and extension—good, bad,

and indifferent; but my experience with the extension I have seen here has led me to believe that it has very fully justified itself, both in the form of general cultural courses and of technical courses."[8]

JAMES HARDY ROPES

Chairman of Commission on Extension Courses
Dean of University Extension
1910–1922

CHAPTER IV

The Formative Years
of University Extension

James Hardy Ropes, Dean (1910-22)

James Hardy Ropes proved an ideal choice as the first dean of University Extension at Harvard. Ropes had an impeccable set of academic credentials. He had attended Phillips Academy, Andover, before matriculating at Harvard College, where he excelled as a scholar, graduating *summa cum laude* and being elected to *Phi Beta Kappa* his junior year. He went on to Andover Theological Seminary and graduated in 1893. After two years of postgraduate study and travel in Europe, he joined the faculty of the Harvard Divinity School as instructor in New Testament criticism and interpretation. He was promoted to assistant professor in 1898, Bussey Professor of New Testament in 1903, and in 1910 he was appointed Hollis Professor of Divinity, the oldest endowed academic chair at Harvard. That same year he also became dean of University Extension and chairman of the Commission on Extension Courses. As an interpreter of the New Testament, he was one of the foremost scholars in the field, with several books and many articles to his credit. Although primarily a member of the Faculty of Theology, he also offered courses on the English Bible in the Faculty of Arts and Sciences. Ropes served as dean of University Extension from 1910 to 1922, but remained Hollis Professor of Divinity until his death in 1933. In 1929 Harvard conferred upon him the honorary degree of Doctor of Sacred Theology in recognition of his distinguished academic and administrative career.[1]

When in the spring of 1910 the local press received word of the plans for a Commission on Extension Courses, they played up the story as a major feature item. Coverage by the *Boston Journal* was typical: "New Plan for People's College. Eight Institutions of Higher Education Unite to

Help Bostonians. Nominal Fee for University Course. Both Men and Women to be Taught Without Interference with Employment." According to the article, "the overseers of Harvard University at their last meeting created a department of University Extension and appointed Professor J.H. Ropes dean." The *Journal* sent a reporter to interview Professor Ropes, who responded: "Our aim will be to give the young people of Boston who have heretofore been prevented from securing a college education the same instruction they would receive were they undergraduates at Harvard."

Ropes went on to distinguish the Harvard extension program from that at Columbia University, where "the University Extension work is carried on almost exclusively by the younger teachers," whereas Harvard's aim was "to supply the most experienced teachers that can be secured." The Commission would not be able "to give so many courses as Columbia does, but the instruction in those we do give will be the very best we can provide." Ropes outlined the extension work already being offered by Boston University and the Lowell Institute's collegiate courses held in the afternoons, evenings, and on Saturdays, and how they must all be incorporated into the newly formed Commission. He concluded by announcing "a charge of $5 will be made for courses. . . . In short, we will endeavor to supply a thorough university training to those who have previously been denied one and supply it at a very low figure."[2]

The impact of the newly established Commission on Extension Courses in the Harvard and Boston communities was reflected in the press. In March 1910, the *Harvard Bulletin* applauded this cooperative venture in University Extension "of great importance," concluding that the "association . . . of the various colleges and universities in this vicinity shows that they are rivals only in the sense that each is trying to do all it can for the benefit of the public." The *Boston Advertiser* on April 8, 1910, carried an article headed: "Harvard Establishes the Degree of 'Associate in Arts.' Entrance Examination Not Required, Nor Residence—Otherwise Equivalent to A.B." By June 1910, the Boston press gave full play to the story. On June 15 the *Boston Evening Transcript* carried a long and laudatory feature article under the headline "Real University Extension," which cited a recently published article by Dean Ropes in the *Harvard Graduates'*

Magazine as asserting that "the first duty of . . . an institution is to give its own students the best education it can supply; but, this being done, there remains a certain portion of available power which is not needed for direct instruction or administration, and which is applied in various ways, largely for the general benefit. University Extension is one of the newer ways, its purpose being to provide technical or culture instruction for persons who are unable to spend four years in college."

The article by Dean Ropes had appeared in the June 10, 1910 issue of the *Harvard Graduates' Magazine* and it was titled "The Possibilities of University Extension in Boston." In choosing Ropes as his new dean for University Extension, President Lowell not only called upon a distinguished Harvard colleague related to him by marriage (Mrs. Ropes was Alice Lowell), but also an articulate and committed proponent of extension work in higher education. As Ropes wrote in his well-timed article: "All such [extension] work as this has now come to be regarded as a part of the proper and obligatory task of the universities and colleges and other institutions which crown and complete the American system of public education. It is all of the nature of University Extension." After reviewing how the Harvard Faculty of Arts and Sciences appointed a committee in 1909 to consider an expanded program in Extension that could lead to a degree, how the committee report was adopted by the faculty in November, how the intercollegiate Commission on Extension Courses was formed in January, and how the enterprise would be implemented the following academic year, Dean Ropes observed: "Many persons who wish that they had a college education will be able to get gradually an effective substitute for it—in some respects more effective than the ordinary college education because of the greater eagerness and maturity of such students. Some young people of talent, zealous for improvement, who are already earning their living, may, it is hoped, be stimulated to begin studies which will lead them to a development of latent power sufficient to open wholly new careers of far greater dignity and usefulness than they could otherwise attain."[3]

The dual theme of educational opportunity and latent talent among segments of the working community so eloquently expressed by Dean Ropes obviously struck a responsive chord in the Boston press. The June

20, 1910 issue of the *Boston Journal* began an article on extension with the query:

> Given a young man or a young woman, who, for any reason left
> school early in life and who, forced to gain a livelihood, cannot
> afford the time to devote to study at regular institutions of learn-
> ing, but who has a desire for greater learning, and an ambition
> to secure a college degree and the willingness to work for such
> an end, how can this be done and the necessary time and atten-
> tion be given to study without interfering with daily duties?

The answer naturally was "in the new plan for University Extension provided by the Commission on Extension Courses," which offered a new
opportunity in education that promised no less than to create "better civic
conditions and assure a higher material efficiency, mental sanity, and
moral stability on the part of the citizens of Boston."

The printed circular "University Extension Courses in Boston for 1910-
11" marked the official beginning of the new program, whose headquarters
were in the office of Dean Ropes in University Hall. The institutional representatives of the Commission were Dean Ropes of Harvard, chairman;
the presidents of Boston College, Boston University, Simmons College, and
the Massachusetts Institute of Technology; the deans of Wellesley College
and Tufts College; and the director of the Boston Museum of Fine Arts.
This august board of directors ensured that institutional participation and
cooperation would be of the highest order, and it was. Twenty-two instructors were listed with their institutional affiliations (Harvard contributed
Charles Townsend Copeland and Chester Noyes Greenough in English,
Douglas Wilson Johnson in physiography, Winthrop J.F. Osterhout in
botany, and Robert M. Yerkes in psychology). Classes were scheduled for
evenings, late afternoons, and Saturdays; all courses were held in Boston in
keeping with the terms of the will of John Lowell, Jr. (It wasn't until 1912-13
that some of the courses were held in Cambridge.)

One can surmise Ropes's dedication to his administrative work as
dean from his twenty-fifth Harvard class report for 1914:

> Since 1910, I have had charge of the University Extension work of
> Harvard (including the Summer School for the years 1910-12),

and have been the executive officer of the co-operative effort to bring opportunities of college instruction to the people of Boston upon which the various colleges and universities of Boston have entered. This last work has been of very great interest. About 1,000 persons annually take the courses given by professors from Harvard, Boston University, and other institutions; and it has appeared to meet increasingly a public need. The ideal which has been aimed at in this work (for which the Lowell Institute supplies most of the funds) has been to secure, as we have done, the friendly co-operation of all the collegiate institutions in and about Boston to maintain high standards of college work, and to have the work done by professors of the highest standing.... and, taking into account the quality of the instruction, Boston is now as well supplied with opportunities for popular adult education as any city in this country, unless it is New York.[4]

On January 20, 1910, a conference on University Extension was convened in Boston to address "the amount of money necessary for the scheme of extension courses." Professor Ropes served as chairman, and the presidents of four of the member institutions of the Commission on Extension Courses were present. It was decided that a total of $10,000 was needed for the first year, with the Lowell Institute Fund, the fees of the Lowell Institute collegiate courses, and the Chamber of Commerce collectively covering the costs. Student fees would be set at "$5.00 per semester for a one-hour course, and $10.00 per semester for a two-hour or a three-hour course." Instructor salaries were set at "$200 per year for a one-hour course, $375 per year for a two-hour course, $500 per year for a three-hour course," with the proviso that "larger salaries might be paid in special cases."

In his annual report for 1909-10, Dean Ropes reviewed the role of University Extension at Harvard: "The opportunity and need of providing instruction for the community outside the walls of the University, and especially for the body of school-teachers in and near Boston, has occupied the Faculty of Arts and Sciences for several years, partly in consequence of the earnest efforts of a committee of Boston public school-teachers." In response to the persistent petitioning of Miss Leadbetter and her associates, courses for teachers were offered on a regular basis on Saturdays and in the late afternoons; but as the Lowell Institute collegiate courses taught by Harvard faculty were introduced by the personal efforts of A. Lawrence Lowell from 1907 on, the school teachers found them more attractive, especially since they were accepted toward the Harvard and Radcliffe degrees. The creation of the Commission on Extension Courses enabled all the cooperating institutions to offer courses, including the Lowell collegiate courses and the Teachers' School of Science courses at MIT. "The outcome of this," according to Ropes, "is that there is now in operation in Boston a kind of extension college, giving courses which lead to an adequately guarded degree, and administered by the joint action of the neighboring colleges and other appropriate institutions. With further experience the arrangement ought to meet well the needs of Boston and the suburbs, so far as collegiate extension instruction is concerned. Not the least valuable and promising aspect of the movement is the fact that it has been possible in this matter to unite in full cooperation for this public service eight separate institutions."[5]

In his first annual report to the president "on the work of University Extension for the academic year 1909-10," Dean Ropes summarized for the record the impetus behind the establishment of the Commission on Extension Courses:

> The opportunity and need of providing instruction for the community outside the walls of the University, and especially for the body of school-teachers in and near Boston, has occupied the Faculty of Arts and Sciences for several years, partly in consequence of the earnest efforts of a committee of Boston public-school teachers. In 1906 plans were made for Afternoon and Saturday Courses for Teachers ... for a fee of $15 per course."

Ropes explained that the eighteen courses offered in 1906-07 and the sixteen in 1907-08 "were not intended to correspond closely to college courses, and were given in Cambridge. At the same time ... the Lowell Institute established free evening collegiate courses, given by Harvard instructors," which were all "given in exactly the same manner as the corresponding undergraduate courses ... [and] were consequently accepted for the degree of AB and S.B. by Harvard and Radcliffe." Ropes went on to cite "one of the courses of the Teachers' School of Science and one public collegiate course at the Boston Museum of Fine Arts have been recently given by members of the Harvard faculty." Also since 1906-07 Boston University had been sponsoring in Boston "an important series of Courses for Teachers" by its faculty to "a steadily increasing attendance."

All these assorted educational initiatives, especially by Harvard and Boston University, "brought out the need of cooperation, and in December, 1909, pursuant to a vote of the Harvard Faculty of Arts and Sciences ... President Lowell and President Huntington of Boston University united in calling a meeting of representatives of the institutions in the neighborhood of Boston from which instruction might be supplied, and in January, 1910, the 'Commission on Extension Courses' was organized." The following were members:

Harvard University	Boston University
Tufts College	Museum of Fine Arts
Massachusetts Institute of Technology	Wellesley College
Boston College	Simmons College.

The member institutions of the Commission, except Boston University, agreed upon the degree of Associate in Arts "to be given on identical terms, and to be maintained equal to the Harvard degree of Bachelor of Arts in number of courses required, but without the exaction of any entrance examination or any academic residence."

For its first year of operation, the Commission on Extension Courses arranged for "a system of courses, given mainly by officers of the cooperating institutions, in which the Lowell Collegiate Courses and the courses of the Teachers' School of Science are included." Ropes went on to explain that the tripartite funding for the Commission's course program would result from student fees, the fund of the Lowell Institute, and gifts secured through the education committee of the Boston Chamber of Commerce. The happy conclusion of all these efforts by Dean Ropes, President Lowell, and the heads of Boston's leading educational and cultural institutions was the operation in Boston now of "a kind of extension college, giving courses which lead to an adequately guarded degree, and administered by the joint action of the [Commission]."

As dean of University Extension Ropes had administrative responsibility for the Summer School of Arts and Sciences, the Commission on Extension Courses, and the Special Students at Harvard. In his second annual report to the president of the University in 1910-11, he covered all three areas, noting that "since the general administration sources for the courses of the Commission were provided by Harvard, it is proper here to make record of the work of the Commission of 1910-11." Accordingly, he listed all sixteen courses taught by the Commission, including those taught by non-Harvard faculty, citing 863 enrollments and 395 certificates or "about 46 percent of the whole enrollment." He made it clear that "the students in these courses are not members of, nor even directly affiliated to Harvard University, but the courses authorized by the Commission having been approved by the Harvard Administrative Board for University Extension, were accepted by the Faculty of Arts and Sciences (on recommendation of the Faculty's committee on instruction) to be counted towards the degree of Associate in Arts." He went on to report that "the Boston School Committee has accepted the degree of Associate in Arts from Harvard, Radcliffe, Tufts, and Wellesley as the equivalent of the AB in the qualifications of teachers, so that the courses of the Commission are now fully available for the purposes of Boston schoolteachers." Apparently the petitions of Florence E. Leadbetter, in her capacity as chairman of the committee on college credit of the Boston school teachers, to A. Lawrence Lowell as trustee of the Lowell Institute and, in 1909, as president of Harvard, had come to fruition in the creation of the Commission on Extension Courses and the acceptance of the Associate in Arts degree by the Boston School Committee.

Miss Leadbetter proved herself a formidable champion of Boston teachers in their quest for educational opportunities and credentials. In a letter from Roxbury High School dated June 5, 1909, to President Lowell she wrote: "Our Committee on College Credit takes pleasure in the record of nearly a thousand teachers pursuing courses of study this year, almost two hundred of them for college degrees, but we realize that many of these teachers have done so at a greater expense of money or strength than they could afford."

Although President Lowell was supportive of Miss Leadbetter and her committee on college credit, others were not, and they doubted that the school teachers would enroll in the courses or, if they did, they doubted they had the strength and stamina to complete their studies. To those naysayers Miss Leadbetter wrote in the *Boston Evening Transcript* of June 15, 1910:

> The teachers needed no urging toward this work, but rather watchful restraint, lest they undertake too much. In spite of all restraints, however, some remarkable records have been made. To give a single instance: An elementary school teacher, taking the Harvard courses in English 22, covering the English A, the Lowell Institute course in Government, a half course in English literature at Boston University, and two science courses at the Teachers' School of Science, has thereby completed with excellent grade the equivalent of four college courses— the standard amount for a regular college student. At the same time, this teacher has carried her class through two years' work in one, forty-five of her pupils receiving a double promotion. In the face of these facts and the good health of this teacher-student (she says that she never felt better in her life and never enjoyed a year's work more) arguments against study on the part of teachers because of detrimental effects upon the physical condition of the teacher and upon her class room work cannot stand.

When Miss Leadbetter wrote to Dean Ropes questioning Harvard's decision to award an Associate in Arts degree, rather than the traditional Bachelor's degree, for the new University Extension program, he responded on April 8, 1910:

> Moreover, as President Lowell reminds me, the choice of studies of a candidate for a degree ought to be adjusted, so far as possible, to her intellectual needs, not to rules made for an entirely different purpose....
>
> The establishment of the Associate in Arts degree has been prompted by the desire to enable the teacher to work for a valuable degree, and, at the same time, to leave her free to make the

wisest choice of her studies without being hampered by rules
which were intended for another set of persons.[6]

The Harvard faculty committee on supplementary instruction, at the
request of President Lowell, had met to discuss the implications of the
Commission on Extension Courses on faculty workload, course availability, and credit for the new program. It concluded:

> This degree at Harvard (and Radcliffe) should require the same
> number of courses as the A.B. or S.B., but might well have dif-
> ferent conditions of admission (e.g., by certificate or by actual
> service in teaching) and of residence (e.g., not requiring the full
> year of residence). The name of this new degree should be con-
> sidered in conference but when conferred by Harvard should
> not be the A.B. or S.B.

At a meeting of the Faculty of Arts and Sciences on November 30, 1909,
it was voted that Harvard join the new "plan of cooperation" with "other
institutions of higher education in or near Boston," and that courses
count for a new degree at Harvard (and Radcliffe), not the Bachelor of
Arts or Science.

Obviously, the primary reason that the Associate in Arts designation
was chosen was to differentiate it from the regular Harvard undergraduate degree, which required course choices in the sophomore, junior, and
senior years from a large curriculum designed for concentrations in academic areas that simply were not possible in the very limited thirty or
fewer courses available through the Commission on Extension Courses.

Despite its designation as an Associate in Arts degree, instead of a
Bachelor of Arts or Science degree, Harvard quickly gave currency to the
new degree. On June 1, 1910, the dean of the Graduate School of Arts and
Sciences at Harvard, C.H. Haskins, wrote letters both to Dean Ropes and
to President Lowell, stating that "the Administrative Board of the Graduate
School of Arts and Sciences voted to admit to the Graduate School men
who hold the new degree of Associate of Arts from Harvard University."

It was Miss Leadbetter's initiative with President Lowell that
prompted him to write to the president of Boston University, William
Edwards Huntington, on October 28, 1909, about "making the University

more serviceable to the public in extension work, and ... proposing in that connection a co-operation among the various colleges in or near the city, to work upon a combined plan, and save duplication of effort." Miss Leadbetter had sent Lowell a "list containing the courses given by Boston University" as a model of the sort of courses Harvard might emulate.

In the early years of the Commission on Extension Courses President Lowell also played an important role as peacemaker among the cooperating institutions. When the *Boston Transcript* on March 28, 1911, carried a short article under the headline "Harvard University" for a summary of the first half-year of courses offered in Boston by the Commission, the president of Boston University wrote President Lowell the very next day: "Some of our professors who are interested in Extension courses this year, have come to me in a good deal of indignation over the enclosed notice, which appeared in last night's *Transcript*. I presume the authorities at Harvard, Dean Ropes and others, had nothing to do with this...." But, President Huntington went on to explain, the reporter's text was "evidently making the public think that the Extension courses are managed by Harvard alone." To placate the offended Boston University contingent, Lowell wrote back to President Huntington that Dean Ropes had already written to explain that Harvard always refers to others in such articles, and Lowell promised to "strive to prevent anything from appearing in the papers which does not fully recognize the share of all institutions engaged in this work."

Ropes, for his part, enjoyed an easy relationship with his kinsman by marriage, A. Lawrence Lowell. In the fall of 1910, he wrote a personal letter to Lowell, offering, "in view of the present financial situation in the Summer School, and the general reduction of salaries," to have his salary for 1910-11 "reduced to $750.00, or to some smaller amount." In the summer of 1912 Lowell wrote Ropes to confirm his having "a leave of absence for the first half of 1912-13. I do hope that you will get a good rest. Of course you have been overdoing, and I recognize that it is my fault, for I have been overworking you. I did not realize that I had been doing so, for I am pretty tough, and an indolent animal."

In the fall of 1914, Ropes again wrote to Lowell to say that he was being overpaid and asked that the president discontinue his "salary of $400 as

Dean," to which Lowell promptly wrote that he was "wholly unwilling to discontinue [Ropes's] salary of four hundred dollars as Dean in charge of University Extension.... It is a highly important part of the University work, and ought to be so treated. It is perhaps unnecessary to say, what you know, how well I think you have done it, and how much credit to the University the Extension Department has been under your guidance." He signed the letter, uncharacteristically, "Yours affectionately."[7]

Starting in 1914, Dean Ropes sponsored an "annual Reception for the students in the University Extension courses ... at Boston University," an event that he deemed "was of distinct value in the enterprise, and was greatly, almost touchingly, appreciated by the students." The Boston press covered the first reception for students enrolled in University Extension courses in the spring of 1914 at Boston University with a statement that "about 490 attended and it was most successful. It was largely arranged by Dean James H. Ropes to create a closer social and educational bond among the students and professors." That evening the speakers were President Lowell of Harvard, President Murlin of Boston University, Director George H. Barton of the Lowell Teachers' School of Science, Superintendent of Schools Franklin B. Dyer, and Dean Ropes. Ropes outlined additional courses in international law and diplomacy, the history of drama, and the geography of Boston that would be offered the following year. President Lowell informed the audience of the history of the Lowell Institute and its founder before launching into a spirited defense of the members of the Commission as "endowed institutions." "But we are just as much organized for the public benefit as any others.... In fact we hold a trust for the community, for the public, and we are nothing but a successive series of servants to the public." President Murlin joined Lowell by stating it took time for educational institutions to realize they had an obligation to offer extension courses to those outside the college walls and "the almost unanimous testimony" was a "fine appreciation of service rendered" to the public. Superintendent Dyer endorsed the courses offered, stating the teachers of Boston "are just hungry for them," and "commended the splendid cooperation" of the Commission members.

One can sense the commitment Ropes brought to his role as chairman of the Commission on Extension Courses and his sincere regard for the students who attended the evening courses by the tenor of his letters inviting dignitaries to the annual receptions. For example, on April 9, 1915, he wrote to President Bumpus of Tufts about the students who attended: "The object is to make them feel that they have a share in a movement of large significance and to have a little thrill of community feeling and also to bring them into contact with some of the representatives of the colleges,—a privilege which they greatly appreciate." The rhetorical appeal of Ropes's invitations was not lost on his recipients, for President Lyons of Boston College replied on April 15, 1915, to such a letter of invitation: "Any opportunity to give aid to these sincere, hard-working, ambitious men and women will be cherished by me as a very great privilege." In the spring of 1915 Ropes wrote to Professor Bliss Perry of the Harvard English department to invite him "to join in that occasion and make a speech of say twenty minutes to the students … to give them a little thrill of enthusiasm and confidence." As an inducement, Ropes was prepared to offer "a small honorarium."

In the fall of 1916, Dean Ropes wrote to the head janitor of Boston University to make arrangements for "a public reading for the students in the University Extension courses" by Professor Charles Townsend Copeland, who, according to Ropes, "will, I think, also confer with you with regard to lighting and ventilation as he is very particular in this respect." Copeland was a masterful public speaker and reader as well as the star performer in his University Extension courses on literature, and he was punctilious about the proper settings for his performances.

In the spring of 1916, Dean Ropes extended an invitation to Mayor James Michael Curley of Boston to attend the annual reception for University Extension students, pointing out that "the occasion is mainly social" with perhaps "three or four short speeches of about ten minutes." Although Mayor Curley could not attend, he sent a representative from his office and Dean Ropes wrote the mayor to thank him for sending Mr. Walsh, "whose speech full of motivation and humor made the hit of the occasion."

As chairman, Ropes maintained a correspondence with the various organizations that supported the courses taught under the auspices of the Commission on Extension Courses, notably the Lowell Institute and the

Boston Chamber of Commerce. In the spring of 1916 the Carnegie Endowment for International Peace in New York City wrote Ropes to express their willingness to subsidize "courses of instruction in the general subject of International Relations." This proposal was in response to a memorandum on proposed courses in International Law drafted by Ropes on January 26, 1916, which outlined University Extension courses on international law given in 1915 that registered 104 persons and "was a notable success." The memorandum underscored that such courses "are attended by persons of a wide diversity of occupations,—teachers, clerks, lawyers, doctors, business men and women." To make its case the memorandum provided a detailed breakdown of the occupations of all 104 students, concluding "that there is special reason for extending in such a community sound ideas about International Law." Ropes's memorandum proved persuasive and the Carnegie Endowment offered "a subvention of $500."

But Ropes also demonstrated his defense of the Commission's independence in educational matters by refusing to comply with the Carnegie Endowment's expectation that a uniform course and syllabus would be approved by all colleges and universities to whom a subsidy would be granted for courses on international relations. As it turned out the Carnegie Endowment sought uniform quality, not content, for the courses, and Ropes held firm that the instructor of the course be chosen from the faculty of the member institutions of the Commission, with the approval of Carnegie officials. Ropes also stipulated the principle of academic freedom: "Once appointed, however, the instructor would be free to express opinions as in his own class-room and would be expected to treat the matter in the same scientific spirit." From 1916 to 1919 Carnegie awarded Harvard and the Commission a $500 annual grant for the course, but in 1920 the grant ceased when Carnegie chose to use its money to underwrite international relations clubs on campuses to promote "the international mind" among undergraduates in the post-World War I era.

The year 1915 had marked the creation of the National University Extension Association (NUEA), with the first annual meeting held at the University of Wisconsin from March 10 to 15, and forty-four delegates representing twenty-four colleges from nineteen states were in attendance. On June 8, 1915, Professor John H. Pettijohn of Indiana

University, in his capacity as secretary-treasurer of NUEA, wrote Dean Ropes "to urgently solicit the Extension Division of Harvard University to become a member of the National University Extension Association," and closing with the expectation of "an early and favorable reply from the Extension Division of Harvard University." Dean Ropes shared the letter with President Lowell, who, on July 21, 1915, responded personally to Professor Pettijohn. Although he approved of the organization and the cost of membership, he expressed his "regret [over] the determination to print the proceedings of the conference" and questioned "whether it is a wise thing, and wise for us to join it."

Professor Pettijohn replied to President Lowell, agreeing that the publication of the proceedings of educational conferences "has been overdone," but noting that "there was unanimous opinion that the papers read and the discussions conducted at that conference should be put in a compressed form to serve as a manual for extension work throughout the United States." Lowell responded that he was "very sorry that the National University Extension Association has determined to publish papers delivered at its meetings," but he agreed to put to the Harvard Corporation "the question of joining the Association ... at its next meeting," and expressing "no doubt that they will agree to join it."

On September 29, 1915, the secretary to the president, F.W. Hunnewell, wrote Professor Pettijohn to report that President Lowell "brought up before the Corporation ... the question of joining the National University Extension Association. The members of the Corporation all felt that it would be most helpful to the extension work we are trying to do here if we joined the National Association." The membership fee of $25 per year was agreed upon and as of October 1, 1915, Harvard University became one of the original twenty-two institutional charter members of NUEA, a membership it would maintain without interruption.

During the tenure of Dean Ropes, the years 1910 to 1922, his annual reports to the president detailed the slow but steady growth of courses offered by the Commission, from sixteen courses at the outset to a high of thirty-three courses in 1918-19 and down to twenty-nine courses in 1921-22. Although the number of courses nearly doubled, enrollments remained high, with some courses each year enrolling more than 100 students and, in 1915-16, when twenty-four courses were offered seven had enrollments exceeding 100, including George Pierce Baker's *History and Analysis of the Drama* and Josiah Royce's *Introduction to Ethics*. By 1916-17 courses were enrolling more than 200 students, with Charles T. Copeland's courses on English literature invariably with the largest enrollments.

In the early years Ropes provided a financial statement with his annual reports. The budgets were always modest, with the first balance sheet for 1910-11 showing income and expenses of $14,600.78, and the Lowell Institute meeting most of the costs not covered by student fees. The annual report for 1915-16 printed the last financial statement, and the total cost of the program was up to $24,616.44, with the Lowell Institute contributing more than $13,000 and other funding sources, such as the Boston Chamber of Commerce, the Boston School Committee, the Old South Meeting House Association, and the Carnegie Endowment for International Peace all contributing to balance the books.

Each annual report also listed the courses taught, the instructors and their affiliations, the number of students enrolled, and the number of certificates of completion awarded as well as an overall proportion of certificates to the total enrollment. The first year of courses (1910-11) "showed an enrollment of 863 with 395 certificates, for a forty-six percent completion rate." But subsequent years recorded growth in the number of students enrolled to more than 1,500 at times, although the completion rate averaged less than thirty-five percent.

An historic note was struck by Ropes in his annual report for 1912-13 when he wrote in his conclusion that "the degree of Associate of Arts was conferred by Harvard University, at the middle of the year, on John Coulson, and by Radcliffe College, at Commencement, on Ellen Marie Greany. These are the first persons to receive the degree since its establishment in 1910." The following year in his annual report Ropes wrote "Tufts College also conferred the degree of A.M. on Ellen Marie Greany (Teacher, Hugh O'Brien School, Boston), who had received the degree of Associate in Arts from Radcliffe in June 1913." There were no Associate in Arts degrees awarded by Harvard in 1914, but Radcliffe College awarded three to women (two of whom were teachers in Boston). And at Commencement 1915 "the degree of Associate in Arts was conferred on

Harvey Mitchell Anthony and Clarence Harrison DeMar (compositor, University Press, Cambridge)."

During the twelve years of Ropes's term as dean of University Extension he witnessed the awarding of the Associate in Arts degree to a total of thirty-six women and men, thirteen by Harvard College and twenty-three by Radcliffe College. It was a modest record of completion, but it was a sure beginning for the new Harvard and Radcliffe degrees of the Commission on Extension Courses.

The Ropes years were characterized by his close relationship with President Lowell at Harvard and his administrative abilities as chairman of the Commission on Extension Courses. He proved himself an effective spokesman for University Extension both at Harvard and in the Boston area. On the occasion of his fiftieth anniversary Harvard class report in 1939, six years after his death, the classmates of James Hardy Ropes honored him with a memorial entry that highlighted both his work in extension and his Yankee character:

> Interested and active in conveying education through the widest channels, he suggested in 1910, a combination of all the institutions for higher learning in and near Boston, to give the public the benefit of college courses, and until 1922 as Dean of the Department of University Extension and Chairman of the joint committee, he carried out his plan, thus originating and developing the policy of University Extension in this community.[8]

His classmates at Harvard remembered him as "a real Yankee Puritan but with warm and unselfish sympathies. There was in him a rare candor and directness ... an eagerness as well as capacity to be of help to everyone under all circumstances." The last word, appropriately, belonged to President Lowell, who in his tribute to Ropes, concluded that "his work was done, the completed work of a scholar who looked out of his window as well as at his books, and his friends can only repeat, 'Well done, good and faithful servant.'"

ARTHUR F. WHITTEM

Chairman of Commission on
Extension Courses
Director of University Extension
1922–1946

GEORGE W. ADAMS

Chairman of Commission on
Extension Courses
Director of University Extension
1946–1949

University Extension at Steady State under Arthur F. Whittem, Director (1922-46), and George W. Adams, Director (1946-49)

Dean Ropes unknowingly initiated the planning process for his successor as head of University Extension as early as October 22, 1914, when he wrote to President Lowell and recommended that Dr. Arthur Fisher Whittem, instructor in Romance languages, be appointed as a member of the Administrative Board for University Extension for the year 1914-15, a nomination that the President and Fellows of Harvard College voted to approve on November 9, 1914.

Arthur Fisher Whittem was a native Bostonian who prepared for college at English High School, entered Harvard College in 1898, and graduated with a bachelor's degree *magna cum laude* in 1902. He received his master's degree in 1903, his doctorate in 1908, and from 1904 to 1915 was an instructor in Romance languages at Harvard, assistant professor from 1915 to 1922, and associate professor from 1922 until his retirement in 1946. A specialist in the French and Spanish languages and literatures, according to the authors of his memorial minute for the Faculty of Arts and Sciences on March 3, 1959, "he chose to emphasize ... activities so typical of an American academic career, and so essential to the success of our universities: teaching and administration."[1]

For his twenty-fifth anniversary Harvard class report, Whittem wrote: "Since graduation I have been engaged in teaching French and Spanish in Harvard University.... A good deal of my time has been devoted to administrative work of various kinds. In 1915 I became a member of the Administrative Board for Special Students, the Summer

School, and the University Extension. Since 1922 I have been dean of this department—work that offers particular opportunities for extending the influence of the University beyond its walls."[2]

In 1922 Whittem began his tenure as Dean of University Extension, an umbrella title for administrative oversight of three academic departments: the Summer School of Arts and Sciences and of Education, the Commission on Extension Courses, and the Special Student office. He served as secretary of the Administrative Board for Special Students and University Extension, dean of Special Students, and director of University Extension, but he signed his annual reports to the president, on behalf of the academic programs under the rubric of University Extension, "A.F. Whittem, Dean."

He assumed the duties of chairman associated with assembling the annual course program for the Commission on Extension Courses as did his predecessor, James Hardy Ropes. This entailed the financial, logistical, and curricular aspects of the Commission's work. Whittem was responsible for the rental of rooms for Commission classes at Boston University, a duty he discharged faithfully. He also had responsibility for paying Commission instructors, and when faculty stipends had not been raised since the beginning, he took the initiative and wrote President Lowell in 1928 to inquire "if it would be possible to increase the remuneration paid for giving courses under Extension." He proposed increasing from $500 to $600 for a half course, and $1,000 to $1,200 for a full course "if we wish to get good men." The Lowell Institute had been providing a subvention of $17,000 a year, and "this increase would amount to about $3,000 per year."

A week later President Lowell acceded to Whittem's request, stating, "I shall be very glad to increase the compensation of the men giving extension courses to $600 for a half-course and $1,200 for a full course, and to contribute for this purpose $3,000 a year more from the Lowell Institute." Whittem wrote Lowell to thank him. In June he wrote Augustus P. Loring, who was in charge of the finances of the Lowell Institute, the customary annual request "for a contribution from the Lowell Institute funds to our University Extension Courses" in the amount of $18,000. Whittem also mentioned that "Mr. Lowell has agreed to an increase in salaries for next year," which would entail "an increase of at least $3,000 in our budget."

The following year, on June 11, 1930, Loring wrote Dr. Whittem that "a check for $21,000" was enclosed for University Extension courses and "that next year the Institute will make the same contribution, but thereafter the contributions will be $15,000 annually." The next day, Whittem wrote Loring to thank him for the check, but he expressed grave reservations about reducing "expenditures down to $15,000 without seriously impairing the work." He concluded by saying he would "talk the matter over further with Mr. Lowell." The Depression was having an adverse effect on the finances of the Lowell Institute and consequently on University Extension.

On June 16 he wrote President Lowell: "I am much disturbed over the possibility, mentioned by you in conversation and by Mr. Loring in a recent letter, of reducing the contribution from the Lowell Fund to $15,000 in June 1932." He summarized the exchanges of letters he had both with President Lowell and with Mr. Loring, noting that when he asked for the additional $3,000 from the Lowell Institute, Loring "raised no objection at that time." As Dr. Whittem stressed to President Lowell:

> If we can count on only $15,000 from the Fund in 1932 it will mean that we shall have to meet the increase in salary and a further amount of $3,000 by cutting down our courses. This reduction of $6,000 will mean that we shall have to drop about ten of the thirty courses that we are now offering. We have not unduly expanded but have kept about the same number of courses each year. The reduction would mean that we should have to cut down seriously in some departments and have no offering at all in others.

When Whittem received no reassuring response from Lowell, he was understandably distraught about the future course program for the Commission on Extension Courses, not immediately but for the year 1932. On July 15, 1930, he took the liberty of appealing to his predecessor, James Hardy Ropes, at his summer home in Cotuit, where A. Lawrence Lowell also had a home. Whittem enclosed a copy of his June 16 letter to Lowell and even surmised that this financial question was "a matter which Mr. Lowell may have already discussed with you." Apparently the Depression had radically altered the finances of the Lowell Institute, and Loring must have informed the trustee that there had to be a reduction in the subvention available for the Commission courses. After Dr. Whittem wrote to Loring, asking for $21,000, "Mr. Lowell came into [his] office shortly afterward and said he felt that $21,000 was more than he could spare from the Fund." When Whittem explained "that plans were already made for 1931 and instructors engaged," Lowell "agreed to $21,000 from the Fund in June 1931. He said, however, that we should have to cut down to $15,000 in June 1932." Whittem explained his "disappointment" at Lowell's reduction from the Fund "since no objection was raised regarding lack of funds available for instructors when we increased the salaries." The draconian cut to $15,000 "meant cutting a third of the courses."

Whittem asked for Ropes's advice about raising the fee of the Commission's two composition courses to $10 because the cost of assistance was high. He also hoped, indirectly, that Ropes would prevail upon Lowell and return the subvention of the fund to at least the $18,000 level prior to the increase in instructor stipends. He apologized for bothering Ropes with these financial matters, but felt he should know about it and perhaps offer suggestions.

On January 6, 1931, Whittem again wrote Lowell and made reference to his letter of June 16, 1930, to which there obviously had been no reply. He reported that he brought the financial crisis "to the attention of the Administrative Board for University Extension ... and they voted to 'authorize the Director of University Extension to increase the fee in the English Composition courses for 1931-32 from $5.00 to $10.00, these being half-courses running throughout the year.'" Since there was a Lowell Institute policy—President Lowell even referred to it as a "statute"—that in keeping with the will of John Lowell, Jr. the cost of a course should not exceed "the value of two bushels of wheat," no half-course could cost more than $5 and no full course more than $10. The increase of the cost of the half-course composition courses to $10 meant they were no longer eligible for Lowell Institute funding. The administrative board was aware of this consideration when they voted to raise the fee to $10, as Whittem informed Lowell. He also reported that "the Board further requested that I consult you in regard to taking legal advice in the [Harvard] Corporation with reference to the possibility, under terms of the endowment of the Lowell Institute, of raising fees for Extension courses generally, or charging an examination fee to these students who take courses for credit. It was felt that the public might be asked to pay more of their share of the fees," but he cautioned that "there was some hesitation" on the examination fee lest it cause "any hindrance in the taking of the courses for credit."

He closed his letter with yet another appeal "that some way may be found so that it may not be necessary to cut the contribution from the Lowell Lecture Fund to $15,000." If the subvention could go back to $18,000 a year, then the course offerings would not have to be cut "so drastically." The letter must have impressed Lowell because within two days, on January 8, he replied: "I have read your letter with care, and I am ready to allow, after the current year 1930-31, $18,000 a year for the Extension courses." He agreed that "the conferences in the English Composition courses" could be charged an additional $5 "to those who want them." But he was opposed "to make an extra charge for examinations in courses" so as not "to discourage students from taking the examination and obtaining the certificate." This crisis over the Lowell Institute subvention for the Commission on Extension Courses came to a satisfactory conclusion when Dr. Whittem typed up a memorandum of a conversation he had with President Lowell on February 4, 1933. Although registrations had declined because of the Depression, the Commission planned "to continue the same scale of salaries if [they] might count on the same funds from the Lowell Institute ($18,000). Mr. Lowell said by all means to continue the present salary scale."

This episode highlighted the difficulties Dr. Whittem faced in his capacity as chairman of the Commission on Extension Courses to maintain his course program and to ensure the best quality of faculty during the Depression. He proved himself an effective administrator and succeeded in continuing the high academic standards initiated by his predecessor. The financial constraints under which Dr. Whittem operated each year to mount a minimal academic program of thirty courses were evident from the budget he presented for the Commission on Extension Courses for 1934-35. The estimated income came from the Lowell Fund ($18,000), tuition from students ($5,662), and the Old South Meeting House

Association contribution ($650), for a total of $24,312. The expenses included instructor salaries ($18,000), compensation for assistants ($2,800), secretary salary ($900), classroom rentals ($1,050), NUEA dues ($50), plus other incidentals to balance the income. Each year the chairman of the Commission had to operate on such a shoestring budget that was totally dependent on the contribution from the Lowell Institute Fund.

Yet despite the tight budget and the modest instructor salaries, Dr. Whittem succeeded in attracting top faculty from the member institutions of the Commission, with the majority of the teachers recruited from Harvard each year. During Whittem's term as chairman, he succeeded in recruiting such Harvard luminaries—or soon to become luminaries—as Charles T. Copeland, Theodore Spencer, and B.J. Whiting in English literature, William Yandell Elliott and Payson S. Wild Jr. in government, William L. Langer and Oscar Handlin in history, Kenneth B. Murdoch and Perry Miller in American literature, William Ernest Hocking and Raphael Demos in philosophy, John Kenneth Galbraith in economics, and Frank M. Carpenter in zoology, among many others.

The year 1933 would present Whittem and President Lowell with another crisis, this time regarding the Extension degree of Associate in Arts. On February 1 President Lowell sent Whittem an uncharacteristically impassioned memorandum: "What is the proper word for a person from whom his good name has been filched? For thou art that man. Read the enclosed and you will see that the name of Associate in Arts has been degraded, probably beyond recovery, by wicked, thievish, and otherwise disreputable institutions.... I wonder whether we are not compelled to invent a new degree which may retain its dignity until somebody by imitation steals it."

The stimulus for President Lowell's heated response was the introduction of a bill to the state legislature by the junior college of Connecticut "to allow them the right to grant the degree of Associate in Arts—which degree is to be allowed for two years study." There was an assumption that the associate in arts degree was being granted by seventy-five American junior colleges, an assumption that Dr. Whittem, in his reply to President Lowell the next day, very much doubted. But he appreciated that "it would certainly be unfair to holders of our degree to have the Connecticut Junior College or similar institutions grant it for two years work instead of four."

Dr. Whittem went on to inform the president that the associate in arts degree was also under attack "much nearer home by one we have felt was our friend." His reference was to the president of Radcliffe, who "expressed doubt whether Radcliffe wishes to continue granting the degree," since they now wished "to have the AB their only undergraduate degree and ... they object to granting a Radcliffe degree to one who has not spent time in residence there."

A search of the records by the secretary of the Faculty of Arts and Sciences in early February 1933 revealed that between 1913 and 1933 a total of 120 Associate in Arts degrees were conferred by Harvard and Radcliffe: fifty-eight men by Harvard and sixty-two women by Radcliffe. Dr. Whittem, in his capacity as chairman of the Commission, responded to a member of the Connecticut Legislature requesting data on Harvard's associate degree with this information. Since this person had been the one to alert President Lowell about junior colleges adopting the associate in arts degree for two years of work, Whittem concluded his letter: "Since your original letter to Mr. Lowell, he has made inquiries concerning the degree of Associate in Arts and we have been surprised to find that the degree is granted by a number of institutions on only two years of work. This cheapening of the degree had not before come to our attention."

On April 28 President Lowell had written Whittem: "now that Radcliffe has announced that it will not give the degree, it seems to me we had better confer it on women as well as on men," a proposal Whittem endorsed as fair to women candidates and "easier of administration ... [to] center the whole matter here" at Harvard. For his annual report for 1932-33, Dr. Whittem noted that "this is the last time that the degree of Associate in Arts will be conferred, since by a vote of the Faculty on May 8, 1933, the title was changed to Adjunct in Arts. It had been learned that a number of Junior Colleges were conferring the degree of Associate in Arts for only two years of work. It seemed best for us to have a new title since our degree had always stood for at least four years' work. By the same vote the Harvard degree of Adjunct in Arts ... is now open to women as well as men." On June 26, 1933, Dr. Whittem wrote to Mr. James Moyer of the Massachusetts Board of Education as a member of the Commission on Extension Courses that the degree had officially been changed to "Adjunct in Arts (Adj.A.), with no change in the requirements. Radcliffe and Wellesley have voted to no longer grant the degree; it will be given by Harvard and Tufts to both men and women."

By 1933 the original Commission on Extension Courses that Dean Ropes first chaired in 1910 had lost most of its viability as a consortium, but it continued to operate in name to promote the mission of the Lowell Institute through its trustee, the president of Harvard. Enrollments in the Commission's courses were influenced by external economic and political factors. Whereas the number of instructors and courses remained relatively stable during Dr. Whittem's term as chairman, with twenty-one to twenty-six faculty on average each year teaching twenty-eight to thirty courses, enrollments fluctuated from a high of 1,690 students in 1930-31 to a low of 871 in 1934-35 and another low of 808 in 1942-43. Obviously the first low was owing to the Depression and the fact that "more specialized courses were offered instead of the survey courses of the year before." The second low was attributed to World War II: "The average loss in University Extension courses all over the country," according to Whittem's annual report, was 30 percent from the previous year. "The departure of young people for service in the armed forces, demands on the time of older people in various war activities, gas rationing, the dim-out, all contributed." But although the Harvard Summer School closed down during World War II, University Extension continued its operation uninterrupted.

Whittem took a special interest in the composition of the students enrolled in the Commission on Extension Courses. Each year he analyzed the registration forms to ascertain the male-female ratio, the occupational breakdown of the students, and the course completion rate. For the year 1934-35, for example, he was curious to understand the "unusually large" decrease to 871 students, and who the students were who registered. He found that 29 percent were men, that 147 gave no occupation (housewives, unemployed), that forty-eight were students, and that "the remaining 585 were engaged in seventy-one different types of business or professions," the largest numbers being teachers (210), clerks and stenographers (161), nurses (twenty-two), librarians (eighteen), physicians and surgeons (seventeen), managers and foremen (fourteen), and attorneys (thirteen). The course completion rate was nearly 44 percent, which was about average. Judging from the occupations listed, many students had advanced degrees and didn't need undergraduate credit.

Whittem did a follow-up analysis of the seventeen physicians and surgeons to determine their degrees and the Extension courses they enrolled in that year. Four of the doctors were women, at least seven listed Harvard degrees, and they distributed themselves among predominantly humanities courses, such as music analysis and appreciation (four), elementary German (four), elementary Italian (three), and elementary French (two). This breakdown helps to understand the diverse and well-educated audience that Harvard Extension courses attracted over the years, and why the completion rate was always well under 50 percent.

In the spring of 1937 Whittem prepared a report for the visiting committee on University Extension in which he promulgated the conceit "that Harvard in 1936 celebrated its Tercentennial . . . [and] that 1936 also marks the 100th anniversary of University Extension at Harvard" because John Lowell, Jr. in 1836 "by his will established the Lowell Institute from the funds of which University Extension derives the major part of its income." He went on to point out that "the year 1935-36 also closed the first twenty-five years of the Commission on Extension Courses."[3]

His report was designed to present a quarter-century overview and summary of University Extension:

> In these twenty-five years 686 courses have been offered, representing a course registration of 37,939. During this period 144 degrees have been granted to 69 men and 75 women. That it has been possible each year to offer a considerable variety within the limits of these few courses (an average of 27) is perhaps evidenced by the fact that one person has taken courses for 26 consecutive years, while two others have been enrolled for 24.
>
> In most fields certain fundamental courses are given every year or in alteration with more advanced subjects. . . . The total registration [in 1935-36] . . . was 1302.

According to an analysis of the previous year's enrollment forms, the majority of Extension students (56 percent) "had never attended college." A total of eighty-eight occupations were cited, including teachers (191), secretaries and stenographers (166), housewives (118) students (forty-five), and library workers (thirty), "while 153 stated on their registration blanks that they had no occupation," which was interpreted to mean "unemployed" or "housewives." A quarter of the enrollees were men and more than half were taking Extension courses for the first time, indicating "that new groups were constantly learning of the opportunities offered by the Commission." Whittem concluded his report by invoking the spirit and will of John Lowell, Jr. by whose "vision and generosity many people enjoy educational opportunities which might otherwise be denied them."

On December 8, 1937, Dr. Whittem responded to a request from Harvard President James B. Conant for information "regarding Extension activities of the University which are of especial benefit to the public" by sending him a paper he recently composed on Harvard's "Extension work in Greater Boston in the last one hundred years." The paper summarized the educational opportunities provided by University Extension, namely, the Summer School, the Commission on Extension Courses, and the Special Students office. As Whittem explained to the president, "I tried to show that our offering, while small, is unusual in quality and lowness of fees, that Harvard has cooperated with other institutions, and has avoided duplicating the many opportunities already available in Greater Boston." To highlight how distinctive the low fees were for Harvard Extension courses, Whittem pointed out that "the extension courses of Boston University, Boston College, and a number of the institutions which offer courses of college standards and length cost usually at least $10 per semester hour or about $60 per course," whereas at Harvard "the cost of all the courses for the degree [Adj. A.] might be less than $100."[4]

In 1938 Whittem undertook an extensive survey of all the recipients of the Associate in Arts and Adjunct in Arts degrees awarded by Harvard and Radcliffe since 1913. A total of 150 questionnaires were mailed and 91 were returned completed (nine graduates had deceased). The results must have been gratifying to Whittem because fifty-eight respondents (64 percent) indicated that they had done graduate work—a figure significantly higher than graduates of Harvard College—and a total of sixty graduate degrees had been awarded, including thirty Master of Arts, twelve Master of Education, six Doctor of Philosophy, one Doctor of Medicine, one Bachelor of Law and two French degrees. Another fourteen respondents indicated that they were at present candidates for graduate degrees. The various professions of these degree holders numbered forty-three, with educators (forty), lawyers (five), and clergymen (three) among those cited most frequently. Although educators constituted the largest number, the variety of the respondents' occupations was impressive.

One female respondent was especially noteworthy, for she was very well educated with an associate degree from Radcliffe as well as graduate study in Switzerland (University of Lausanne) and at Harvard (Graduate School of Education) before earning her master's degree from Radcliffe College in 1925. Her present occupation was "Head of the History Department, Jamaica Plain High School, Boston." Under the heading of remarks she wrote: "I once heard a professor of a certain college ask a prominent Harvard professor what the Associate in Arts degree stood for. The Harvard professor replied 'Amateur's Attempt.' This was said to be witty, but, nevertheless, shows in what light the degree is held by the faculty of Harvard University."

After leaving the presidency of Harvard in 1933, A. Lawrence Lowell continued his relationship with Dr. Whittem in his capacity as trustee of the Lowell Institute. But it must have been difficult for Whittem as chairman of the Commission on Extension Courses to rely on Lowell's memory of decisions made in earlier years. When Whittem presented the list of Extension courses and the budget for 1937-38, Lowell wrote him on June 7, 1937, that he considered the list of courses "excellent" but questioned "the fee of ten dollars for the two English composition courses. I do not quite see how I am to reconcile this with the limit imposed on me by the Will (and now by statute) not to charge more than five dollars a year." Two days later Whittem painstakingly responded by reminding Lowell that the fee of $5 "dates back to 1931-32," that in 1928 he had agreed to "an increase in the compensation" for Extension instructors, that in 1930 the administrative board for University Extension voted "to authorize the Director of University Extension to increase the fees in English

Composition courses for 1931-32 from $5.00 to $10.00," that in January 1931 Lowell agreed to a charge of "$5 additional for the conferences to those who want them," and that on February 16, 1931, the administrative board had officially voted "to authorize the Director of University Extension to institute a conference fee of $5.00 in English Composition and Advanced English Composition." After summarizing the major correspondence and meetings he had with Lowell over nearly a decade, Whittem concluded his letter by saying he was "glad the list of courses for next year meets with your approval."

When Dr. Whittem sent birthday wishes to Lowell in December 1938, he responded promptly from his home on Marlborough Street in Boston to thank Whittem, but also to express his high regard for University Extension: "you are carrying on one of the things that seem to me worth while—that is the Extension Courses, suggested to me at the very beginning of my career as President by James Ropes, and managed by him for some time. These courses have given a service to the public, through the University and the participating institutions of higher learning about Boston, which seems to me of the utmost importance." It had been five years since he left the presidency of Harvard, but as trustee of the Lowell Institute he still valued the *pro bono publico* services provided by Dr. Whittem and the Commission on Extension Courses. It is also noteworthy that he credited Dean Ropes with the creation of the Commission late in 1909, when Lowell had just assumed the presidency of Harvard.

Arranging courses and generating a budget for the Commission courses each year was a precarious process for Dr. Whittem by his total reliance on the trustee of the Lowell Institute for approval of the faculty and courses as well as the Lowell subvention. But during World War II, when President Conant was away on government business, Paul H. Buck, dean of the Faculty of Arts and Sciences and later provost, also had to give his approval each year to the appointment of Harvard faculty as teachers of Commission courses. On May 21, 1943, Dean Buck wrote a scathing letter to Whittem:

> I must confess that I was quite disturbed to find at the meeting Tuesday when the list of extension courses was presented that not one of the members of the Faculty of Arts and Sciences

listed as giving extension courses had cleared the matter
through my office. This is a direct violation of a Corporation
rule which requires every member of a faculty to secure the permission of his dean before assuming any outside teaching
responsibility. I am at a loss to understand how the situation
would have developed as it has this year when the procedure
was explained so clearly to you last year and when it was further explained that I had been directed by the Corporation
specifically to enforce the rule, that had been somewhat casual-
ly observed in the past.

   The purpose of writing this letter is to advise you that I cannot consider your list as final until the members of the faculty
scheduled to give extension courses have secured the necessary
permission from me. I might say that after studying the list
there are several instances where I am quite dubious whether
permission will be granted.

Duly chastened by this severe reprimand, Whittem for the remainder of
his term as chairman of the Commission and director of University
Extension had to seek approval from Dean Buck prior to approaching
members of the Faculty of Arts and Sciences about teaching evening
courses. On February 20, 1945, he dutifully wrote Dean Buck: "Have you
any objection to my approaching the Harvard men listed below for possible teaching under University Extension in the academic year of 1945-46?"
He concluded his letter by assuring Buck that he will consult him "before
making any definite commitments. It is understood, of course, that in
every case they must apply to you for permission."

   On March 14, 1945, after "a short vacation" delayed his reply, Dean
Buck finally wrote Whittem and rejected four senior Harvard professors
who had taught in University Extension successfully for many years, stating simply that "for one reason or another I should not like to see [them]
teach under University Extension next year, and it is dubious whether I
could give my approval to their doing so." Other names on Whittem's list
Buck also rejected because their appointments would not be renewed. Buck
concluded his letter by stating he had "no objection" to Whittem approaching four others on his list who were primarily foreign language teachers.

Dr. Whittem in April appealed to Dean Buck for permission to approach one of the professors who had not been approved because it was essential to the course program and the professor, who "has always taken a personal interest in the University Extension courses and in the students under him," would be "willing to do it." Since the professor was not listed among the Harvard faculty teaching in Extension the following year, it is evident that Dean Buck did not accede to Whittem's appeal. The exchanges between the chairman of the Commission on Extension Courses and the dean of the Faculty of Arts and Sciences highlight the diminished status of Extension teaching during the final years of Whittem's tenure owing to World War II, the low enrollments, the absence of President Conant from Harvard, and the unsympathetic and dictatorial role of Dean Buck.

The academic year 1942-43 was a low point for University Extension under Dr. Whittem, as his annual report for the year clearly shows. Even the Summer School of Arts and Sciences and of Education, which since 1871 had offered summer courses at Harvard, was "discontinued in the summer of 1943" by vote of the Harvard Corporation. The Commission on Extension Courses, which since 1910 had offered courses in Boston, enrolled only 808 women and men, the lowest enrollment in its history. Whittem noted that "A. Lawrence Lowell, sole trustee of the Lowell Institute for many years, died on January 6, 1943. Ralph Lowell ... succeeded him." Until his death, "A. Lawrence Lowell kept his interest in the various forms of adult education aided by the Lowell Institute." Whittem summarized Lowell's role as president of Harvard in 1910 in establishing the Commission on Extension Courses and the degree of Associate in Arts, now the Adjunct in Arts. "The usefulness of this degree has been proved in the years since its establishment [and] ... more than half of those who have taken the degree have gone on for advanced work and have obtained higher degrees."

Whittem assumed many administrative roles at Harvard, including director of the Summer School, chairman of the committee on admission and chairman of the department of Romance languages twice, but his abiding commitment was to his work in University Extension. According to his faculty memorial minute:

Whittem felt keenly his responsibility for the success of adult education in the Boston area. He took great pride in Harvard's contributions, many of them the results of his own initiative. His reports reveal a particular satisfaction with the number of recipients of the degree of Adjunct in Arts who continued on to higher degrees. In a statement covering the first quarter-century of the degree, he points out that 64 percent of those holding it went on to graduate work—"a higher percentage than is usual in college classes"—and that many of these attained advanced degrees in education, theology, law, medicine, and arts (including six PhD's).

Dr. Whittem was remembered by his Harvard colleagues for his "friendly manner and unfailing courtesy, and the genuine wit that rendered him a master in the art of conversation." But it was his administrative talents that made him indispensable at Harvard in his time: "No problem of administration was too small to receive his full and undivided attention, and it was always obvious that his direct, forceful attack on any problem, minute or weighty, bore the mark of a strong hand and a clear mind." Arthur F. Whittem died on February 13, 1958, at the age of seventy-eight.[5]

The end of World War II marked a return to normalcy in University Extension, as indicated in the annual report for the academic year 1946-47, which was written by Dr. George W. Adams, the successor of Arthur F. Whittem. Registrations in the courses of the Commission rose from 1,243 in 1945-46 to 1,528 in 1946-47 or a total of 1,156 women and men enrolled.

In 1944 a brief report on the Summer School and University Extension had been presented to the Harvard Board of Overseers by a subcommittee of nine members that described the effects of World War II on these academic programs. The Summer School had "discontinued its courses in the arts and sciences last summer" and probably would not reopen "until after the war." University Extension courses, however, "have continued even during the war," but registration was off "about 30 percent from the previous year." The committee looked to England and was impressed by "a remarkable vitalization of adult education" taking place there. They did not prescribe "what Harvard should do in adult education after the war," but they proposed that "conceivably Harvard might find it should undertake a program more ambitious than it has been able to carry out with the Lowell Institute funds."

George Worthington Adams succeeded Arthur Whittem as dean of Special Students and as director of University Extension in 1946, and in 1947 he also assumed the duties of director of the Summer School of Arts and Sciences and of Education. A native of the Midwest, he attended Illinois College in his home town of Jacksonville, Illinois, and thus was the first head of University Extension not to have graduated from Harvard College, but he received his graduate degrees in history from Harvard, a master of arts in 1928 and a doctorate in 1946. His academic career included teaching positions at the Massachusetts Institute of Technology, Harvard and Radcliffe Colleges, MacMurray College for Women, and Lake Forest College, before he returned to Harvard after World War II to become assistant counselor for veterans and secretary of the Graduate School of Arts and Sciences, prior to succeeding Whittem. Paul Buck, provost and dean of the faculty, was instrumental in the appointment of Adams because both were historians of the American Civil War and Buck was impressed by Adams as an academic administrator. In 1946 Adams had completed his two-volume doctoral thesis, "Health and Medicine in the Union Army, 1861-1865," and the thesis was published as a book in 1952 under the title *Doctors in Blue: The Medical History of the Union Army in the Civil War* to critical acclaim. His tenure at Harvard, however, was short-lived because in 1949 he accepted a position at Colorado College as dean of the college and professor of history.

In his second year, on April 9, 1947, Adams undertook a survey of the adjunct in arts recipients to ascertain how many had gone on for graduate work at Harvard, Radcliffe, or other institutions, as did Whittem in 1938. A total of fifty-six questionnaires were sent out, thirty-two were returned completed, and twenty-three respondents reported having done graduate work, including seven at Harvard. Among the graduate degrees received between 1938 and 1947, were eight different designations: AM, MEd, MSS, MS, LLM, DSc, PhD, and STB. The PhD recipient was Leland E. Cunningham, who received his doctorate from Harvard in 1946 and was currently assistant professor of astronomy at the University of California at Berkeley. According to a letter from Whittem to the chairman of the Overseers Visiting Committee on University Extension dated March 30, 1950, six Extension graduates had earned a doctorate and two from Harvard had distinguished themselves in academe:

> The Harvard PhD's include Harry Berman who became Associate Professor of Mineralogy here and had already gone far in a distinguished career when he was killed in an airplane crash in Scotland during the war; and Leland Cunningham, who became an astronomer of note and discovered a new comet while he was at the Harvard Observatory.[6]

During his three-year tenure Adams, as chairman of the Commission on Extension Courses, maintained the twenty-nine or thirty courses offered each year, and he witnessed a heartening increase both in course registrations and number of students enrolled, with the year 1947-48 recording a total of 1,955 registrations, "the highest total enrollment of any year since the Extension program began," and the total number of students reaching 1,562.

The financial situation for Harvard's University Extension courses in 1948-49, the final year of George W. Adams' tenure as director, and the year enrollments reached 1,951 (the second highest enrollment in history), was not significantly different from what Arthur Whittem faced some twenty-five years earlier. Only thirty courses were offered and the fees remained at $5 a course, with conference fees of an additional $5 for the two English composition courses and laboratory fees of $2.50 for the botany, geology, and zoology courses, for a total of $10,675 in tuition and fees collected. The expenses for the year included instructor salaries of $19,600, course assistants $1,257, secretarial staff $2,374, clerical assistants $861, printing and stationery $1,087, postage $239, dues for NUEA $112, classroom rentals at Boston University $315, and other incidentals for a total of $26,761 in expenses. The difference between the tuition and fees collected and the total expenses came from the annual subvention of the Lowell Institute Fund. Clearly the constraints on the courses that could be sponsored and the faculty salaries were the result of the literal interpretation of the will of John Lowell, Jr. in 1836 stipulating that the tuition for the courses sponsored by the Lowell Institute not exceed the value of two bushels of wheat—or $5 a course. The time had not yet come for University Extension at Harvard to "undertake a program more ambitious than it has been able to carry out with the Lowell Institute funds," as the Harvard Overseers Visiting Committee on University Extension had floated, presciently, as an idea in 1944.

On June 13, 1949, Ralph Lowell, as trustee of the Lowell Institute wrote Adams to say that he had just read in the Sunday *Herald* the news that he was going to be dean of Colorado College and to congratulate him "most heartily." On June 17 Adams wrote to Lowell to thank him for his "congratulatory note" and to describe his Harvard experience as "a happy one," especially his relationship with Ralph Lowell. He also used the occasion "to make the customary request for the contribution of eighteen thousand dollars ($18,000) from the Lowell Lecture Fund toward the expenses of our University Extension Courses for the current academic year, 1948-49," and to enclose "a preliminary list of the courses as arranged for 1949-50 with the hope that the offering will appeal to you."

Adams also shared with Lowell the news of his proposed successor:

> Mr. Buck is requesting that Professor Reginald Phelps of Columbia University be appointed to succeed me in my Graduate School appointment and in the Special Student and Extension Office. Professor Phelps should do an excellent job. He is a Harvard summa and PhD and was formerly one of the Assistant Deans in University Hall. After war-time service with the OSS he accepted an appointment at Columbia University in the German Department. If the Overseers see fit to confirm him, I am sure that you, as the Lowell Trustee, and your successor as Chairman of the Visiting Committee will both enjoy working with him.

Adams was scheduled to assume his new duties at Colorado College in September and Phelps succeeded him, as predicted, in the dual role of dean of Special Students and director of University Extension as well as a dean in the graduate school. Phelps wrote the annual report to the provost of the University for the academic year 1948-49 after Adams' departure, concluding with a warm tribute to his predecessor:

It is with great regret that I report the departure from Harvard of Dr. George W. Adams, who served as Dean of Special Students and Director of University Extension from 1946 to 1949, and as Director of the Summer School from 1947 to 1949. His devotion, efficiency, and general expertness in dealing with his many duties, will not soon be forgotten by those who had the privilege of working with him.[7]

REGINALD H. PHELPS

Chairman of Commission on Extension Courses
Director of University Extension
1949–1975

CHAPTER VI

A New Beginning
for University Extension

The Early Years of Reginald H. Phelps,
Director (1949-60)

The thumbnail sketch of Reginald H. Phelps that George W. Adams sent to Ralph Lowell as an introduction to his putative successor as director of University Extension at Harvard was succinct and accurate. Phelps was born in Southwick, Massachusetts, on August 20, 1909, attended high school locally before matriculating at Harvard College and graduating with a bachelor's degree *summa cum laude* in 1930, a master's in 1933, and a doctorate in 1947. He specialized in German literature and history, teaching German and holding administrative posts at Harvard, including assistant dean of Harvard College and secretary to the faculty, from 1931 to 1944, when he served in the Office of Strategic Services in Washington, London, and in Germany at the end of the war. He returned to Harvard to complete his doctoral dissertation on the Weimar Republic in 1947 before moving to Columbia as assistant professor of German for two years, after which he was recalled to Harvard to assume his assorted administrative and teaching duties: director of University Extension, dean of Special Students, associate dean of the Graduate School of Arts and Sciences, and lecturer on German. For his fiftieth anniversary Harvard class report, he wrote that "administration can be boring, and I probably had too much of it, but a good dose of it is valuable." He found his teaching "generally a pleasure," and among all his administrative activities, he summed up: "I found Extension the most rewarding. Partly, this was, no doubt, because I could run a rising program with practically no interference; partly it was the feeling that a second chance in education for people passed by in the normal run of school and college is one of the finest

67

aspects of American education; and partly it was the chance to establish and maintain friendly relations through our program with black people in Boston, who would otherwise not have had any contact with Harvard."[1]

Among the many credentials and experiences Phelps brought to his new post as director of University Extension was his three semesters of teaching in Columbia's School of General Studies between 1947 and 1949. He knew evening students first hand as a teacher, and he valued their ability and motivation to learn, while also understanding "the handicaps for people who had worked all day coming up against stiff intellectual requirements—and of their capacity to overcome those handicaps."

In retrospect, Phelps noted that University Extension at Harvard was *sui generis* because "it was not a faculty, or a school, nor for that matter a Division of Arts and Sciences," and therefore there existed "the opportunity for free wheeling.... And in the absence of tight and constant Departmental control, Extension could to an astonishing degree go its own way." As a native New Englander, Phelps saw in the University Extension program he returned to Harvard to direct the "New England virtues of simplicity, thrift, and concern for quality," virtues he fully appreciated and proceeded to nourish. As he later wrote: "In 1949, on returning to Harvard, I found that the Extension office in Weld Hall consisted of two full-time members—the unforgettable Genevieve Welch as Assistant to the Director, and a secretary.... The size of our budget would have thrown any high-spending educator into fits. The uncomplicated apparatus which dealt with over a thousand individual students, the minimum of paper work, regulations, and chit-chat, the direct contact with the Extension faculty, all look like the state of primitive bliss from which mankind fell, and they demonstrated that the best administration is that which administers least." In surveying Extension at Harvard in 1949, Phelps saw an academic program "of high-quality courses and faculty, a large proportion of students with some previous college training, and very few graduates—slightly more than 200 in forty years—and a nearly unchanging number of enrollments." Phelps was determined to overcome the stasis of University Extension and, as he recalled later, "early in the 1950s I began to see that we could, with careful expansion, reach far more adults without incurring additional expense for Harvard or the Lowell

Institute. For twelve consecutive years, 1951 to 1963, annual enrollments increased, as did in most years the number of courses."[2]

As early as 1937, A. Lawrence Lowell had nominated his cousin Ralph Lowell, as a co-trustee of the Lowell Institute. In the summer of 1938 he announced at the annual meeting at the Boston Athenaeum that he had chosen Ralph as his successor. Since Ralph Lowell was the grandson of John Amory Lowell, the first trustee of the Lowell Institute, it was historically apt that this decision was made to restore the trusteeship to the original Lowell line a century after the creation of the Lowell Institute. Upon the death of A. Lawrence Lowell in January 1943, Ralph Lowell became the new trustee.

He was, like his predecessors, an extraordinary person. He was born in Newton, Massachusetts, on July 23, 1890, and followed family tradition by matriculating at Harvard College in 1908 and graduating *magna cum laude* in 1912. After graduation he and his roommate, the Harvard football quarterback and future Congressman Richard Wigglesworth, embarked on a grand tour similar to that undertaken by John Lowell, Jr. Upon returning to Boston, he went to work as a banker in the investment business and eventually became chairman of the Boston Safe Deposit and Trust Company. In his fiftieth anniversary class report for Harvard he characterized himself as "a Proper Bostonian," devoting himself to his growing family, to his many memberships on civic, academic, and corporate boards, and to Harvard University. As he wrote, "Harvard has always been of paramount interest to me and one of the proudest moments of my life was the day I was elected president of the Board of Overseers, that pride being exceeded only on Commencement Day at our 40th Reunion when I was given an honorary LL.D. by Harvard."[3]

Despite a remarkably busy career that earned him the sobriquet of "Mr. Boston" for his community involvement, Ralph Lowell's abiding interest was in promoting radio and television communications in his native city. As he wrote in his class report:

> The project in which I have been most involved and perhaps which means more to me than any other is the WGBH Educational Foundation. In 1943 I inherited the trusteeship of the Lowell Institute from President A. Lawrence Lowell; and

in 1945 in that capacity as trustee President Conant suggested
to me that I form the Lowell Institute Cooperative
Broadcasting Council for the purpose of presenting educational programs on the air. The council as originally set up consisted of Boston University, Boston College, Harvard University,
Massachusetts Institute of Technology, Northeastern
University, and Tufts College. This grew rapidly until we had
our own FM station and later, on Channel 2, our television station. The membership of the council has since been increased
to include Boston Symphony Orchestra, Brandeis University,
Museum of Fine Arts, Museum of Science, and New England
Conservatory. I am happy to say that our station is now
acknowledged to be the outstanding educational TV and FM
station in the country.

A news release from the Lowell Institute Cooperative Broadcasting
Council on Sunday, December 4, 1949, carried the headline: "Boston
University, Harvard, Northeastern Professors Broadcast Direct from
Classroom in New F-M Experiment." The news release announced that
starting December 5 New Englanders could go to college six nights a week
at 7:30 p.m. without having to leave their homes. They could join college
students in the classroom virtually "and listen at leisure as outstanding
professors lecture on psychology, world history, and economics."

This was an historic event for educational radio courses in the United
States, and the news release from the council highlighted the major role
played by the Lowell Institute in presenting this new venture with the
cooperation of the university members: "three college courses, recorded
right in the classroom on magnetic tape, will be broadcast exclusively by
FM over station WBMS-FM (104.1mc) six evenings a week, Mondays
through Saturdays from 7:30 to 8:00.... This will be the first time complete courses have been brought by radio from our leading universities."

The first course offered on the radio was *Introductory Psychology* by
Professor Peter A. Bertocci of Boston University's College of Liberal Arts:

> Lecturing in a classroom at Harvard University, where his
> course is presented under the Commission on Extension
> Courses, Professor Bertocci will explore with his class the

workings of the human mind, the nervous system, the various
sensations humans are normally capable of experiencing, and a
detailed examination of human needs and drives. Scaling the
problem of heredity versus environment, the listener will move
to a study of the learning process and various theories of learning, and examine the mind in its various functions of thinking,
remembering, and imagining.

The choice of Professor Bertocci to inaugurate the radio courses of the
Lowell Institute Cooperative Broadcasting Council was a wise one
because he was already established as the most popular professor teaching
in the Commission on Extension Courses. Over a thirty year period,
between 1946 and 1976, Bertocci, professor of philosophy at Boston
University, taught a cycle of five popular courses for the Commission on
Extension Courses: *Philosophy of Personality*, *Personality and the Creative
Life*, *Psychology of Personality*, *Philosophy of the Good Life*, and *Introduction
to Psychology*. His enrollments never fell below 100, and frequently reached
300 and even, on occasion, 400 students. His combined student enrollment over the years approached 7,000, surely a record in the annals of
Extension at Harvard. Whereas Charles T. Copeland of Harvard was the
star Extension performer during the early years, Peter A. Bertocci of
Boston University was the most popular teacher during the middle years.

Radio listeners also were invited to join students in a night classroom
at Northeastern University to hear Professor Joseph Skinner of the history department in the College of Liberal Arts lecture on the history of civilization Tuesdays and Fridays: "the listener can hear about Egypt, Greece,
Rome, the Middle Ages, the Renaissance and the growth of Science and
Industrialism in Europe and America, gaining a broad picture of the
meaning and progress of world history from the beginnings of recorded
time to the atomic age of today, with attention to the rise of our present
scientific, cultural, and industrial institutions."

Lastly, to understand one's place in society in economic terms, listeners could tune in on Wednesday and Saturday evenings to hear Professor
Seymour E. Harris of Harvard's economics department deliver his
Economics for the Citizen lecture in his Harvard classroom. The course covered economics "in all its aspects—different systems, government regula-

tions, foreign trade, how an economy operates, economic diseases and social security":

> Using the economic growth of the United States as a spring-board, Dr. Harris traces the effects of population and natural resources on our economy, following up with the nature of various economic systems such as capitalism, socialism, and communism. The class will then study such factors as stability and security, industrial relations, the nature of the market, competition and monopoly, science and economics, and government in modern economic life.

Professor Harris, like Professors Bertocci and Skinner, was a recognized authority in his field and a popular lecturer at Harvard.

This historic initiative in FM radio educational courses was designed by the council "to fulfill the needs of a substantial cross-section of Americans of voting age, as pointed up recently in nationwide surveys. The curriculum to be presented by the universities—psychology, history, and economics—features three of the courses that rate the greatest popularity among those who would like to attend adult education courses, as revealed in a survey by the American Institute of Public Opinion."

This essay into educational radio broadcasting by the council proved successful and the program was expanded in succeeding years. In his capacity as chairman of the Commission on Extension Courses, Dr. Phelps received a letter on September 25, 1951, from Parker Wheatley, director of the Lowell Council, announcing that when WGBH went on the air in early October they would have a radio station available for broadcasting "more University Extension Courses than in the past." The plans of the council were "to have either a regular college course or a University Extension course every afternoon at 3:30 and every night at 7:30, excepting Saturdays and Sundays." Arrangements had already been made to broadcast three University Extension courses: *Introduction to Psychology* by Edwin B. Newman of Harvard University on Tuesdays and Thursdays from 3:30 to 4:20 p.m.; *Our Changing Earth*, a geology course by Professor C. Wroe Wolfe of Boston University on Mondays and Thursdays from 7:30 to 8:20 p.m.; and *The Epic* by Professor John H.

Finley of Harvard University on Saturdays from 3:30 to 4:20 p.m. The expectation for the success of these three courses was "excellent."

Mr. Wheatley had discussed with Ralph Lowell the "ambitious plans" of the council in developing educational radio courses with the Commission on Extension Courses, and Lowell clearly supported these plans wholeheartedly. Dr. Phelps was informed that "there are additional University Extension Courses which we tentatively want to record and possibly broadcast subsequently," such as

> *Economics of Control and Planning*, by Lewis F. Manly, Tufts
> *Masters of Modern Drama*, William B. Van Lennep, Harvard
> *History of American Literature*, K.B. Murdoch, Harvard
> *Expansion of Europe Since* 1815, R.G. Albion, Harvard
> *Problems of Modern Philosophy*, Henry D. Aiken, Harvard
> *International Politics*, Leo Gross, Fletcher School, Tufts

Wheatley closed his letter by hoping that Phelps had acquired an FM radio since they last corresponded because "it is our expectation that there will be some good listening for serious-minded listeners of all kinds over WGBH." He enclosed "several press releases and fact sheets about this new project."

A press release for October 1953 highlighted the WGBH-Commission on Extension Courses nexus and commemorated the third year that offerings from the Commission were broadcast over WGBH. The program plan was that each year there would be educational radio courses in each of the traditional academic triad of the humanities, social sciences, and natural sciences. In the academic year 1953-54 WGBH listeners could hear Professor C. Wroe Wolfe on Mondays lecture on mineralogy, Professor Albert Guerard of Harvard lecture on the modern novel on Tuesdays, Professor Daniel Cheever of Harvard on Wednesdays cover foreign policy, and on Saturdays Professor Richard Frye of Harvard taught *The Civilization of the Middle East* and Professor Everett Burtt of Boston University taught *New England Economic Trends*.

In addition to these lecture courses, three new experimental courses drawn from the Commission on Extension Courses were broadcast over WGBH: Professor William N. Locke of MIT offered *Oral French* (this was the first foreign language course to be broadcast), Professor Genevieve

Birk of Tufts presented the course *English Composition* over the radio for the first time, and Dr. Richard McLanathan of the Museum of Fine Arts had his course *The Arts in America to* 1865 broadcast over the radio as well.

The impetus behind the educational radio courses offered by the Commission on Extension Courses and WGBH was Ralph Lowell, trustee of the Lowell Institute and the creator of the Lowell Institute Cooperative Broadcasting Council. In these dual roles he was able to utilize the resources of the Commission in pioneering a radio outreach to New England in keeping with the spirit of John Lowell, Jr., the founder of the Lowell Institute. The news release about the WGBH and Commission cooperation in 1953 concluded with a salute to John Lowell, Jr. in words that sounded very much like those of Ralph Lowell:

> The broadcasting of several courses by WGBH is something of a symbol of the way in which John Lowell's generous ideas have been followed and adapted with what he might have called the wants and taste of the age. From the Lyceum and the various forms of instruction used in the last century, to modern classrooms, laboratories, lectures and conferences, and FM broadcasts, is after all no great distance, as long as all the methods combine toward the achievement of his purpose of helping in the education of the inhabitants of New England.

The success of educational radio courses was also featured in the annual report Phelps filed at Harvard for the academic year 1953-54. For three successive years Extension courses had been broadcast over WGBH with encouraging results, as Phelps attested:

> The Director mentioned at a meeting of the New England Extension Workshop our method of taping recordings of "live courses" in the classroom for broadcasting; there was some incredulity that this could be effective, in comparison with courses specially devised for the radio; yet our experience shows that this method works, and that there is a radio audience for courses of the college level presented on the radio as they are in the classroom itself. This is encouraging and important and completely in accord with the purpose of our program.

With the advent of television, it was inevitable that Ralph Lowell and the Lowell Institute Cooperative Broadcasting Council would begin to experiment with the educational potential of that mass medium. As Phelps hinted in his annual report: "It is expected that the attempt will be made in 1954-55 to broadcast a few courses by television over the new Lowell Institute station. Here the difficulties and complexities are much greater than with broadcasting courses by radio, but it should be possible for us to advance in this field of adult education also."

Phelps was eager to begin innovating with the Commission curriculum, and his first initiative was to introduce Harvard courses in general education into the evening program in 1950-51: under the natural sciences he added Professor I Bernard Cohen's *The Nature and Growth of the Physical Sciences*, and under the social sciences Professor Samuel H. Beer's *Western Thought and Institutions*. These courses had a combined enrollment of nearly 200 students, which prompted Phelps to observe in his annual report for the year that "the Director believes that courses of this type, with their stress on a general rather than a departmental approach, and their emphasis on aspects of education most significant for the citizen of the twentieth century, are especially well adapted to a program of adult education. It is his hope that such courses will become an increasingly important part of the Extension offerings, at the same time that the traditional types of courses within the various areas are maintained and strengthened."

The following year Phelps announced that the registration in the thirty courses was 2,062, "the largest in the history of these courses," and that Harvard courses in general education were again included: in humanities, *The Epic* by Professor John H. Finley; in natural sciences, *Introduction to Atomic and Nuclear Physics* by Professors I Bernard Cohen and Gerald J. Holton; and in social sciences, *Western Thought and Institutions*, Part II, by Professor Samuel H. Beer. As Phelps noted, "Once again, the enrollment in these courses was large, and the response of students indicates that this type of course has an important place in a program of adult education." A survey revealed that nearly half the students lived in Cambridge or Boston, more than half cited a profession, notably teaching, more than half had more than two years of college, and three quarters enrolled out of general interest.

As Phelps gradually expanded the curriculum and the mode of delivery for courses, the enrollment increased apace, reaching 2,141 registrations and 1,569 students in thirty-three courses in 1952-53. Six people earned the adjunct in arts degree, bringing the total to 228 men and women graduates since 1913. But as Phelps explained in his annual report, the Extension program operated under several financial constraints because of the terms of the founder of the Lowell Institute:

> The increase in our enrollment over the past few years leads to the question of what our ceiling should be. It is, to be sure, gratifying that more people than ever before are taking these courses, yet it is astonishing that despite the growth of the community and the University, and the vast increase in interest in adult education in this country, we have only three or four hundred more registrations than we did thirty years ago!
>
> Expense is, of course, a major factor in keeping our program, and consequently our registration, limited. Hardly half a dozen courses in the past four years have really paid for the cost of instruction by income from tuition, and the program as a whole is possible because of the generosity of the Lowell Institute, which pays more than half the total expenses. In addition, one course in American History is provided for annually by the Mary Hemenway Foundation of the Old South Association in Boston. Last year's schedule of 33 courses brought us our largest enrollment, but it also brought a deficit for the first time, and it emphasizes the fact that a program involving much over 30 courses is at present financially impossible. Tuition fees have been set in accordance with a provision of the will of John Lowell, establishing the fee for a course at approximately the value of two bushels of wheat. The current $5.00 tuition fee for all courses was established in 1948. A half-course under Extension, in fact, cost just as much in 1911 as it does now— something probably unique in contemporary American education. If it should be found possible, on consultation with the Lowell Institute, to raise the tuition fees, the higher income from tuition might enable us not only to increase the course

offerings but also to attempt, for example, more work in laboratory sciences from which the cost of equipment and supplies now excludes us.

On the other hand, it is important to keep the cost of tuition low, for adult education should on principle be in the reach of every qualified person, and its functions are not properly fulfilled if it costs the same or nearly the same as regular college courses.

Many problems of purpose, curriculum, and cost have not been surveyed on a large scale for a long time. Neither have the requirements, or the name itself, of the degree of Adjunct in Arts. The number of courses needed, and the distribution requirements, for this degree are still what they were forty years ago. In those days, the Faculty was unwilling to accept Extension credit toward a Bachelor's degree. It may be time to raise again such questions as these, as part of the broader problem of Harvard's place in adult education. The Director would welcome a review of the organization and goals of Extension courses at Harvard.

It is evident from Phelps's extended discussion of the state of University Extension that the Harvard evening program had been unable to grow significantly in enrollment over the past thirty years because the reliance on the Lowell Institute for funding and the mandated low tuition fees limited the number of courses that could be offered to no more than thirty a year on average. And if there were an increase in courses, and in enrollment, the result was a budget deficit, as the director experienced the preceding year. Phelps wisely called for a comprehensive review by Harvard and by the Lowell Institute to address the "many problems of purpose, curriculum, and cost" as well as "the requirements, or the name itself, of the degree of Adjunct in Arts." Despite his timely and persuasive call for a review, he was unsuccessful, restating in his annual report for the following year that the director "would welcome a re-examination of the purposes and organization of University Extension at Harvard."

Unable to persuade Harvard or the Lowell Institute to change the *modus operandi* of University Extension, Phelps devoted himself during the 1950s to championing the distinctive nature of his academic program while raising enrollments, increasing the number of graduates of the program, and innovating with modes of delivery through radio and television courses. As he wrote in his annual report for 1955-56:

> ... our program is rather that of an evening college than the more miscellaneous and less academic programs that are now generally described as University Extension; and even in the category of evening colleges, we are unusual in having no professional courses, and in limiting ourselves entirely to a liberal arts program in essence like that of an undergraduate college. If, despite this, our program has been able to expand in numbers, it is an indication of the continuing interest of adults in a substantial educational experience, and of the continuing vitality of classroom instruction as a means of teaching adults. Such a program as this offers great possibilities. It gives adults a chance to attain, at minimum cost, an education of quality comparable to that of a good liberal arts college—and this is a point which may become increasingly important as the pressure to enroll in colleges increases. It offers adults who are not concerned with a degree but have retained genuine educational interests the benefit of fine instruction in a university environment. It may enable persons with some training and interest in teaching, who have dropped that career, to refresh their knowledge and skill sufficiently so that they can return to a profession where they are desperately needed. From the Faculty's point of view, Extension courses offer a valuable challenge to the cut-and-dried pedagogic methods, a chance to experiment with effective ways of teaching large courses, especially in the languages, and the possibility of participating in new forms of teaching through radio broadcasts of lectures and, it is expected, through television.

Dr. Phelps fortunately had a strong supporter of University Extension in the office of the dean of the faculty, McGeorge Bundy, who wrote him on October 11, 1956, that he had "read with interest this year's installment on the success story of University Extension," and that he was sending it on to the president with his personal recommendation that it be included in the president's annual report: "It is really very heartening to find this quietly managed part of Harvard's work goes on from strength to strength, and everyone who knows anything about it knows how much is owing to the man who makes it all happen." Surely such communications were welcome motivators to Phelps as he worked at developing "the success story of University Extension."

By 1956-57 enrollment had soared to 2,890, with 2,246 women and men (an increase of nearly 58 percent since Phelps took over as director in 1949-50), and thirty-seven courses in twenty subjects were offered. "There were no courses broadcast over WGBH-FM radio during 1956-57," Phelps reported, but "the most interesting innovation of the year was the presentation of a course in Anthropology: Primitive Technology, by Professor J.O. Brew, as a combined television and classroom course":

> Professor Brew's classroom was the studio of WGBH-TV; here his class sat during his one-hour telecast on Monday evenings, with the opportunity to see him, and his numerous illustrative materials, before them in the flesh, as well as to catch close-ups on either of two monitor television sets at the sides of the room. After the telecasts, the class remained for a half hour as a regular discussion group. The dual purpose of the course was met admirably by Professor Brew, aided by the staff of WGBH-TV, and it is expected that this pioneer venture will be followed by other telecasts of Extension courses.

This historic first educational television course replaced the pioneering efforts in educational radio courses, and the following year two more television courses were sponsored successfully: "Professor C. Wroe Wolfe gave 'Introductory Geology' in the fall term, and Dr. William Van Lennys gave 'Masters of Modern Drama' in the spring term, both presenting the courses at the WGBH Studio, with the first half-hour of each class telecast, followed by an hour of classroom lecture and discussion."

Whereas University Extension courses had since 1910 been full-year courses, Dr. Phelps in 1957-58 persuaded the administrative board to introduce one-term courses, with the approval of the instructor, into the cur-

PROFESSOR J.O. BREW
HARVARD UNIVERSITY (ANTHROPOLOGY)

Professor Brew teaching "Primitive Technology,"
the first presentation of the Commission on Extension Courses
to be telecast by WGBH (1956–57)

riculum, "thus making the program more flexible and particularly widening the opportunity to begin courses at mid-year." This option soon provided a boon to working adults and helped to increase enrollments. In keeping with the traditions of the Lowell Institute's early years, when courses were offered only in Boston, Dr. Phelps did not limit University Extension courses to Harvard buildings in Cambridge, but also "presented courses in Boston at the Museum of Fine Arts, Boston University, and the Old South Meeting House, and in Cambridge at the WGBH Studio."

Toward the end of the decade, Dr. Phelps had persuaded Ralph Lowell as trustee of the Lowell Institute to approve a tuition rate of $5 per term rather than per year, which enabled him to "be able to present a boarder range of middle-group courses" and thereby increase the number of courses offered each year. By 1959 the number of courses had grown to forty-four and the number of individuals went to 3,307 with a registration of 4,538. Phelps saw the growth as a reflection of the overall growth of adult education in the country, especially the special segment of the movement described as "evening college [or] adult education." University Extension was devoted to the liberal arts exclusively, but the curriculum evolved continuously and, in its innovations demonstrated its adaptability, notably in continuing the radio and television formats: "Elementary Russian, given on Channel 2 as a combined television and classroom course, and rebroadcast twice over WGBH-FM, is an example of its adaptability, as is the presentation of courses in Mathematics and Physics."

The year 1959-60 marked both the end of the decade and the fiftieth anniversary of the founding of the Commission on Extension Courses. To commemorate the occasion Dr. Phelps assembled fifty-six courses in twenty-two fields, by far the largest program to date. It enrolled nearly 4,000 students who accounted for more than 5,500 course registrations— all new records.

On August 5, 1959, Phelps sent a news release from the Harvard News Office to the editor of the *Cambridge Chronicle-Sun* announcing that the year marked "the 50th Anniversary of the establishment of the Commission on Extension Courses … [and] during that time the Commission has offered some 1,400 courses and has had nearly 85,000 enrollments." What made the date and the program newsworthy were the facts that after a half century the program would be "the largest since the Commission began and will include for the first time offerings of Television courses for credit." The news release promised that "Bostonians sitting in front of their television sets can take college courses for credit" on WGBH-TV. The new television instructors were two of Harvard's distinguished historians: Robert G. Albion, Gardiner Professor of Oceanic History, and Crane Brinton, McLean Professor of Ancient and Modern History. To take the courses for credit towards the Harvard adjunct in arts degree, viewers simply had to register at Harvard and "pay the usual fee of $5 per term." Professor Albion's two television courses, *The Old Empires* and *The New Imperialism* as well as Professor Brinton's *The Anatomy of Revolutions* course had robust enrollments that indicated strong interest in these subjects and in this new medium of instruction.

Dr. Phelps announced in 1960 that "the most significant development was the creation of the new Extension degree of Bachelor of Arts in Extension Studies, recommended by the Faculty in May and voted by the Governing Boards in June. The degree is conceived specifically for adult students." It was designed to approximate the Bachelor of Arts degree of Harvard College by requiring at least four full-year courses in one area (humanities, social sciences, or natural sciences), competence in a foreign language and in English composition and sixty upper-level credits to provide greater coherence and concentration than the previous elective system afforded students. Phelps explained in his annual report the significance of the new degree:

> This new degree indicates one main purpose of University Extension at Harvard—to provide an adult college education combining independence with a minimum framework of requirements. Historically, the creation of an adult college program was our earliest task; and it is becoming even more important as Americans see increasingly the need of substantial higher education. Equally significant is our second task—to reinvigorate the intellectual lives of the already-educated. People in our profession are not always aware of how dull the once sharp edge of intellect may become through simple disuse, and how little college graduates may know about changes and

advances in education since their own time, or may realize that—particularly through sciences and technology—a new world has been opening that was closed when they were in college. What better device for creating an enlightened citizenry than "continuing education" through Extension?

To celebrate the first half-century of University Extension at Harvard, Dr. Phelps maintained a seemly sense of New England modesty by arranging for an exhibition at Widener Library, sponsoring a brief television program at the beginning of the academic year over WGBH-TV, and hosting at Harvard a joint regional meeting of the Association of University Evening Colleges and the National University Extension Association to address the theme of "Quality in Continuing Education." After little more than a decade as head of University Extension, Dr. Phelps could conclude his annual report for the year 1959-60 on a decidedly upbeat note: "The second half-century has started auspiciously; the national climate is a bracing one for this kind of education, and the country should be the richer for it."

POLARIS UNIVERSITY EXTENSION PROGRAM

Top: U.S.S. *Little Rock*, at that time the flagship
of the United States Sixth Fleet, near Gaeta, Italy.
Bottom: The cover of the Polaris program course listings, 1967.

CHAPTER VII

The Commission on Extension Courses, WGBH-TV, and the US Navy Create Collegiate Programs

From "Polaris University" to PACE (Program for Afloat College Education), (1960-72)

D r. Phelps recorded in his University Extension annual report for the academic year 1960-61 that "the most dramatic innovation of the year was the presentation of television courses for submarine crews of the Polaris Fleet." The genesis of this singular collaboration between Harvard's Extension program and the Navy's Polaris submarine fleet dates from March 4, 1960, when Lieutenant Commander Guy Leonard, chaplain of the US submarine base at New London, Connecticut, came to Cambridge to meet with Phelps and discuss how Harvard might provide collegiate courses for submarine crews, especially the Polaris nuclear submarines that spent months submerged. Chaplain Leonard had attended Harvard Divinity School in 1956 and saw great potential in the educational resources of University Extension for the US Navy.[1]

On March 14, 1960, Dr. Phelps wrote McGeorge Bundy, dean of the Faculty of Arts and Sciences, about his meeting with Chaplain Leonard and outlined how "kinescopes of television courses could easily be presented and repeated" for Navy personnel. He felt that Harvard could find appropriate professors and teaching fellows "to handle classroom instruction and to give examinations entitling students to Extension credit." Since the Navy was very interested in promoting this initiative, and willing to pay WGBH for the kinescopes and to pay the salaries and travel expenses of the teaching fellows, it was irresistible to Phelps not to pursue "this fascinating project of undersea Extension." He concluded his letter to Dean Bundy enthusiastically: "All in all, it's an extraordinarily appealing idea, combining education, patriotism, experiment, and enormous possibilities in relation to teaching the Armed Forces." Within a few days Dean Bundy responded affirmatively: "I see no reason why we should not try this sort of thing, if only to see how it works."[2]

On June 2, 1960, Dr. Phelps prepared a draft memorandum for Dean Bundy to present to the Harvard Corporation for approval of the proposal to present kinescopes of the telecasts of Professor Crane Brinton's *The Anatomy of Revolutions* course to crews on Polaris submarines, supplemented with traditional readings and examinations, for Extension credit. If this experiment proved successful, the Navy was eager to have other collegiate courses prepared "in subjects such as mathematics, of particular importance to the Navy and the crews," also for credit. A few days later Dean Bundy forwarded the memorandum with a strong letter of endorsement to President Pusey, calling for the Harvard Corporation to authorize the plan at its June 15 meeting so that a formal contract with the US Navy could be negotiated. The Corporation approved the plan on June 15, 1960, and the program for the Polaris fleet was officially launched.

On September 2, 1960, a news release was issued jointly by Harvard University, WGBH-TV, and the US Navy announcing that "new members of the Navy's Polaris missile-firing submarine, USS *George Washington*, will have a chance to work for Harvard University credits when the atomic powered submarine goes on operational patrol this fall." This was another historic event for University Extension because the submarine crew members would "be the first students to take a Harvard extension course away from the Boston area."

The news release outlined the details of this first Polaris University course:

> Through films of lectures telecast last spring by Boston's educational station WGBH-TV, the Polaris submariners will study the meaning of modern revolutions. The course, "The Anatomy of Revolutions," was one of the first Harvard extension courses to be given for television credit. The 15 kinescope-

recorded lectures by Crane Brinton, McLean Professor of
Ancient and Modern History at Harvard, will be shown while
the submarines are cruising undersea on patrol.

Assigned reading for the lectures will be available in the submarine's library. When crewmen return to the U.S. Submarine
Base at New London, Connecticut, the students will meet with
a Harvard teaching fellow for classroom instruction. Those
who pass the final examination will receive one-quarter course
credit (approximately two semester hours of college credit).

The news release indicated that "plans are being made for a similar course
in college mathematics and subsequent courses in other fields," thereby
promising that "crew members of other Fleet Ballistic Missile submarines
will have the same opportunity" to participate in a full-fledged Polaris
University.

Predictably, as Phelps wrote President Pusey on June 7, 1961, "the
beginnings of this fascinating educational venture have been very encouraging and . . . the Navy has demonstrated its real interest by the requests
to repeat the courses" for another submarine crew. The new visibility
afforded University Extension by the Navy contracts prompted President
Pusey to ask Dr. Phelps for a detailed accounting of his financial situation,
to which he responded with a five-page letter on June 29, 1961, outlining
Extension's origins under President Lowell in 1910 and its close ties with
the Lowell Institute over the years. The approval of Ralph Lowell in 1958
"to a tuition fee of $5 per term" and "to additional fees for credit students
and for registration" enabled Phelps to expand the course offerings and to
raise teaching stipends to $900 for a half course. The Navy contracts cov-
ered the costs of expenses at WGBH-TV, the kinescopes, and the instructional and related costs and overhead to Harvard. Phelps could take a New
Englander's pride in the financial picture he presented to the president:
"To summarize: Extension has so far lifted itself by its financial boot-
straps, and provided a growing and improving program under its own
power." Admittedly, Extension was still "a modest program, compared, say,
with Columbia's School of General Studies," but Phelps resisted the
temptation to expand and to cut ties with the Lowell Institute "for reasons
of sentiment and tradition," preferring to offer "excellent instruction at a

really low cost—and to keep our strange but useful Commission structure, and to grow organically."

The following spring Dr. Phelps met with President Pusey to discuss a proposed two-year collegiate curriculum of television courses by the Commission on Extension Courses for the US Navy. On April 20, 1962, he wrote the president to confirm his understanding that Harvard approved of this plan, "provided it is financed fully by the Navy and by income from tuition; and that you are also willing for me to negotiate for release time for faculty members to prepare these courses." A week later the president responded by letter approving "the proposed United States Navy two-year curriculum of television courses," and wishing Phelps success "in finding the men to prepare the courses."

Phelps had drafted a detailed memorandum on the Navy's two-year curriculum of televised courses for the Polaris Fleet. It consisted of courses in expository English, mathematics, chemistry, and physics in the first year; courses in engineering sciences and metallurgy, mathematics and physics, and foreign language or electives in the second year, with TV instruction supplemented by classroom and laboratory instruction. WGBH would prepare five to six television courses a year, with the Navy covering the costs of production and faculty released time. Upon completion of the two-year curriculum, Navy personnel would receive a Harvard certificate of completion, as would other students who completed a similar two-year science curriculum. In time this program would be called the Polaris University Extension Program.[3]

The Polaris University Extension Program proved so successful, and so many kinescopes of the televised courses were produced for the Navy by WGBH-TV, that on October 7, 1966, the National Center for School and College Television (NCSCT) wrote to Dr. Phelps expressing its "general interest in distributing the television units" and outlining its qualifications for doing so, with a willingness to "bear all costs of catalogs, promotion, preview, duplication and distribution" as well as a readiness to pay "the Commission fifteen percent of the total user fees received from the rental and lease of lessons." Since the Navy had agreed to allow Harvard and WGBH to arrange for an expanded use of the films educationally and none of the films made had been copyrighted, the dean of the Faculty of

Arts and Sciences, Franklin L. Ford, wrote President Pusey on November 14, 1966, that he recommended, on behalf of the administrative board for University Extension, that the board be authorized to pursue "the expanded use of the Polaris filmed courses by governmental and nongovernmental bodies" generally, and also to contract "with such an organization as the National Center for School and College Television for distribution of the films" specifically. (NCSCT was a US Office of Education NDEA project of the Indiana University Foundation with offices in Bloomington, Indiana.) The Harvard Corporation at its meeting on December 19, 1966, voted its agreement in principle with the proposal, and the terms were set forth in the contract with NCSCT that ensured "to protect the interests of WGBH, of the Faculty members who prepared the films, and of the Commission on Extension Courses."

In the January 1967 issue of the Navy monthly periodical *All Hands*, the editor, John A. Oudine, wrote a feature article titled "Ivy League On and Under the Sea: The Story of PACE and Polaris University," a history of the collaboration between the Commission on Extension Courses and the US Navy in creating the Polaris University filmed courses with the technical support of WGBH-TV as well as the PACE Program (Program for Afloat College Education) that succeeded it. As the editor pointed out, it was the initial success of the Polaris University Program for the first five years that "drew such critical praise that the Secretary of the Navy's Task Force on retention recommended its expansion to the surface ships of the Navy," hence the creation of the PACE Pilot Program "to find out whether the concept could be adapted as successfully to the diverse types of surface ships (with many home ports) as it had worked with *Polaris* submarines."

To accommodate the PACE Program's need for home ports across the United States, other universities joined Harvard in providing instruction. Harvard was designated to coordinate the academic instruction at the ports of New London, Boston, and Newport. The University of South Carolina handled instruction at the naval installation at Charleston. On the West Coast the San Diego area became the responsibility of San Diego State College. And in the anticipation of greater growth of the PACE Program, "other universities at or near Navy installations will be approached as participants," notably the University of Hawaii for the naval base at Pearl Harbor.

Pilot programs had already been carried out successfully in two surface ships, the guided missile cruiser USS *Boston* in the Atlantic Fleet at Boston, and the aircraft carrier USS *Constellation* from the Pacific Fleet at San Diego. Five more surface ships were scheduled to participate in the PACE Program in the fall of 1967: the destroyer tender *Cascade* in Newport, R.I., and the remaining four in San Diego—the guided missile cruisers USS *Galveston* and *Canberra*, the guided missile frigate *Mahan*, and the destroyer tender *Piedmont*.

The article singled out for praise the pivotal role played by Reginald H. Phelps as director of University Extension at Harvard. According to a Navy status report, without his perceptive vision of the program's educational potential, "Polaris University would never have progressed from experiment and trial to its present status of the most imaginative general education program in the Department of Defense."

The following year, in 1967-68, the Commission on Extension Courses printed a mini-catalogue, "The PACE Program," in recognition of the availability of the entire two-year collegiate curriculum and the growing popularity of the program in the Navy. By this time Polaris University had been superseded by PACE and submarines were supplemented by surface ships. The distinctive educational components of the PACE Program were outlined by Phelps in the catalogue: "since the films can be viewed, texts read, and problems worked at sea, and live classroom instruction provided at the bases—New London, Newport, Boston, and overseas—the program has proved to be an effective and practical means of education for hundreds of Navy men." The catalogue listed the complete curriculum as well as the individual courses, with detailed course descriptions, recommended prerequisites, and the name of the course film lecturer. The final page provided a roll call of all faculty members who prepared kinescopes for the PACE Program with their university affiliations as members of the Commission on Extension Courses. All the member institutions of the Commission were represented, but as expected Harvard had the largest number of faculty involved.[4]

In the spring of 1968 a news release from Harvard announced that a film produced by WGBH-TV for the Commission on Extension Courses as a college-level course, *Principles of Behavior,* by Professor Bernard W. Harleston for the US Navy had received a special mention award in the Japan Prize competition, marking the first time a US entry had been a winner in this international contest sponsored by the Japan Broadcasting Company to further the role of educational broadcasting.

In his annual reports on University Extension during the 1960s, Dr. Phelps recorded the progress of the Polaris University program, which he first announced in 1960-61. By 1963-65 he could report "notable advances in the plan for instruction of the Polaris fleet," especially the operation of the two-year certificate program, "based almost wholly on filmed television courses combined with classroom sessions in New London." By this time seventeen courses had been prepared by WGBH-TV for the Polaris University: five in mathematics, four in chemistry, three in physics, and one each in metallurgy, American literature, critical reading, world history, and Professor Brinton's original *Study of Revolutions.* Another four courses were in preparation, and more would be offered the following year, in anticipation of having a total of thirty-two courses available within a few years.

One educational benefit of the filmed courses for the Polaris program was that they could also be made available for University Extension students studying in Cambridge. In 1963-64 six courses were telecast by WGBH-TV and four of them "were originated for the Polaris program." In addition to these televised courses, three courses were offered to Navy crewmen: *Expository English* on the submarine *Robert E. Lee*, *Introduction to Modern Algebra* on the *George Washington*, and *Chemistry I: Basic Principles* on five other Polaris submarines, for a combined enrollment of 90 submariners. The following year the number of courses was increased to seven and total enrollments soared to 440. The eight courses broadcast over WGBH-TV all originated as courses prepared for the Navy.

By 1965 Dr. Phelps could announce that the Navy program for the Polaris fleet was in the initial stages of expansion to include surface ships, with the crew of the USS *Boston* being offered four courses during the summer and fall. In his annual report for 1965-66, Phelps could draw a distinction between submarine and surface crew enrollments, as 276 were from Polaris submariners in New London and another 144 were members of the USS *Boston* crew. He cited this inclusion of filmed courses on a surface ship as "an important example of the use by other parts of the Navy of the courses originally prepared for the Polaris fleet. Nine different courses received a total of 13 presentations on the USS *Boston*; English Composition, World History, Mathematics, Physics, and Computer Science were the subjects offered." The same practice of showing the filmed courses at sea and then providing classroom instruction and final examinations on shore was employed successfully. Subsidies from the Navy permitted Phelps to dispatch five instructors to the Mediterranean to teach crewmen onboard ship as part of the PACE Program of the Navy.

The following year he could record in his annual report that registrations in the Navy programs increased dramatically to 803, with 529 enrollments from Polaris crews in New London and 274 from surface ships in Newport. As he summarized:

> The program conducted for the Navy—originally for the Polaris fleet, and renamed this year the PACE program (Program for Afloat College Education) as it has been expanded to surface ships—continues to grow and to prove its effectiveness. Following the pattern begun years ago for television courses here, filmed lectures are viewed while crews are on patrol, and are supplemented by regular classroom instruction at New London, Newport, and Boston; occasionally, and most spectacularly, by instruction on board ship or at bases abroad, with members of the teaching staff flown to the Mediterranean and transported to the deck of the U.S.S. "Little Rock" during the spring crisis in the Middle East.

A feature story titled "Hub Educators Educated, Profs Hit Carrier in Search of Their Class" appeared in the July 30, 1967 edition of the *Boston Sunday Globe*. It described the adventures of five Extension faculty members who "arrived in Italy at the height of the mid-East drama [the Arab-Israeli War], expecting to find classes of Navy sailors at the Sixth Fleet port of Gaeta." The Harvard team had been sent from Boston to rendezvous on the flagship USS *Little Rock* to teach sailors as part of PACE (Program for Afloat College Education). The team of faculty consisted of "Robert G. Albion, professor of history *Emeritus*; Max R. Hall, editor for the Harvard University Press and a writing instructor in extension courses; Howard L. Kramer, Harvard physics instructor; Carroll F. Miles, professor of government at Simmons College, and Francis Scheid, professor of mathematics at Boston University."

When the University Extension faculty arrived in Gaeta, the harbor was empty and the cruiser *Little Rock* was at sea under emergency war orders. The teachers waited three days in a villa, expecting to be sent home, but the Navy sent a plane to fly them to Athens and then to the Mediterranean over the island of Crete, finally making a tail hook and cable landing on the carrier *America*. They were then ferried to the fleet oiler USS *Truckee* by helicopter and finally to the cruiser *Little Rock* by bosn's chair over the choppy waves. The band of the *Little Rock* played "High Above Cayuga's Waters" as the Harvard team was chaired across the surging seas and they were met by the commander of the Sixth Fleet, Admiral William I. Martin, who awarded each intrepid teacher a certificate of membership in the "Order of the Salty Highliner" for their perilous passage.

"The educators held review sessions in physics, mathematics, world history, American history, and English for some 60 sailors who themselves were making history on the fringe of the war." Final examinations were administered, and the faculty completed its work and returned to the United States as word was received of hostilities erupting in the Middle East. The article concluded: "Five Harvard professors in search of a class returned to the US—one by ship—with a new chapter added to their self-education. Admiration for the US Navy was intense."

For the remainder of the 1960s Phelps reported regularly on the expansion of the PACE Program, which by 1968 had all forty planned filmed courses completed, constituting the equivalent of two years of college work. The number of surface ships joining the PACE Program increased sharply as registrations approached 1,000 in a year and courses offered rose into the seventies. Meanwhile the reach of the PACE Program extended as far as Antarctica when five instructors, including Professor Frank Friedel of the Harvard history department, were flown by the Navy to McMurdo Base to teach several courses in February of 1968. There were regular requests in writing in the late 1960s from the director of University Extension to the dean of the Faculty of Arts and Sciences for approval of payment to faculty members for teaching their courses under the PACE Program on location, such as on the *USS Boston* in port in Marseilles or in Boston or in Naples.

By 1970, however, enrollment in the PACE Program dropped precipitously from 959 the previous year to a low of 404. The reasons cited for this decline were "reductions in Navy personnel, and uncertainties and transfers affecting men still on duty." In 1970-71 Phelps could cite "a gratifying increase" in enrollments as the figure rose to 681, but "the Director and the Navy are aware that many of the films prepared for these courses are beginning to date."

The note of optimism struck the year before was unfortunately a false one because the annual report for University Extension filed by Dr. Phelps in 1971-72 contained the following message:

> With regret, the Director reports that our connection with the PACE program is coming to an end. Since the first attempts, in 1960, to combine filmed or videotaped lectures available during patrols with live instruction on shore, Extension has had 5,674 registrations by Navy students, representing about 4,500 individuals, and has offered 428 presentations of courses. Surface ships based at Newport were added in 1965. The concept was sensible. Originally it was developed for the Polaris fleet, with a set of filmed courses equivalent to two years of college-level work being planned in 1962. The films were completed in 1968. The peak year was 1967-68, with 992 registrations. Many students have used PACE as an introduction to college work, and have found the experience valuable in itself, and helpful when applying to college after leaving the Navy. There might, and should, have been larger enrollments, but the "turbulence" arising from frequent transfers and discharges of personnel, the difficulties of scheduling, and undoubtedly the heavy emphasis on science and mathematics—which seemed appropriate when the program was planned—combined to prevent most students from going on to the more advanced courses prepared for PACE. Still, the figures

above give evidence of its quality and effectiveness. Other institutions have participated in it, and all of the more than thirty courses created for PACE have been used, several of them repeatedly, in the Cambridge/Boston program, through telecasts on Channels 2 and 44. Presumably a few course presentations begun in 1971-72 will be completed this year, and final figures for PACE will thus appear in next year's report.

As promised, Phelps in his annual report the following year offered a valedictory for the PACE Program:

> We have had 5,903 registrations by Navy students, for 443 presentations of courses, with Extension instructors traveling not only to New London and Newport but to the Mediterranean and Antarctica—doubtless the farthest range that Harvard education has had on this earth! The quality of the filmed courses prepared for the program with the Navy's support was high. All have been used, and some are still being used, in the home program, through telecasts on Channels 2 and 44; and it is pleasant to report that a survey of undergraduate credit course television tapes, issued in September, 1973, shows on the basis of replies from the member institutions of the National University Extension Association and the Land Grant universities that the PACE program is by far the largest and most complete of any there recorded.

Nearly a decade after his retirement from Harvard, Dr. Phelps was interviewed about his many eventful years as director of University Extension. He reflected on the eight years that Harvard played a lead role in the Polaris University and PACE Programs, noting that there were "close to 6,000 registrations" during that period, yet only one Navy seaman came to Harvard, graduating with a *magna* in economics and then going on for an MBA at the Harvard Business School. Phelps estimated that the forty televised courses prepared by WGBH-TV and the Commission on Extension Courses constituted "the biggest television program in higher education in the 1960s."

When asked why the PACE Program ended, Dr. Phelps responded that "the Navy decided it was costing too much and didn't have big enrollments." The Navy had anticipated mass enrollments, but the turbulence of the times, notably the Vietnam War, had a deleterious effect on seamen having the time to study for their courses or even to sign up for them in the first place. The Navy did a cost-benefit analysis of the PACE Program and decided that the cost per student did not justify its continuation. The original design of a curriculum heavily weighted to science and technology resulted in low enrollments, whereas courses in the social sciences and humanities proved much more popular with seamen. For Phelps it was disappointing that more sailors did not avail themselves of the PACE Program, and that no one completed the equivalent of two years of collegiate work to qualify for the certificate, but, he added, "it was not a flop by any means" because of the pioneering role played by University Extension in educational television.[5]

The prime mover behind University Extension's essay into educational radio and especially educational television was Ralph Lowell, who created the Lowell Institute Cooperative Broadcasting Council as an electronic counterpart to his cousin A. Lawrence Lowell's creation, with Dean James Hardy Ropes, of the Commission on Extension Courses, in 1910. When Ralph Lowell died on May 15, 1978, at the age of eighty-seven, his obituary in the *Boston Globe* the following day highlighted his distinguished career and his many honors, but the headline rightly recognized him as the founder of WGBH-TV. Whereas all the Lowells who had served as trustees of the Lowell Institute "made some advance in adult education," it was Ralph Lowell, who, "in taking to the airwaves, made, of course, the biggest contribution of them all. Acting on Conant's suggestion, he formed the Broadcasting Council. Originally it consisted of Boston University, Boston College, Harvard University, Massachusetts Institute of Technology, Northeastern University, and Tufts College. Later the Boston Symphony Orchestra, Brandeis University, the Museum of Fine Arts, the Museum of Science, and the New England Conservatory were added to the ranks. In 1952, WGBH-FM took to the air, and two years later WGBH, better known as Channel 2, followed suit. These are perhaps the greatest single contributions this very Proper Bostonian of vision and dedication made to the community."

HARVARD UNIVERSITY UNDER SIEGE, 1969

CHAPTER VIII

University Extension's Community Outreach in a Time of Crisis (1968-75)

The *sui generis* nature of Harvard's University Extension program was becoming increasingly evident in the early 1960s as other extension programs in the United States were forced to modify their liberal arts curricula. The dean of University Extension at UCLA, Paul H. Sheats, wrote Dr. Phelps on January 31, 1963: "I do think that your willingness to give liberal arts education top priority in your extension offerings is certainly quite defensible at Harvard, but I can tell you from long experience that it is not practicable in an institution such as ours. Not only do we have the strong pressure from professional groups such as the Bar Association and the Medical Association to do postgraduate courses, but ... there is increasing pressure to allocate lower division extension courses to the junior colleges and upper division degree credit work to the state colleges." Dr. Phelps replied to his extension colleague a week later: "I guess that we are in a favored position as far as pressure for offerings outside our special field is concerned. We have had astonishingly little pressure from any groups ... to set up special programs for them. Perhaps the reason for this is that we make it very clear that we don't intend to offer anything excepting the Liberal Arts." Little did Phelps envision the disrupting elements of the late 1960s that would force even Harvard University Extension to bow to the demands, both within and without the University, to rethink this exclusive commitment to the liberal arts.

The late 1960s were a time of social unrest and political upheaval across the United States, and the city of Boston was no exception, especially the Roxbury community. Since 1968 the director of Harvard University Extension had been meeting with various community organizations in

Roxbury concerned with adult education opportunities, "but two major proposals—setting up classes in Roxbury to accompany an expanded program of televised courses, and using the Commission on Extension Courses as a framework for a consortium of Greater Boston institutions to offer courses in the Boston Model Cities Area—[had] ... not been realized." The one positive outcome was a specially designed workshop course by Professor Peter H. Elbow of the Massachusetts Institute of Technology and the Commission, *Critical Writing Skills,* for Roxbury.

In February of 1969, a major Harvard University committee, appointed by President Nathan M. Pusey and chaired by Professor James Q. Wilson of the government department, filed a report, "The University and the City," as a collective and informed attempt by the University to cope with the growing tensions among Harvard's student body, faculty, and the community at large. The Wilson committee looked to University Extension as a significant resource of the University to contribute to potential solutions of Harvard's relations with the community:

> The Extension program is clearly one of the most important community-serving activities undertaken by Harvard. Almost all the courses, however, are offered in or near the Harvard Yard, and relatively few are addressed to current "urban" issues. We would urge the Director of University Extension to review the structure, offerings, and location of his program to see what opportunities may exist for broadening the scope of the courses and improving the access of more distant parts of the community to those courses. Large segments of the Boston-Cambridge community may be unaware of Extension offerings, or may feel slightly intimidated by the prospect of entering the Yard to enroll.

It recommended that University Extension not limit itself to the traditional liberal arts courses, but to broaden the scope of its curriculum by sponsoring courses and programs "more responsive to the needs and interests of the local population," such as urban politics and government, urban economics, race relations, and urban history, as well as improving the means of "access of more distant parts of the community" to such applied courses. It suggested that the Commission on Extension Courses, which had been operating in name only since the 1920s, be reactivated by returning to the original historic consortium of local universities to address community issues and needs. And it urged that Extension courses be offered away from Harvard Yard in points around the city.[1]

Given the success of the Polaris University and PACE initiatives with the Navy, Phelps proposed to Richard McCann of the Office of Education in Boston that some of the filmed Navy courses could, for a modest sum, be offered in Roxbury. McCann supported this proposal and suggested that he apply for a small project grant to meet the costs of broadcasting four televised courses, the salaries of instructors, and the administration of the project, including an evaluation of the results. Dr. Phelps drafted "A Study of the Effectiveness of College-Level Filmed or Televised Courses, with Supplementary Classroom Instruction in an Urban Area," which was designed to present some select filmed college-level courses from the PACE inventory for presentation in the Roxbury area. The dean of the faculty approved the proposal and endorsed the project on June 4, 1969.

In his annual report for 1969-70, Dr. Phelps drew attention to the course listings under such rubrics as Urban Studies, Roxbury program, and Jamaica Plain project to highlight that University Extension had "done something to meet the new needs for courses directly pertinent to the community," specifically that "contacts with Roxbury continued; an interesting experimental workshop was conducted by Professor Belensky [Boston College] in Jamaica Plain [on Community Youth Workers]; and several courses on urban problems were added," yet Phelps added a major caveat:

> But it would be absurd to regard this as sufficient. Extension might, and should, do an enormous amount to help the University and the community to improve their somewhat mixed relations. The Director suggests that this is a task for which more manpower and more money are needed than we can now furnish, and that the task had better be done well and fast.

The concern of Dr. Phelps about the magnitude of the community's needs and the limited resources of University Extension was raised again in the following year's annual report. A review of the many programs and projects initiated by Harvard only "heightened this concern":

> ... we set up, in cooperation with the School of Education and the Summer School, a TTT program (Training Teachers of Teachers) enabling students, thus far all from Roxbury, to combine pursuit of an A.B. degree with fulfillment of state requirements for teacher certification. We offered three courses in the Model Cities Cambridge neighborhood, and in the spring we provided instruction and credit for inmates at the House of Correction on Deer Island in three of our televised courses. The Roxbury Program, begun in 1968-69, continued satisfactorily. Other developments over the summer, well outside our traditional framework, will be discussed in next year's report. But in the meantime, the Director's view should be repeated here—as it has been to the appropriate Harvard officials and to the Visiting Committee—that the structure of Extension as a function of the Faculty of Arts and Sciences, essentially a liberal arts evening college, is not adequate for the role it should play in the present complex educational world of the metropolis. Our charter is too narrow, our staff too small, we cannot even be aware, under these circumstances, of what we should and could be doing. President Bok has appointed a committee to review the structure and purpose of Extension, which, at the time of writing in early October 1971, is heavily engaged in this necessary task.

It was abundantly evident to Dr. Phelps that University Extension was being stretched programmatically from a traditional liberal arts evening college into a community vocational arm of the University, with expanded course offerings under the rubrics of Urban Studies, enrolling 321 students, Roxbury program enrolling twenty-eight students, Cambridge Model Cities program enrolling fifty-four students, TTT program (Training Teachers of Teachers) enrolling forty-six students, and even Radcliffe Seminars, devoted to community outreach in such courses as *Child Care, Alternative Schools, Urban-Suburban Boston—A Sociological*

Portrait of a Metropolis, and *Child Development*, all enrolling a total of seventy-six students. With nearly 400 registrations in these community-oriented courses supplemented by another 266 registrations in Afro-American studies and American-Indian studies, Dr. Phelps expressed his concern over the direction University Extension was taking away from its liberal arts core competency.

As the PACE Program was coming to an end in 1972, the course program for University Extension was continuing to show a split between its traditional liberal arts program, which reportedly was doing well, and the "notable increase in courses of direct community concern, e.g., on Population Biology, Day Care, and the Portuguese Community." Dr. Phelps noted an expansion of the Roxbury Program to six courses. The Training Teachers of Teachers (TTT) Program, "enrolling students to work toward state educational certification while they are degree candidates," was effective and in its second year of operation. The Cambridge Model Cities Program featured a successful course in elementary Spanish. The Cambridge Economics Opportunities Committee (CEOC), enabling "employees in public service positions to work toward a degree while improving their professional skills," joined with University Extension to provide such courses by Harvard faculty as *Language and Communication*, *Human Growth and Development*, and *Health and Nutrition* for more than 100 Cambridge city staff. The teachers of North Providence, R.I., were provided with a special course, *Black Experience in America*, by a Harvard faculty member. All these initiatives led Dr. Phelps to conclude that "we are moving into different kinds of programs ... " but, whereas the traditional liberal arts courses were "of high quality," the newly developed courses "directly concerned with the community [were] somewhat different in nature from the others." Although some programs "may well be models for combining liberal arts with training toward a profession," Phelps was decidedly uneasy about other aspects of the community programs academically, so much so that he called for "a thorough review of our part in continuing education at Harvard; of the desirability of a general, if loose, University organization to deal with this area; and of the possibility of developing the Commission on Extension Courses into an active consortium for higher education in Boston." This was recommended by the Wilson Committee proposal to return to the original founding of the Commission by President Lowell and Dean Ropes in 1910 to draw upon the combined resources of the major colleges and universities in Boston to form a consortium for providing adult education to the public locally.

Unfortunately, the Commission had already lost some of its vitality by the time Dean Ropes retired as chairman in 1922, and when A. Lawrence Lowell left the presidency of Harvard in 1933, it functioned mainly as an umbrella for a course program that was run by University Extension at Harvard. Dr. Phelps maintained the "tradition" of the Commission on Extension Courses in his role as chairman, but it was his role as director of University Extension that was his primary responsibility. Despite his call for reactivating the Commission in 1972, it was no longer a reasonable possibility, given the different directions that the other member institutions had taken in the intervening years.

As the annual reports filed by Dr. Phelps on behalf of University Extension in the early 1970s make clear, he and the administrative board were looking for a resolution to the growing split between the historic liberal arts programs and the pressures to introduce more vocational and applied courses and programs. In his annual report for 1973-74, he discussed a review he had undertaken of the curriculum in recent years, only to find that "the direction appears to be toward 'practical' courses and away from the traditional literary and historical fields." As he correctly surmised, this shift had occurred as a result of University Extension's "efforts to reach a broader population," and the most successful approaches to new groups, "particularly minorities," had been programs like Training Teachers of Teachers (TTT) and the Cambridge Economic Opportunity Committee (CEOC), which addressed the needs of public schools and public services. At the time of his writing the annual report in 1974, Dr. Phelps and the administrative board were at work on developing an expanded CEOC program "concentrating on health services." This shift in the curriculum was by this time regarded as a necessary move by University Extension to address career opportunities for a new class of students, thereby "realizing an ideal of broad educational opportunity for a great many people to whom traditional academic approaches do not appeal." But University Extension could not perform this added role by itself; it necessitated "participation by other Harvard faculties," notably the Graduate School of Education, which played a major role in the TTT program designed to enable black teachers in Roxbury to get credentials through University Extension.

The course listings for the year showed significant increases in rubrics and enrollments for community-related courses offered by University Extension: Urban Studies with 162 enrollments; Roxbury-Cambridge Program with 143 enrollments; C.E.O.C. Program with 177 enrollments; Cambridge Model Cities with thirty-five enrollments; plus related courses among the Radcliffe Seminars, Cambridge Learning Center, Portuguese, English for Foreign Students, and American-Indian Studies.

For his final annual report as director of University Extension in 1975, Dr. Phelps cast a backward glance at his twenty-six years in office, acknowledging that "with community needs in mind, Extension has moved a long way from the traditional path." He cited that the Roxbury program had been in continuous operation since 1968, and that two of the "most important ventures," Training Teachers of Teachers and Cambridge Economic Opportunities Committee, "showed that we could combine academic and practical requirements in impressive new degree programs." Despite the many pressures of community outreach for the past seven years, "Extension has kept a strong traditional program," while also responding to the community "with nontraditional offerings." The experiences of recent years had convinced Phelps that University Extension had to have a commitment to community involvement, "and we need to reach far more of the poor than we do."

In retrospect Dr. Phelps saw the years of 1968 to 1975 as the most exciting time of his tenure at University Extension because of his personal involvement in community outreach. At one time Harvard College had a robust and substantial commuter population reaching 16 percent of the undergraduate body, but by the late 1960s Harvard College was almost all residential, and commuters only attended University Extension at night. Phelps joined Charles Whitlock, advisor to the president on community affairs, in visiting local communities, especially Roxbury, to meet with community leaders and learn how Harvard could assist them. At first it was thought that the Navy televised courses could be shown in community centers, but soon it was clear that something much more basic was needed, and the first success was owing to Professor Peter Elbow's writing workshop in Roxbury, which provided a model of the sort of course that was needed.[2]

Repeated trips to the Roxbury Community Center established good relations between University Extension and two dynamic women, Ledonia Wright and Bernice Miller, who were recruited to offer for Harvard Extension credit the courses *Community Dynamics* and *Child Care*, respectively. Mrs. Wright was affiliated with Boston College and Mrs. Miller was affiliated with the Harvard Graduate School of Education; later Mrs. Wright became affiliated with the University Without Walls in Roxbury and taught *Public Policy and Its Effect on Community Organizations* for Extension credit. Dr. Phelps would defer to the officials at the Roxbury Community Center in selecting the courses local people wanted offered and even finding the appropriate teachers to teach them on site.

The dream that a new consortium of the Commission on Extension Courses member institutions could combine to create a curriculum for Roxbury never materialized, despite many meetings with Charles Whitlock, Reginald Phelps, and Paul Park, who became the first president of Roxbury Community College. Rather than having Commission faculty come to Roxbury to teach, Paul Park insisted that the residents of Roxbury be bused to Commission campuses at Harvard, Tufts, or Wellesley. In time the right solution resulted in the creation of Roxbury Community College with its own campus, administration, faculty, and students. This outcome was immensely gratifying to Dr. Phelps, who regarded it as "one of the two or three best things I did in Extension."[3]

It was to Dr. Phelps's great credit as an educator that he could champion the traditional liberal arts curriculum that had been the hallmark of the Commission on Extension Courses since its inception, while also acknowledging the critical needs of the communities in Greater Boston for more applied courses during the time of crisis. By the time he retired in 1975, he could assert with conviction that "community involvement" ranked at the top of his priorities. He had learned that there were constituencies beyond Harvard Yard, and he had demonstrated his commitment to serving them through the outreach programs of University Extension he administered between 1968 and 1975.

RALPH LOWELL

Trustee of the Lowell Institute
1943–1978

CHAPTER IX

The Second Half-Century

The Later Years of Reginald H. Phelps, Director (1960-75)

Throughout his tenure as director of University Extension, but especially during the 1960s, Dr. Phelps was mindful of the low status generally accorded deans of evening extension programs in the United States. Since he wore several administrative hats at Harvard, serving as associate dean of the Graduate School of Arts and Sciences as well as director of University Extension, he often described himself wryly as a combination of "a daytime and a nighttime dean." He was also an active member and participant in national organizations, such as the Association of University Evening Colleges (AUEC) and the National University Extension Association (NUEA).

When he returned from the annual meeting of the Association of University Evening Colleges in November 1960, he wrote to Dean Bundy that "the perennial theme of the status of evening colleges" was addressed, with the invidious distinction drawn between "evening college deans [and] graduate deans." But Phelps noted "that status is a malleable thing in the hands of a good dean," and, unfortunately, "evening college deans have let themselves be entrepreneurs for academia, or the outside world, at the cost of achieving distinction in the substantive aspects of education." As the head of Harvard's evening college, Dr. Phelps was regarded by his national colleagues in the associations as representing "distinction" in the field and serving as a countervailing force to the low esteem felt by many. On February 2, 1962, he received a typical letter concerning status from John P. Kidd of the University of Toronto: "I found the AUEC interesting, although there seemed to be, in some sessions, a militant sadness and defeatism with respect to the status of the university evening college within the university community. It didn't quite become a wailing wall but came close to it on occasion."

In 1962 Dr. Phelps had succeeded in persuading Ralph Lowell and the Lowell Institute to allow him to charge "a credit fee of $5 per course each term," thereby generating enough additional income to expand the academic program to seventy courses and achieve a record enrollment of 7,448 from more than 5,000 individual students. The following year he announced in his annual report a further increase in the courses offered and new records for total enrollments (8,435) and individual students registered (6,037). The year 1963 marked the end of a remarkable run of twelve consecutive years of steady growth in enrollments, amounting to nearly a three-fold increase during that span. And at Commencement fourteen women and men received the new AB in Extension Studies, "the largest number of Extension graduates in a single year," bringing the total number of degree recipients since the program began to 299.

In the autumn 1963 issue of *Harvard Today*, the editor Frank Pemberton wrote a feature article titled "Education After Dark," which highlighted the academic success of University Extension. It praised Reginald H. Phelps for assembling a teaching staff that he personally referred to as "the dream faculty of any institution anywhere," a grandiose claim that the facts fully supported. "Of 75 members of the teaching staff, there are 34 full Professors, 12 Associate Professors, 12 Assistant Professors, and 11 Lecturers. There are five instructors, and one Dean who teaches a course in Expository English. He is John U. Monro, Dean of Harvard College."[1]

Although the academic program of University Extension in 1962-63 included veteran faculty from the member institutions of the Commission on Extension Courses, notably Boston University, Simmons College, Boston College, MIT, and Tufts University, the overwhelming majority of the courses offered were staffed by distinguished Harvard professors ranging across the departmental disciplines. According to Phelps, the motivation to teach in Extension was twofold: "They get paid for it … enough to make it worthwhile, but not enough to make anyone do it merely for the money involved"; but "the principal reason they even teach in Extension is because they find it stimulating."

Students also were motivated to attend the Extension School by a strong desire to learn and to benefit from the teaching of such an outstanding faculty drawn from Harvard and other local universities. By 1963 enrollments had reached an all-time record, and even with the added fees allowed by Ralph Lowell and the Lowell Institute for Extension credit, the cost was kept "as low as possible, $25 per course for credit students and $15 for non-credit. At this rate, a college education leading to a Harvard degree costs in University Extension just about $1,000." As Dr. Phelps was quoted in the article: "That is a bargain that simply cannot be matched anywhere in the field of education." The prospects for growth were almost without limit when this article appeared.

By 1964, however, total enrollments and total number of students registered declined, even though the number of courses presented increased slightly, and "the long record of yearly increases" finally came to an end. But within a year, Phelps could announce in his annual report that "the total enrollment was 8,693, the highest we have recorded," and a record twenty-two students were awarded the Bachelor of Arts in Extension Studies. To help meet the needs of Extension students, a part of Lehman Hall, a building in Harvard Yard, was made available to Extension students, providing them with conference and study rooms, a television viewing-room, library facilities, and a dining hall during the evening hours.

Dr. Phelps in his annual reports regularly commented on the number of degrees awarded, watching the growth of the bachelor's degree, first approved in 1961, increase from year to year. By 1968 he could write with satisfaction: "Forty-eight students received Extension degrees, the largest number yet awarded (35 in 1966, 31 in 1967). This brings to 452 the total of Extension degrees awarded since the establishment of the Commission. Of these, 173 or 38.3 percent have been awarded in the seven years since the first conferral of the degree of A.B. in Extension Studies."

The growth in Extension degree recipients and the creation of an Extension Center in Lehman Hall resulted in "a notable event," according to the annual report for 1967-68: namely, "the formation of the Harvard Extension Alumni Association" (HEAA), a decisive move to provide the graduates of the Extension program with a legitimacy enjoyed by other graduates of Harvard through their own alumni body. As Phelps noted, the Extension alumni now "have their own enthusiastic organization." This significant development was owing to the efforts of two energetic alumni, Ella Smith '66 and Edgar Grossman '66, who worked with Dr. Phelps in the planning stages and, once officially recognized by the Harvard Alumni Association, held a celebratory first meeting prior to Commencement with Edgar Grossman elected the first president.

Starting in 1965, Radcliffe Seminars were made available to Harvard Extension students and that first year three seminars enrolled twenty-four Extension students. In subsequent years more Radcliffe Seminars were open for credit to Extension students, with the number of Extension student enrollments increasing from year to year. By 1970 the number of Radcliffe Seminars open to Extension students was eleven and more than one hundred registered. Most of the seminars were taught by faculty associated with either Harvard or Radcliffe. In his annual report for 1970-71, Dr. Phelps cited "sixteen Radcliffe seminars were open to Extension Students, of whom 176 enrolled, by far the largest number that has taken advantage of this fine opportunity." For his final annual report in 1975, Phelps noted that "39 Radcliffe Seminars were open to Extension students—more than twice the number in the previous year," and they accounted for a record total of 335 enrollments. The Radcliffe Seminars were a singularly rich array of courses taught mostly by distinguished women scholars representing many local institutions and they added a valuable educational element to the curriculum.

The social and political unrest of the late 1960s and early 1970s had convinced the Harvard administration and faculty that it would be appropriate to offer a two-year degree in the Extension School to complement the traditional four-year bachelor's degree so that members of the surrounding community could aspire to a Harvard degree in less time than ordinarily was needed. Dr. Phelps accordingly announced in his annual report for 1971 that "the Faculty and Governing Boards approved in the spring the establishment of an Associate in Arts degree in Extension Studies, representing the equivalent of two years of full-time study, and permitting up to half of this work to be in 'professional subjects,' such as a practicum in teaching, taken under Harvard auspices. The first group of Associate in Arts in Extension Studies, numbering twenty-four, received degrees at Commencement. Thirty-eight bachelor's degrees were conferred during the year, and now over half of the total of 577 Extension degrees awarded by Harvard from the beginning of the program in 1910 have been granted in the decade since the establishment of the A.B. in Extension Studies." Since he was responsible for the introduction of the AB degree, it was surely gratifying that the majority of degrees awarded in the history of University Extension were the result of his initiative as director.

Gradually, the Faculty of Arts and Sciences recognized the academic quality of the Extension graduates, now both the two-year Associate in Arts and the four-year Bachelor of Arts in Extension Studies. In the spring of 1972, the Faculty and the Governing Boards approved the awarding of the AB degree with honors, and Phelps noted that "22 Honors degrees were conferred" in that first year. In subsequent years some AB degrees could be awarded *cum laude* in recognition of the academic achievement of the candidates. The year 1972 was also noteworthy for the great growth in the number of degrees awarded (98) because of the forty-four recipients of the Associate in Arts and the fifty-four Bachelor of Arts. All told, the year 1972 "was a record-breaking year" with a total of 144 courses offered, more than 10,000 registrations, and 6,885 students enrolled.

In announcing the end of the PACE Program in 1972, Dr. Phelps had singled out for special recognition "the notable work of Ms. Alice Kendall, who has handled details of the PACE Program since its inception." He also acknowledged the retirement of Miss Genevieve Welch, who was "remembered with affection by thousands of our students." Immediately after graduating from Simmons College in 1927, she went to work for the Commission on Extension Courses and remained until her retirement in 1972, a remarkable span of forty-five years, during which time she assumed responsibility for almost every phase of the operation of the office and knew personally most of the faculty and many of the student degree candidates. In the words of one Extension alumna, "she *was* Extension."[2]

For his final annual report Phelps focused on the number of Extension degrees awarded, noting that seventy-nine students earned degrees: thirty-seven Associate in Arts and forty-two Bachelor of Arts, including twenty-five who graduated *cum laude*, "the highest number and proportion so far. Since the beginning of University Extension, 915 degrees

GENEVIEVE ANNETTE
WELCH

Worked for Harvard
Commission on Extension
Courses from 1927 to 1972.

ELLA SMITH, ABE '66

Co-founder and past-President
of the Harvard Extension School
Alumni Association, Harvard
Alumni Association Appointed
Director, and recipient of the
2008 Harvard Alumni
Association Award.

have been conferred." It must have been a source of satisfaction to Phelps that all but about 200 of the degree recipients came during his tenure as director of University Extension, and that in the previous forty years so few degrees had been awarded.

In an attempt to summarize "the aims and achievements of Extension in the past twenty-six years," Phelps cast a backward glance at the program from its inception by President Lowell to 1950, observing that throughout this extended period it remained "a small program of high academic distinction, with the faculty drawn from Harvard and the other institutions belonging to the Commission on Extension Courses. The incredibly low tuition fees, made possible by the support of the Lowell Institute, were based on the value of two bushels of wheat, a currency specified in the will of John Lowell, founder of the Institute." The expansion in the number of courses under the leadership of Dr. Phelps was made possible, as he noted, "by adding small fees for registration, conferences, laboratory, and credit—to retain tuition rates scarcely matched even by public institutions and still to expand the program enormously, largely through tuition income," with the result that "now we provide for more than four times the number of courses and some five times the number of students that we did in 1950."

Among the educational accomplishments cited by Phelps were the addition of the Radcliffe Seminars for Extension students "to undertake specialized study," the creation of the PACE Program for the Navy, the pioneering work with the educational radio and television courses for college credit dating from the 1950s and 1960s, and the outreach efforts to the Greater Boston community, especially Roxbury, through the Training Teachers of Teachers and the Cambridge Economic Opportunities Committee initiatives. University Extension maintained its "strong traditional program, and it has moved into the community with nontraditional offerings."

Much was accomplished, but many years later, in retrospect, Phelps reflected on what he aptly termed "architecture that wasn't built" during his tenure. He listed nine *desiderata* as a wish list that never materialized. First, he cited the need for "an Extension community center." Although Lehman Hall offered a partial solution, he felt the program needed a dedicated space for a "community-university meeting place." Second, through his experiences during the crisis period when he engaged in outreach programs to the community, he became convinced that University Extension should make a "regular procession of programs outside Harvard Square." Since all the successful programs resulted from outside funding, usually government support, "it was impossible to develop permanent programs," such as courses in community centers or local schools or government offices. Third, he wanted to combine the traditional liberal arts curriculum with preprofessional training, especially for careers in "education, health, and public service," but this required "not only government support but faculty commitment within Harvard," both of which were not forthcoming. Fourth, he had hoped for greater "collaboration of Harvard faculties in extra-mural education generally," but only the Harvard School of Education had come forward as a partner, and except for participation from individual faculty from other schools, no other partnerships ensued. Fifth, he had lobbied for part-time graduate degree programs, both in arts and sciences and in education or business, but there had been no support for this initiative.

As a sixth *desideratum*, Phelps had envisioned "a core faculty, not full-time in Extension, with, say, five-year appointments" to ensure continuity in the curriculum from year-to-year as well as "to cultivate special talents and experience in teaching adults." But this idea, however sensible and practicable, never was realized. Seventh, he had hoped for "closer academic and social relations with Harvard College and Radcliffe," yet there remained a great gulf between the day and the evening students. Eighth, Dr. Phelps never relinquished his title as chairman of the Commission on Extension Courses, and he dreamed of a "revival of the Commission" to plan and provide a comprehensive program of adult education to Greater Boston as a modern means of realizing "Mr. Lowell's vision." And lastly he had a vision of Harvard University "combining its many strengths and, *viribus unitis*, living wholly with the community . . . , not a series of affairs interrupted by sorry quarrels." The *desiderata* and the concluding utopian vision were characteristic of the mind and heart of Reginald H. Phelps as director of University Extension. They constitute a worthy complement to the House of Intellect he built during his long tenure, even though, as he observed wistfully, they turned out to be the "architecture that wasn't built."[3]

MICHAEL SHINAGEL

Director of Continuing Education and University Extension,
then Dean of Continuing Education and University Extension
1975–

CHAPTER X

University Extension Unbound and Transformed

The Early Years of Michael Shinagel, Director and Dean (1975-85)

The retirement of Reginald H. Phelps, who had served as director of University Extension for a quarter century, scheduled for July 1975, prompted a comprehensive review of continuing education in the Faculty of Arts and Sciences at the recommendation of President Derek Bok and Dean Henry Rosovsky. Accordingly, a committee consisting of Professor Patricia A. Graham, Dr. George W. Goethals, and Dr. Peter McKinney, chairman, was appointed in October of 1974 by Dean Rosovsky, and on April 11, 1975, they filed their report on the future of continuing education in the Faculty of Arts and Sciences.

Their charge had been twofold: to propose the appropriate administrative structure and to recommend staffing for this structure. They identified continuing education in the Faculty of Arts and Sciences as comprising the following programs: University Extension, Summer School, Special Students, and Alumni College. The committee acknowledged that while these programs "do not fall among the highest priorities of this Faculty," they do serve "an important function in the University-community relationship" and also "provide alternative education patterns, both degree and non-degree, for a broad spectrum of students."

The recommendations of the committee were, administratively, that all the programs "should be drawn under a single full-time director" who would report directly to the dean of the faculty; financially, these programs should be self-sufficient and also "produce a surplus above the full direct costs of the programs," both for "program development" and for "unrestricted income" to Faculty of Arts and Sciences. Finally the search process should be national and the candidate "should probably not be a professional in continuing education" given the unique culture of Faculty of Arts and Sciences and its ambiguous relationship with nontraditional programs.

The report was accepted, and a search committee was formed to screen candidates responding to an advertisement in the *Chronicle of Higher Education* with the intention of having a new director in place by September 1, 1975. More than 300 candidates applied and the search committee, headed by Dr. Peter McKinney, worked during the summer months to present its final two candidates to the president and the dean for consideration.

The person finally hired was Michael Shinagel, a *Phi Beta Kappa* graduate of Oberlin College and a Woodrow Wilson Fellow to Harvard for a doctorate in English literature earned in 1964. He was an assistant professor of English at Cornell University from 1964 to 1967, then he went to Union College as associate professor of English and chairman of the department, eventually becoming a full professor and having served in assorted administrative capacities. What made his candidacy more relevant was his having taught for four years with John U. Monro, dean of Harvard College, in his *Expository English* course at University Extension from 1959 to 1963, as well as having held several academic and administrative posts at Harvard during the years he worked for his doctorate, such as associate director of the office for graduate and career plans, freshman advisor, member of the admission staff for Harvard College, tutor in the English department, and a teaching fellow in freshman English. Shinagel was an experienced academic administrator who knew Harvard in general and University Extension in particular. He assumed his new position on September 2, but his teaching commitments for the fall term at Union College had to be honored, so he shuttled between Cambridge and Schenectady until the end of the year, when he could devote himself to his new role full time.

In his first annual report for 1975-76, Dr. Shinagel highlighted an expanded curriculum and increased enrollments as nearly 200 courses were offered, including forty-eight Radcliffe Seminars, and 6,206 students and 9,705 registrations were recorded (the second highest totals in Extension history). Extension TV courses, five in number, were sponsored, marking the seventeenth consecutive year that televised courses were a part of the curriculum.

Extension degrees were conferred on eighty-two students, bringing the total of degrees earned to 1,000 since the beginning of University Extension in 1910, and the total of women and men enrolled by the school to nearly 160,000. Surveys conducted during the fall and spring confirmed the diversity of the students: two-thirds were women, more than half had a bachelor's degree, half lived in Cambridge and Boston, nearly two-thirds were thirty years or under, almost half were new to the program, 7 percent were Harvard staff, and 5 percent were active degree candidates.

Harvard Extension maintained its outreach to the community by sponsoring courses at various non-Harvard locations: the Boston Public Library, the Museum of Fine Arts, the Old South Meeting House, and the Center for Afro-American Artists in Roxbury. Students and faculty from Roxbury High School and students from the Cambridge Pilot School enrolled on tuition scholarships. In subsequent years University Extension would expand its tradition of community outreach by offering courses at other locations, such as the New England Aquarium and the Museum of Science, as well as offering tuition-free scholarships to Roxbury High School and Cambridge Pilot School students.

Growth became the operative word for University Extension in its first few years of operation under the directorship of Shinagel. For his annual report for 1977-78, he summarized:

> The dramatic growth of University Extension in the past few years can be seen if we compare this year's courses and enroll-ments with those for the academic year 1974-75. That year there were only 135 courses (including Radcliffe Seminars), 6,060 individual students, and 9,677 course registrations, of which only half were for credit. In the brief span of three years we have witnessed a doubling of courses offered, an increase in enrollment of nearly 1,150 students, an increase of nearly 2,000 course registrations, and a marked increase (30 percent) of stu-dents taking courses for credit.

Obviously the demographic composition of the student body was changing, and the computerized registration data bore this out, for current students were "younger, better educated, and more motivated." Now nearly
two-thirds of the students had a bachelor's degree, including a quarter
with a graduate degree as well, and two-thirds were women. Significantly,
the majority of students "reported family incomes of $15,000 or less, thus
placing [them] below the national average of $16,000 for family incomes
... [and] making our program accessible to the majority of students who
otherwise would not be able to avail themselves of a Harvard education."

Soon after Dr. Shinagel became director of University Extension, he
noted that Harvard University had ignored an important constituency in
its community service efforts: namely, Harvard staff. In recent years the
University had expressed concern over its support staff retention practices
and results. Support staff, according to Harvard's personnel office reports,
had been staying at the University only an average of less than two years,
which meant a loss of millions of dollars annually in recruitment, training,
and retention expenses. With the director of human resources he worked
to establish the Tuition Assistance Plan (TAP) for Harvard staff that
made available to them study and degree opportunities at the University.
But since release time for day courses presented problems, the logical educational resource for the TAP users was University Extension and, to a
lesser extent, the Harvard Summer School. Special cases allowed for study
at other Harvard schools and even at local institutions, such as Simmons
for library degrees, but the majority of TAP enrollments would devolve on
Harvard University Extension.

In his annual report for 1977-78, Dean Shinagel cited the new TAP
program:

> The creation of the Tuition Assistance Plan by the University
> Personnel Office in 1976-77 has encouraged Harvard employees
> to enroll in Extension courses. In its first year of operation,
> TAP sponsored 238 employees to take Extension courses. In
> 1977-78 we saw a total of 360 Harvard employees in the fall and
> spring semesters. This increased participation by employees is
> an encouraging sign, for it means that our program is serving a
> growing number of men and women who, in addition to work-

ing at the University, also find a valuable educational resource available to them here, and it may make job and career opportunities at Harvard more attractive at a time when the market for prospective employees is becoming increasingly competitive with the private sector.

The success of the TAP program could be measured by the growth in enrollments in subsequent years: 360 in 1977-78, 525 in 1978-79, and 571 in 1979-80. In his annual report for 1979-80, Dean Shinagel wrote: "It is gratifying to note that more than seven percent of the enrollment in the 1979-80 Extension program was by Harvard staff members, for in a tangible way we can serve the educational interests and needs of our co-workers at the University through evening Extension courses and degree programs." Among the eighty Extension degrees awarded that year, four went to Harvard staff members. The following year Harvard staff enrollment increased dramatically to nearly 800, and by the time Shinagel composed his annual report for 1981-82, he cited "a record 834 staff members enrolled for 1,043 course registrations, of which 150 were in the CSS [graduate Certificate of Special Studies in Administration and Management] and 205 in the ALM [Master of Liberal Arts]. We are gratified to note that thirty-seven Harvard staff members are active Extension degree candidates (twenty-eight ALB and nine ALM). Another five are admitted candidates for certificate programs."

Within five years of its introduction, the University's TAP program had demonstrated its success. Harvard staff were availing themselves of the educational opportunities it provided in growing numbers, especially in University Extension. TAP was proving itself as a valuable recruiting tool for Harvard in attracting support staff to the University, and it also proved itself an equally valuable tool in retaining staff for longer tenures as they pursued educational opportunities, including degree and certificate options, while working at Harvard. The University's plan had effectively solved the support staff retention problem of the mid-1970s and the Extension course and degree and certificate options were instrumental in its success.

Upon the death of his father, Ralph Lowell, on May 15, 1978, John Lowell became trustee of the Lowell Institute, although he had worked closely as a co-trustee during the declining years of his father's life. John

Lowell had prepared at the Noble and Greenough School and entered
Harvard College in 1938. He graduated in 1942 and served on destroyers
in the US Navy during World War II. He remained in the US Naval
Reserve and retired with the rank of lieutenant commander. For his occupation, he followed his father into banking and the investment business,
serving as vice-chairman of the board of directors and chairman of the
investment policy committee of the Boston Safe Deposit and Trust
Company. Like his predecessors as trustees of the Lowell Institute, John
Lowell held offices in many corporate, civic, and political organizations
and was a member of numerous Boston clubs and societies.

The retirement of Dr. Phelps in 1975 and the succession of Dr.
Shinagel as director of University Extension resulted in a significant shift
in the relationship with the Lowell Institute. John Lowell, in his capacity
as co-chair, was not as punctilious as his predecessors in interpreting the
"two bushels of wheat" stipulation in the will of the founder, John Lowell,
Jr. Under his energetic direction, the Lowell Institute was sponsoring or
underwriting a cornucopia of cultural activities for the citizens of Greater
Boston, including public lectures and exhibits at the Museum of Science,
the New England Aquarium, the Old South Meeting House, the Boston
Public Library, the Museum of Fine Arts, the Cambridge Forum, and the
Ford Hall Forum, among others. The Lowell Institute Cooperative
Broadcasting Council, a consortium including Harvard that resembled
the original members of the Commission on Extension Courses, continued "to promote the general education of the public" through its many
radio and television programs. The institute also supported academic programs and lectures at MIT, Boston College, Simmons College, and
Harvard. With such a broad range of public lectures, academic programs,
exhibits, and other public service activities available to the people of
Greater Boston, the Lowell Institute was already amply fulfilling the
terms of the will of John Lowell, Jr.

The Lowell Institute continued its association with University
Extension at Harvard, providing an annual contribution to support outreach efforts to the community, but there were no longer any restrictions
on the cost of the courses or the need to control the number of courses
offered annually or the salaries of the faculty. The Commission on

Extension Courses was no longer involved for historic purposes, and University Extension could grow as a financially self-supporting academic program. The annual contribution of the Lowell Institute soon was devoted to the support of the Lowell Scholarship Program designed to encourage local high school students and faculty to enroll in Extension courses.

Among the *desiderata* of Dr. Phelps was the approval by the Faculty of Arts and Sciences of a master's degree program for University Extension. It never came to pass during his tenure, but the pressure for such a graduate degree was growing both among students and alumni of University Extension and outside Harvard at other universities across the country.

From the outset of his tenure as director of University Extension, Dr. Shinagel knew the importance of graduate education and graduate degrees to this audience. He lobbied with the president and the dean of the faculty to have a committee study the feasibility of graduate degrees for Harvard Extension, and in late November 1977 Dean Rosovsky appointed a blue-ribbon committee "to consider the academic aspects of those programs in Continuing Education for which the Faculty of Arts and Sciences is particularly responsible." The members of the committee were Professors Andrew Gleason (mathematics), E.L. Keenan (history), John D. Montgomery (government), John Murdoch (history of science), Richard E. Schultes (botany), and Glen W. Bowersock (classics), chairman.

In his letter of charge to Professor Bowersock, who was also dean of undergraduate education at the time, Dean Rosovsky pointed out that "this committee grew out of conversations between Michael Shinagel and the Academic Deans," and that "Shinagel has very ambitious plans: he would like for Extension to offer work at the level of the master's degree." The principal questions for the committee to address centered on what academic aspects earn Faculty of Arts and Sciences degree credit; who teaches in the Extension programs and how they are selected; what quality control procedures are in place; whether the degree requirements are appropriate; and how Faculty of Arts and Sciences might participate more effectively in Extension and Summer School.

On February 28, 1978, President Derek Bok wrote to Dean Rosovsky:

> Over the past few months, we have had lively discussions with
> Mike Shinagel at the Council of Deans and before the

Corporation. These occasions have helped to increase the 'visibility' of continuing education and to alert the Fellows and the Deans to the large number of students enrolled in our non-traditional programs. While the discussions have elicited enthusiasm for the initiative and vigor displayed by Shinagel, they have also evoked a concern that we provide sufficient supervision to ensure that his programs are of satisfactory quality and that they are reasonably related to the mission and purposes of the University.

President Bok proceeded to enumerate a list of questions for the Bowersock committee to consider as part of its review of continuing education at Harvard: specifically, what are the purposes of each program and how are they related to the University as a whole? Are adequate procedures in place to review the content and quality of each program? Are faculty selected according to appropriate standards? Is open enrollment suitable for the nature of the program? Since continuing education came under the jurisdiction of the Faculty of Arts and Sciences, President Bok directed his questions to Dean Rosovsky and Dean Bowersock, urging them "to address these issues reasonably soon" and offering to discuss them further.

To assist the Bowersock committee in its deliberations, Shinagel provided the members with a "working paper" of a proposal for a Master of Liberal Arts (MLA) in Extension Studies that included a timely article, "The New Master's Degrees," that appeared in the October 1978 issue of *Change* magazine and highlighted the growth of terminal liberal master's degrees at institutions like Georgetown, Wesleyan, and Johns Hopkins. Whereas these established master's degree programs all required a total of thirty units of credit beyond the bachelor's degree, Dr. Shinagel proposed that the Master of Liberal Arts in Extension Studies require a total of forty units of credit or ten regular semester courses, seven of which would be in a designated field of study and at least one seminar with a Harvard faculty member in that field. To ensure that the MLA degree was truly a Harvard degree, at least eight courses or thirty-two units of credit would be with Harvard-affiliated faculty. A bachelor's degree from an accredited institution would be required for admission, and students could only apply honors grades (B minus or better) toward the degree, which they should complete in no more than five years, while maintaining a grade point average of B or better to remain in good academic standing.

The Bowersock committee responded favorably to the proposal, noting from the supporting articles and newspaper clippings "that there is considerable demand for an advanced degree in continuing education and that such a degree is full of opportunities for a university to enhance its role in the community." The report concluded "Dean Shinagel's proposal … makes good sense to us, [but] in conformity with usual Harvard practice (AB, AM, etc.) this degree would be known as ALM (*artium liberalium magister*), rather than MLA as originally suggested by Dean Shinagel.… We urge that it be acted upon favorably."

At the regular meeting of the Faculty of Arts and Sciences held on April 10, 1979, President Bok recognized Dean Shinagel to move the recommendation for a University Extension master's degree. Before presenting his motion, Dean Shinagel provided the faculty with background on University Extension, from its founding by President Lowell and the involvement of senior Harvard faculty over the years to the growth of such terminal master's programs locally in Boston as well as nationally, and the broad interest in such a graduate degree program among many constituencies. He then moved the motion on behalf of the administrative board for University Extension. Dean Bowersock seconded the motion on behalf of his committee, as did other members of the committee. Dean Rosovsky reported that the Faculty Council had voted unanimously for the proposed legislation. The president then called for a voice vote by the faculty and it carried without dissent.

Although the faculty had approved the new master's degree, the president raised a concern about this new graduate degree and its potentially deleterious effect on the Harvard Graduate School of Education, whose own master's degree "was in particularly precarious position because of the loss of Federal funds, and because of the rather poor job market in education which had severely constricted their applicant pool." The president did not want the Graduate School of Education to have its master's degree threatened by competition with the new Extension master's degree, and he proposed having the implementation of the Extension graduate degree delayed for a year or more.

Subsequently a meeting was held in the office of the president attended by Deans Paul Ylvisaker and Blenda Wilson of the Harvard Graduate School of Education, Deans Henry Rosovksy and Michael Shinagel of the Faculty of Arts and Sciences, and President Bok. The president explained why he felt that the Graduate School of Education had to be protected from internal competition at this time, and why he wanted the implementation of the new Extension master's degree delayed for a year, even though the Faculty of Arts and Sciences had voted it. This delay was a blow to Dean Shinagel and to University Extension.

Dean Shinagel left the meeting convinced that the new master's degree had to be implemented without delay, even if only in a very limited manner. He persuaded the Graduate School of Education deans to allow him to offer the degree the following year only to Harvard Extension graduates and Harvard staff, which would not affect the Graduate School of Education's master's degree applicant pool, but which would make the ALM degree at least operational. The dean of the Graduate School of Education agreed to this compromise and signed the agreement that Dean Shinagel personally hand delivered to the Office of the Governing Boards so that the master's degree would be approved and implemented for the following year. It was, and after a year the Graduate School of Education had weathered its financial and applicant crisis so that the Extension ALM could be offered to all who wanted it.

After seventy years University Extension in 1979-80 finally had its graduate degree program approved and operational. And at Commencement in June 1980 the first graduate degree was awarded to John K. Jennings, a naval oral surgeon who completed the graduate degree in its first year of operation by studying full time. The following year, in 1980-81, when the president and dean of the Graduate School of Education lifted the restrictions on the new degree, a total of 741 students accounted for 1,243 course registrations in the graduate program, and three more graduate degrees were awarded at Commencement in 1981. Despite its precarious beginning, the Extension's ALM degree was within a year's time well launched and well subscribed.

To commemorate the seventieth anniversary of the creation of the Commission on Extension Courses and University Extension at Harvard, the academic year 1979-80 saw record numbers of courses offered and students enrolled: 316 courses, 7,702 students, and 12,567 course registrations, with nearly 80 percent for credit. Whereas the general profile of University Extension students had remained constant over the past several years, the majority of students, nearly two-thirds, were new to the program, indicating "a high degree of mobility in the student population from year to year."

A decision by the Faculty of Arts and Sciences to transfer its English as a foreign language program from the English department to University Extension at the start of the academic year in 1979 enabled Harvard Extension to sponsor for the Harvard and Boston communities a revised and expanded series of course offerings at several ability levels in grammatical, speaking, and writing skills. During the year 232 students received instruction in the fall term and 202 in the spring; one-third had a Harvard connection as a student, visiting scholar, spouse, or staff member. From this date onward, University Extension would provide the Harvard, Boston, and international communities with a comprehensive course program in English as a second language at various ability levels.

The expansion of the Extension curriculum in recent years enabled it to offer a complete premedical program to a growing number of adult students eager to prepare themselves for entry into medical schools and eventually for a medical career. On the occasion of the seventieth anniversary year for University Extension the Health Careers Program was officially instituted with a premedical advisory committee, chaired by Gloria White-Hammond, MD, to assist students in evaluating their career choices, planning their premedical course requirements, developing application skills and strategies, and gaining emotional as well as academic support. In March of 1980 a symposium, "Medical School Applications: Strategy Planning," was sponsored by the Health Careers Program. Carola Eisenberg, MD, dean of students, Harvard Medical School; James Morehead, PhD, Tufts Medical School; and Edgar Smith, PhD, University of Massachusetts Medical School, joined Dr. White-Hammond to discuss the application process and to explain the rigors and rewards of a medical career. The Health Careers Program enabled three Extension students, including one Extension degree recipient, to be admitted to medical schools in the fall of 1980. The lone Extension degree recipient, Michael Wood, Bachelor of Arts in Extension Studies *cum laude* '80, became the first Extension student in several decades to be admitted to a medical school directly after graduation. As the Health Careers Program grew in the following years, hundreds of adult learners would be admitted to medical schools, including to Harvard Medical School.

In commemoration of the seventieth anniversary, John Lowell, trustee of the Lowell Institute, established an annual lecture, co-sponsored by University Extension, devoted to major issues of our time. The inaugural lecture, "Americans in the Un-American World: How Not to Think About Foreign Policy in the 1980s," was delivered by McGeorge Bundy on May 5, 1980. Professor Bundy had been sponsored in 1947 by the Lowell Institute when he was a promising junior fellow at Harvard and gave a series of eight lectures. Since then his meteoric career included dean of the Faculty of Arts and Sciences (1953-61) and professor of government (1954-61) at Harvard, special assistant for national security affairs to President Kennedy (1961-64), a senior staff officer on foreign and defense policy to President Johnson, president of the Ford Foundation (1966-79), and then professor of history at New York University. (For a list of the subsequent Lowell Lecturers and their topics, see Appendix A.)

In response to the great demand from students for graduate study opportunities in University Extension, Shinagel as early as 1977 had created a graduate Certificate of Advanced Study (CAS) designed for holders of a bachelor's degree or its equivalent who were interested in a full year of graduate study in one of three areas: humanities, social sciences, and natural sciences. Since two-thirds of the students enrolled each year already had a bachelor's degree, this graduate option immediately proved an attractive alternative to those seeking a master's degree. Candidates for the certificate were required to complete eight courses, six in an area of concentration, including a graduate seminar and an independent research project with a Harvard faculty member. The CAS was skillfully directed by Dr. L. Dodge Fernald from the outset.

The success of this certificate program prompted University Extension to introduce another graduate certificate program in 1980: the Certificate of Special Studies in Administration and Management (CSS), which constituted one full year of study beyond the bachelor's degree. Designed primarily for students with no prior academic background in business or administration, the CSS offered practical and theoretical approaches to managerial issues in the for-profit and nonprofit sectors. The curriculum covered courses in four key areas: policy, planning, and operations; human resources development; finance and control; and quantitative methods. Candidates were expected to take at least one course in each area as well as demonstrate competency in written and oral communication and in the use of computers.

Students seeking an alternative to a traditional master of business administration were attracted to this streamlined and flexible certificate program. In its first year of operation the CSS Program sponsored eighteen courses taught by fifteen faculty and recorded 1,500 course enrollments. In 1984 the CSS achieved national recognition when it was cited as one of the nation's best new continuing education programs by the National University Extension Association. By 1985 the program had expanded its curriculum to seventy-eight courses taught by fifty-nine faculty and recorded 3,400 course enrollments.

This great growth was owing in large part to the initiative of the CSS Program's director, Raymond F. Comeau, assistant dean of University Extension, who personally sought to attract outstanding faculty to teach in the new evening graduate program. Dr. Comeau was especially successful in recruiting Harvard Business School professors *emeriti* to join the faculty, notably the original seven distinguished professors who collectively held ten Harvard degrees and accounted for more than 200 years of teaching experience in their fields of business. This illustrious company consisted of Bertrand Fox, Jacob H. Schiff Professor of Investment Banking; E. Robert Livernash, Albert J. Weatherhead Jr. Professor of Business Administration; Robert N. Anthony, Ross Graham Walker Professor of Management; Henry B. Arthur, Moffett Professor of Agriculture and Business; Jesse W. Markham, Charles Edward Wilson Professor of Business Administration; and Professors of Business Administration Lawrence Thompson and Edward Bursk.

The responses of the students to these seven teachers were predictably positive. Many students ranked them as among the best they had ever had.

The former Harvard Business School professors reciprocated the high regard of the students by citing their singular motivation, readiness to participate in class discussion, and considerable work experience they brought to their studies. They regarded the CSS students as comparable to many of the executive education students they had taught at Harvard and elsewhere. By the time of University Extension's seventy-fifth anniversary, the graduate management program was a respected and established feature of the academic curriculum.[1]

With the approval and implementation of the Master of Liberal Arts (ALM) in Extension Studies degree, the Certificate of Advanced Study (CAS) had served its purpose in the five years of operation, as thirty-nine students had earned their certificates. Students in the certificate program could transfer to the master's degree program with half their credits, and by 1985 the CAS was phased out.

In the fall term of 1982 a new graduate certificate was launched. The Certificate of Advanced Study in Applied Sciences (CAS) was designed by Dr. Paul Bamberg, director of science instruction, to "include both fundamental courses in areas such as computer science, laboratory electronics, and mathematics taught mainly by Harvard-affiliated instructors, and specialized courses such as software methodology and database management, taught by practicing professionals from industry as well as from Harvard." The aim of the program was to help meet the growing demand by the local high-technology industry in Greater Boston for well-trained personnel. The immediate response to the program was encouraging as 174 students enrolled in the fall. Within a year the program would have its first graduate, the first of many in the coming years.[2]

With the establishment of graduate programs, the Tuition Assistance Plan of the University, and the premedical Health Careers Program, enrollments in University Extension continued to soar. For the annual report in 1981-82, Dean Shinagel wrote: "A record number of 398 courses were offered (up from 335 last year), a record number of 10,445 students enrolled (up 14 percent from last year), and a record number of 17,032 course registrations were filed (also up 14 percent from last year)." For the first time more than 100 students received Harvard degrees in extension studies, a total of 106, including fifteen Master of Liberal Arts.

According to Shinagel, "The dramatic increase in enrollments is attributable to the growing interest in our graduate programs in Extension. Since the majority of the students attending classes in Extension already have a bachelor's degree, they are naturally attracted to our graduate study options, notably the Master of Liberal Arts (ALM) in Extension Studies. The ALM Program enrolled 954 students who accounted for 1,664 course registrations, increases in students of 29 percent . . . over last year."

Similarly Harvard staff were attracted to Extension courses because of the auspices of the Tuition Assistance Plan: "This year a record 834 staff members enrolled for 1,043 course registrations, of which 150 were in the CSS and 205 in the ALM. We are gratified to note that thirty-seven Harvard staff members are active Extension degree candidates (twenty-eight ALB and nine ALM)," according to Shinagel

For the premedical students in University Extension, orientation meetings and workshops were scheduled for the more than 100 women and men in the program. The Health Careers Advisory Committee supported five students in their medical school applications, and three were accepted for the following year at the University of Massachusetts, New York University, and Tufts University. It was also noteworthy that Harvard Extension graduates were admitted to leading graduate schools of arts and sciences as well as professional schools, including Harvard Law School, Harvard Graduate School of Education, Kennedy School of Government, and Harvard Graduate School of Business Administration.

The expanding role of continuing education programs at Harvard University was highlighted by President Derek Bok in his Commencement address on June 10, 1982:

> In fact, universities have been gradually expanding their audience in recent years by reaching out to groups quite different from the more traditional students gathered here today to receive their degrees. Like many of the most important developments at Harvard, this new growth has taken place not by careful planning nor by conscious decision but through a host of quiet initiatives in many nooks and offices of the university. . . .

> Consider this fact, for example. We enroll about 15,000 students in traditional degree-granting programs. That figure is essentially unchanged from what it was ten years ago. But we currently teach more than 30,000 additional students in a variety of nontraditional ways. And *that* figure has almost doubled in the last decade.

This phenomenon described by President Bok was perhaps most evident in University Extension, which in 1975 enrolled slightly more than 6,000 students and in 1982 saw a record enrollment of nearly 10,500 students.

In his annual report for 1981-82, Dean Shinagel focused on this trend as it applied to the Faculty of Arts and Sciences by proposing that the increase in nontraditional adult learners had resulted in "a dual sense of mission: to educate the best traditional students we can attract to the College and the Graduate School of Arts and Sciences, and also to educate through our Continuing Education programs those nontraditional adult students who now represent such a major part of our overall enrollment." Shinagel argued that Harvard's dual sense of mission was opportune because of national demographic trends that, with the end of the post-World War II baby boom generation, were transforming American society into "a nation of adults." Data from the National Center for Education Statistics projected that by the year 2000 "the United States population will be dominated by persons in their middle years."

The national trend of lifelong learning was explained by K. Patricia Cross in her pioneering study *Adults as Learners*:

> First are the demographic factors that result in larger numbers of adults in the population. Between 1975 and 1985, the number of adults between the ages of 25 and 45 will increase relative to other age groups—from 25 percent of the population to 31 percent. A second influence is social change—the rising educational level of the populace, the changing role of women, early retirement, civil rights, increased leisure time, changing life styles, and so forth. Depending on individual circumstances, education for adults has become necessary for some, desirable for others, and more acceptable and attainable for almost every-

one. The third pressure springs from technological change and the knowledge explosion. Almost any worker in society has the problem of keeping up with new knowledge, but technological change is so fast and powerful that it wipes out entire industries and creates new ones in a single decade.[3]

What had been emerging on both the national and the local levels was the growing awareness that higher education no longer was limited to traditional degree programs, undergraduate and graduate, but that education, broadly conceived, should properly be a *process* spanning an entire lifetime, hence the increasing popularity of such slogans as "lifelong learning" and "learning never ends." As adult women and men began to appreciate the need for acquiring new knowledge and skills to maintain their professional competence or to change careers or live fuller and richer personal lives, they turned to institutions of higher learning, like University Extension, to provide them access and opportunity to fulfill their professional and personal goals. And as President Bok pointed out in his timely Commencement address, the University no longer could ignore the needs of society and had to adopt a dual sense of mission that accommodated the growing number of adult learners. If the United States were to realize its aim of becoming transformed into a true learning society, it would depend on continuing higher education programs as never before.[4]

In 1984-85, the seventy-fifth anniversary of University Extension at Harvard, a new record was set in the number of courses offered, students enrolled, course registrations recorded, degrees awarded, and Harvard staff enrolled for courses and degrees under the auspices of the Tuition Assistance Plan.

Throughout its history University Extension never had its own coat of arms, as did all the other schools of Harvard University. To correct this omission, Dean Shinagel arranged a luncheon meeting at the Harvard Faculty Club with Mason Hammond, Pope Professor of the Latin Language and Literature of Harvard University *Emeritus*, a recognized authority on heraldry and coats of arms. In August 1982 the two met at the Harvard Faculty Club for lunch and discussed a coat of arms for University Extension that would be appropriate, using paper napkins to sketch various designs.

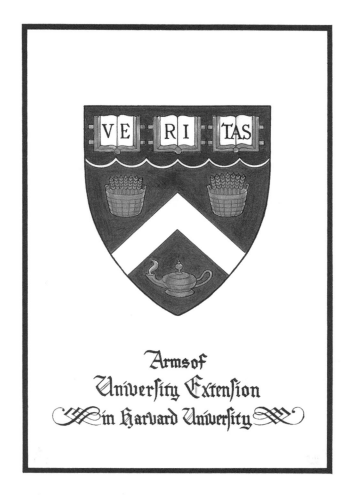

ARMS OF UNIVERSITY EXTENSION

Designed by Professor Mason Hammond and Dean Shinagel,
and executed by D'A. Jonathan D. Boulton, 1982.
Approved officially by the Harvard Corporation, June 8, 1983.

When they had drafted a proper coat of arms, they called upon Marjorie B. Cohn, conservator in the University Art Museums and senior lecturer on fine arts, who executed a colored version of their proposed design in September 1982. Eventually it was presented for approval to the University Committee on Seals, Arms, and Diplomas, which had a reputation for being conservative, and it called for revisions to the design. An Extension faculty member, Dr. D'A. Jonathan D. Boulton, who was very knowledgeable in heraldic matters, agreed to revise the rendering of the coat of arms in color, and it was finally approved on January 21, 1983, and voted by the Harvard Corporation on June 8, 1983. The final color drawing of the coat of arms by Dr. Boulton for University Extension was hung along side all the other official arms of the University in the Harvard Corporation Room at 17 Quincy Street in Cambridge.

The design of the arms had to address three key features of University Extension: it was the creation of President A. Lawrence Lowell in 1910, it offered instruction leading to Harvard degrees at the undergraduate and graduate levels, and its courses were taught in the evenings at Harvard. The coat of arms of the Lowell family already had been assigned to Lowell House when it was created, so it could not be used. But the founder of the Lowell Institute, John Lowell, Jr., had stipulated in his will in 1835 that the courses offered should not cost more than the value of two bushels of wheat. It seemed appropriate to have the coat of arms show two gold bushel baskets with gold stalks of wheat sticking out of them.

To represent graduate education, the top of the shield had the three open books spelling out the Harvard motto of "veritas," the same chief that was used by Harvard's graduate schools to signify their affiliation to the University. But whereas other graduate schools had a straight line at the bottom of the chief, the University Extension design differed by having a series of arcs pointing downward so that the chief was inverted.

Undergraduate education was represented by a silver chevron below the two bushels of wheat with the point separating the two bushel baskets. Historically, the chevron denoting undergraduate education was used by Harvard College from the seventeenth to the late nineteenth centuries, and although no longer in use, the precedent was deemed suitable for University Extension in the later twentieth century.

Finally, a golden lamp of learning was inserted under the chevron at the base of the shield to signify teaching and learning in the evening. The background colors for the shield were the Harvard crimson for the chief, and a midnight blue for the field.

According to Professor Hammond, "the arms may, therefore, be described in English as: midnight blue bearing in chief two bushels of wheat in gold and in base a lamp of learning, also in gold, the three separated by a chevron in silver (white); above a chief of Harvard inverted. The heraldic blazon would be: Azure foncé, between the two bushels of wheat in chief and a lamp of learning in base, all or, a chevron, argent; above chief of Harvard." One hundred fifty years after John Lowell, Jr. drafted his final will and testament in Luxor, Egypt, and fifty years after Harvard celebrated its tricentennial, Professor Mason Hammond's article, "The Genesis and Symbolic Significance of the Extension School's Coat of Arms," appeared in the *Harvard Library Bulletin*. University Extension finally had its own coat of arms and it was officially documented.[5]

The academic year 1982-83 was memorable because it was the last year that the Grossman Library for University Extension was housed in Lehman Hall in quarters that University Extension had long outgrown. The following year it moved to a newly renovated and more spacious location on the third floor of Sever Hall, the most heavily used classroom building by the Extension evening program. The Extension library provided an invaluable service to thousands of Extension students, who recorded more than 16,500 visits to the facility each year. The reserve desk held nearly 1,700 books and articles for Extension courses in a year. After the move to Sever Hall the library recorded a near doubling of student visits to nearly 30,000, and the circulating reserve books increased to more than 13,000.

Commencement in 1983 had the distinction of honoring two Extension graduates. Christopher M. Lohse, ALM '83, was selected to give the Graduate English Oration titled, "Ten Thousand Ghosts of Harvard," a reference to the thousands of Extension students who attend classes in Harvard Yard in the evenings. Thomas Small, ALM '83, received his degree in the ninetieth year of his age, thereby making him the oldest earned degree recipient in the history of Harvard University, a singular achievement that President Bok singled out for special mention when conferring the Extension degrees.

The year 1983-84 marked the fifth year that the Master of Liberal Arts (ALM) in Extension Studies degree program had been in operation. In approving the program, the Faculty of Arts and Sciences had mandated that the ALM undergo a formal review in five years. The dean of the Faculty of Arts and Sciences charged the newly established Standing Committee on Continuing Education to undertake such a review of the program during the year. The standing committee completed its review in the spring and gave its endorsement of the program in its report to the Faculty Council, which in turn was reported to the full faculty by the dean at its May meeting. The master's degree program was now fully accepted by the Faculty of Arts and Sciences.

It was fitting, according to Dean Shinagel, that University Extension should celebrate its diamond anniversary year in 1984-85 by "continuing its recent trend of setting annual records for the number of courses offered (527, up 9 percent from 480 last year), the number of students enrolled (12,822, up 3 percent from 12,431 last year), and the number of course registrations recorded (20,366, up 4 percent from 19,561 last year). By the end of the academic year, an estimated 250,000 women and men had received collegiate and graduate level instruction through Extension courses since the program was started at Harvard in 1910."

A record number of degrees (158) were also awarded during the year, as were another 144 graduate certificates, for a total of 302 degrees and certificates. The growth of graduate enrollments continued unabated as one-third of the students (4,206) and one-third of the course registrations (6,681) were for graduate credit.

The University's Tuition Assistance Plan (TAP) maintained robust enrollments as 943 Harvard staff registered for 1,122 course enrollments. A total of sixty-seven staff members were active candidates for Extension degrees or graduate certificates, and during the year sixteen graduated. The broad appeal of Extension graduate degree and certificate options was evident from the 40 percent of TAP enrollments at the graduate level.

The Health Careers Program continued its estimable work in preparing adult students for admission to medical schools. During the year nearly 150 students participated in the program, taking premedical courses and getting oriented for medical careers. Of the nineteen students who applied to medical schools, fifteen were admitted, a high placement rate for such a program. An historic first was recorded during the year as two students, both women, were accepted by Harvard Medical School.

In the spring term of 1985 University Extension sponsored a new scholarship program for qualified employees of the City of Cambridge to attend the graduate management program of the Certificate of Special Studies (CSS) in Administration and Management. Cambridge city officials greeted the program enthusiastically. According to city councilor Francis Duehay, who led the discussions that eventuated in the scholarship program, "internal management always needs strengthening. It makes sense to Cambridge to utilize opportunities that Harvard offers." Dean Raymond Comeau, coordinator of the CSS Program, noted, "this program is another example of Extension's long-standing commitment to community service." The following year the Leonard J. Russell Scholarships, named in honor of the late mayor of Cambridge, were initiated with three Cambridge employees awarded scholarships each term. These scholarships proved particularly attractive to Cambridge city employees, and in subsequent years the applicant pool was so strong that the selection committee awarded four scholarships instead of the usual three. The Russell scholarships, among other Extension town-gown initiatives, strengthened the ties between the University and the local community.[6]

Another milestone occurred in the spring of 1985, when Roy J. Glauber, Mallinckrodt Professor of Physics at Harvard, offered his Harvard core curriculum physics course to Extension students, Physics E-26 *Waves, Particles, and the Structure of Matter*. This marked the first Harvard course in Extension designed for advanced secondary school students and their teachers from Greater Boston; the first course to offer scholarship help to those secondary school students and teachers; and the first course to enlist teaching assistants who were faculty members from Boston institutions and authors of major books in the field. The enrollment in the course numbered nearly 150, with forty-two area high schools as well as a dozen high school science teachers represented. Professor Glauber used his course to influence the teaching of science in secondary schools, much as he remembered being taught science in the first graduating class at the illustrious Bronx High School of Science. He went on to teach this course to thousands of students and teachers in University Extension for many years for whom it was as much fun to learn physics as it was for him to teach it. There was a happy ending to this story in 2005, when Professor Glauber was awarded the Nobel Prize in physics.

To commemorate the seventy-fifth anniversary of University Extension, the *Harvard Gazette* published an eight-page supplement for its April 26 issue titled "75 Years of Community and Classroom," that celebrated the role of Extension in serving both the Harvard and the Greater Boston communities over the years. Also, *Harvard Magazine* for its May-June issue presented a feature article by Dr. Robert Coles titled "Learning After Hours" that highlighted Extension's educational role in serving the wider community. Finally, University Extension sponsored a special public concert in Sanders Theatre on March 18. The Harvard Chamber Orchestra conducted by Leon Kirchner performed works by Brahms, Britten, and Debussy to a capacity audience.[7]

Administratively, after seventy-five years of a fringe existence at Harvard University, Extension formally became the Division of Continuing Education within the Faculty of Arts and Sciences, comprising the Extension School, the Summer School, and the Institute for Learning in Retirement. And on July 1, 1985, Extension became a formal school as well as a department of the University, thereby achieving a new form of governance and financial and legal status within the University that allowed it to maintain its historic role of serving the community while also earning a more clearly defined role within the Faculty of Arts and Sciences in particular and Harvard University in general. University Extension had finally become an acknowledged and accepted academic and fiscal entity within Harvard.

Thomas Small, ALM '83; Alvaro Uribe, CSS '93;
Mary Fasano, ALB '97; Amit Chatterjee, ALB '02

CHAPTER XI

New Programs, New Constituencies, and an Expanding National and International Reach (1986-99)

The year 1986 marked the sesquitricentennial of Harvard College, a celebratory year for the entire University coming just one year after University Extension celebrated its diamond anniversary. To commemorate this auspicious occasion the Harvard University Marshal, Dr. Richard M. Hunt, commissioned the Boylston Professor of Rhetoric and Oratory, Seamus Heaney, to compose a poem for the convocation exercises scheduled for September 5, 1986, in the Tercentenary Theatre of Harvard Yard. More than 20,000 Harvard graduates and guests of the University assembled to witness this historic event. The highlight of the day was Heaney himself, attired in the scarlet, blue, and white academic gown of his *alma mater*, Queen's University, Belfast, who recited in his richly resonant baritone voice his commemorative poem. His "Villanelle for an Anniversary" captured poetically the spirit of the early Harvard as well as of University Extension, and Extension students were especially moved to hear the concluding quatrain:

> Begin again where frosts and tests were hard.
> Find yourself or founder. Here. Imagine
> A spirit moves, John Harvard walks the yard.
> The books stand open and the gates unbarred.

The spirit of John Harvard and the University Extension tradition of open access to Harvard Yard and learning after dark were encapsulated by Heaney's poem.

Harvard Extension School embarked on its seventy-sixth year of operation by setting new records for the number of courses offered (575),

143

the number of students enrolled (13,320), and the number of course registrations (20,578). The growth of the academic program was matched by the number of graduates: 143 degrees and 195 graduate certificates for a total of 338 new members of the Harvard Extension Alumni Association.

Among the academic innovations for the year was the approval of the new graduate Certificate of Public Health (CPH), sponsored jointly by the Harvard School of Public Health and University Extension. The certificate was designed to meet the educational needs of a wide range of health professionals in Greater Boston. Patterned after the Extension School's other graduate certificate programs, the CPH program constituted a full year of study, or eight courses, including four that were required: *Introduction to Epidemiology, Pathophysiology of Human Diseases, Introduction to Biostatistics*, and a management course. Among the more than fifty interested students who attended the initial orientation meeting, most were in-service health professionals at hospitals, public health agencies, and private health clinics who were motivated to pursue the CPH to advance their careers or to shift the focus of their careers. According to Dr. Dade Moeller, associate dean for continuing education at the Harvard School of Public Health, "the CPH provides an opportunity for graduate training to those with only a bachelor's degree, an option not readily available at the School of Public Health." The CPH had a successful launch in the fall term of 1986 and featured its first graduate in June 1987, Ioulia Pavlopoulou of Athens, Greece, who was trained as a pharmacist and came to the United States in 1985 to work as a research associate at Brigham and Women's Hospital while her husband was a fellow at the Harvard School of Public Health.[1]

Since its inception, University Extension attracted some of the University's most distinguished professors to teach in its evening academic program. In the 1920s and '30s Professor Kenneth B. Murdoch taught courses in American literature at the Extension School, and in his role as dean of the Faculty of Arts and Sciences in 1933-34, he described in his annual report the ideal of the Harvard teacher-scholar whose creative combination of teaching and scholarship "results in the most successful educational leadership." In the year of Harvard's 350th anniversary, six professors *emeriti* of the Faculty of Arts and Sciences were teaching in the

Harvard Extension School, and they all epitomized the teacher-scholar ideal set forth by Dean Murdoch by their distinguished scholarly records and their dedication as teachers in retirement.[2]

Daniel Aaron, Victor S. Thomas Professor of English and American Literature *Emeritus*, was teaching the course *American Literature and Society Between the Wars:* 1912-1943, while also serving as president of the Library of America series, volumes designed to be the definitive editions of all major American authors. Professor Aaron, author of *Men of Good Hope*, *Writers on the Left*, and *The Unwritten War* as well as a founding father of American studies, valued the opportunity to teach a diverse audience of older and younger students in his Extension classes.

Morton Bloomfield, Arthur Kingsley Porter Professor of English *Emeritus*, was offering at the Extension School the same course he taught at Harvard College, Chaucer's *The Canterbury Tales*, a course in close textual analysis considered in literary and social contexts. Professor Bloomfield's scholarly reputation was established by two major works: *The Linguistic History of the English Language* and *The Seven Deadly Sins*. He admired his Extension students for their determination to pursue a broad, humanizing liberal education throughout their lives, despite the demands of family and career.

I Bernard Cohen, Victor S. Thomas Professor of the History of Science *Emeritus*, was teaching his signature course on *The Scientific Revolution*. It was an intellectual and social approach that reflected his own broad interdisciplinary interests in science as evidenced in his recent book *Revolution in Science*. A founding father of the field of history of science, Professor Cohen also published *Birth of a New Physics*, a standard textbook for high school and college students. He taught at the Extension School throughout most of his academic career at Harvard, describing it as "an energy-replenishing experience."

Henry Hatfield, Kuno Francke Professor of German Art and Culture *Emeritus*, offered his popular course *Mann and Kafka*. Among his many publications, Professor Hatfield was noted for his study of Thomas Mann titled *From the Magic Mountain* and *Goethe: A Critical Introduction*. Like Professor Cohen, Hatfield characterized his Extension teaching as "regenerative." He concluded that Extension teaching "is as interesting as regular College teaching, but with a significant difference. Extension students are more eager, more grateful for what they receive."

Albert B. Lord, Arthur Kingsley Porter Professor of Slavic and Comparative Literature *Emeritus*, taught *Heroic Poetry: From Oral to Written Epic and Romance*, a course derived from his seminal study *Singer of Tales*. He valued the Extension teaching because "it is exciting to teach adults who bring such difference to combinations of personal, educational, and professional backgrounds to heroic literature."

Lawrence Wylie, C. Douglas Dillon Professor of the Civilization of France *Emeritus*, taught *Communication with the French*, an innovative course devoted to an analysis of nonverbal communication as compared with verbal communication. A specialist in French body language and an interdisciplinary scholar of such studies as *Village in the Vaucluse* and *Chanzeaux: A Village of Anjou*, which drew on his training in anthropology, communication, and French culture, including a mime school in Paris, Professor Wylie introduced his Extension students to the nuances of French body language by having them practice it in class.

The participation of these six eminent Harvard teacher-scholars in retirement in University Extension during Harvard's anniversary year highlighted the storied role that members of the Faculty of Arts and Sciences had in the appeal of the evening program over the years. The "dream faculty" of which Dr. Reginald Phelps wrote in the early 1970s was still very much in evidence in the mid-1980s, and would continue to remain a distinctive feature of the Extension curriculum in the years ahead.

Thanks to an initiative by the president of Harvard, Derek Bok, an executive committee was created in 1986 to meet once each semester to address problems facing University Extension. The membership included the president, the dean of the Faculty of Arts and Sciences, the administrative dean of arts and sciences, and the dean of the Extension School. The purpose of this newly constituted committee was to enable Extension to tie in more directly with both the FAS and the University. The growth in size and service of the Extension School prompted the president and the deans to recognize the expanded role of continuing education at Harvard.

As part of its outreach to the local community, University Extension for a dozen years offered course scholarships to talented juniors and seniors at Cambridge Rindge and Latin School, which, through its Community-Based Learning Program, selected fifteen or more students for the scholarships and monitored their progress. Although seniors were usually given preference, exceptional students also were recognized. One notable student, Beth Friedman, received her first scholarship when only a freshman, and thanks to subsequent scholarships was able to complete her four-year high school program in only three years. The headmaster of the school, Edward Sarasin, praised the University Extension scholarship program, saying "it provides an opportunity for our advanced students to take college courses in a real college setting." As the student body at Cambridge Rindge and Latin School became more multicultural with the influx of new immigrant groups to Cambridge, Harvard Extension School also provided scholarships to deserving students for its English as a second language program. The first three recipients of these scholarships were King Lam from the People's Republic of China, Nabil Emmad from Yemen, and Bertine Larosiliere from Haiti, all of whom benefited enormously from the scholarship program.[3]

The Lowell Scholarships, which enabled local high school students and their teachers to enroll in Harvard Extension School science courses at reduced tuition, were created to meet the needs of talented and motivated secondary school students whose schools either eliminated or curtailed advanced placement science courses for budgeting or staffing reasons. This program enabled thousands of Boston area students and in some cases their teachers as well to enroll in mathematics and science courses, such as Harvard Physics Professor Roy Glauber's *Waves, Particles, and the Structure of Matter*, which drew more than 200, and *Introduction to the Calculus*, *Introduction to Computing in Pascal*, and *Animal Behavior*, all of which enrolled many students.

In the fall of 1989, after three years of planning, University Extension introduced its newest graduate program: the Certificate in Museum Studies (CMS). The CMS was initiated by the directors of Harvard's many museums who participated in the planning process with senior staff from University Extension. The program was designed to provide both in-service museum workers and beginners with the basic knowledge and training to pursue professional careers in the field. The curriculum called for the completion of eight courses, including two required core courses (*An Introduction to Museology* and *Issues in Museum Administration*) as well as a museum internship. That first year University Extension offered thirty-nine courses in the field, and the *Introduction to Museology* course alone enrolled ninety-one students. Candidates could choose electives from seven fields: museum administration, anthropology museums, art museums, history museums, natural history museums, library/archives, and technical/practical topics. In time the CMS would evolve into a master's degree and the certificate would be discontinued.

In 1982 a member of the Providence, Rhode Island, city council began commuting weekly to University Extension as a candidate for the ALM in government. Joseph R. Paolino, Jr. continued to combine his political and his academic careers, rising to president of the city council and then to acting mayor until 1984, when he became the youngest person elected mayor of Providence. Mayor Paolino completed his requirements for the master's degree in government in March 1989 with a thesis on the housing problem in Providence, using material from three of his Harvard Extension School graduate courses. As mayor he was named by the Providence Junior Chamber of Commerce as the "Outstanding Young Rhode Islander" and by the Italo-American Club of Providence as "Man of the Year." At the June degree-awarding ceremonies on Commencement Day, Paolino gave the graduate student address, "A Time of Choices," a personal account of his family experiences and the challenges he dealt with as mayor of Providence. He was also the recipient of the Derek Bok Award for Public Service from University Extension. Eventually President Clinton appointed Joseph R. Paolino, Jr. as US ambassador to Malta.[4]

When Sarah M. Buel graduated, with honors, with a Bachelor of Liberal Arts in 1987, she also was honored by being selected as one of the "Ten Outstanding Young Women of America," a national distinction reserved for women between the ages of twenty-one and thirty-six who achieved notable accomplishments in both the civic and the professional spheres. Buel had served as the domestic violence, child abuse, and sexual assault program coordinator for the Massachusetts governor's statewide anti-crime council and at the time of her graduation from University Extension was the president of the board of directors of the Victim

Resources Center of Lowell. The selection committee for the award had been particularly impressed with the extensive volunteer work Buel had done nationwide. In addition to working as a paralegal and office worker for many years while a single mother, she volunteered in assorted civic service organizations dealing with child abuse, domestic violence, and civil rights. As a resident in Colorado in 1983-84, for example, she worked in the Women in Crisis Shelter in Arvada, founded the Colorado statewide community legal education committee, was chairperson of the Colorado Civil Liberties Union's women's rights committee, and volunteered with the Legal Aid Foundation of metropolitan Denver.

She was admitted to Harvard Law School following graduation from University Extension and continued her work as an activist in civil rights as a member of the board of Children's Rights Project, a member of the Harvard Law School civil rights-civil liberties action committee, and a member of the Prison Legal Assistance Project. She also served on the staff of the *Harvard Women's Law Journal* and wrote an article on family violence. Her plans after Harvard Law School called for her to organize a poverty law center in Massachusetts. In time Buel became a professor of law at a national law school, grateful to University Extension for her education and for the opportunity to work effectively "for social change" and to provide "poor people with the knowledge that will help them help themselves."[5]

Under the able direction of Sylvia Field, in 1989 the Health Careers Program of University Extension achieved a remarkable 100 percent admission rate to medical schools for the sixteen women and eleven men who applied. These twenty-seven applicants ranged in age from twenty-two to thirty-seven years and had an average undergraduate grade-point average (GPA) of 3.2. The following year twenty-eight candidates applied, ranging in age from twenty-two to thirty-nine years and having an average undergraduate GPA of 3.3. The diversity of the applicant pool was evident from their backgrounds, which included an engineer, an ordained minister, a homebuilder, a former chef, an Olympic rower, and the usual assortment of medical researchers, nurses, and social workers. Their undergraduate colleges included Brown, Cornell, Dartmouth, Yale, Boston College, Middlebury, Vassar, and Wesleyan. Of the twenty-eight applicants, twenty-four were admitted, including three to Harvard Medical School and nine to the University of Massachusetts. The singular success rate of students completing the Health Careers Program and gaining admission to top medical schools established the reputation of this Harvard Extension School program as the "second chance" for those intent on a medical career.

In the fall of 1992 William Fixsen became the new director of the Health Careers Program at a time when enrollments in the premed courses were burgeoning both at Harvard and at the national level. Dr. Fixsen, with a doctorate in biology from the Massachusetts Institute of Technology, also taught *Introductory Biology* at Harvard College as well as in University Extension. His knowledge of the program and the students served to enhance the reputation of the Health Careers Program nationally, especially the singular success rate of graduates in applying to medical school. By the year 1993-94 the program could boast a 90 percent acceptance rate to medical school for the thirty-eight students sponsored by the Harvard Extension School. It was a competitive time when there was a record number of applicants to US medical schools and only one in three was accepted. Five women from the Health Careers Program were accepted to Harvard Medical School, a new record for the program. By the year 2000, a total of 615 women and men had been sponsored for medical school by the Health Careers Program and 582 had been admitted, an acceptance rate of greater than 80 percent.

University Extension celebrated its eightieth anniversary year in 1990 and experienced a record enrollment of 14,300 women and men, accounting for nearly 22,500 course registrations. According to an analysis of the student registration forms, the educational backgrounds of the students were impressive, as more than three-quarters already possessed a bachelor's degree and one-fifth had a graduate degree as well. This helped explain the motivation of the students, for only 25 percent sought to pursue a degree or graduate certificate, whereas 38 percent came out of personal interest and 37 percent for professional development. The majority of the students, as in previous years, were new to the Extension School. The attractions of attending University Extension were the outstanding quality of the faculty and the rich assortment of courses and programs offered. Each year Extension students evaluated their teachers on a course evaluation questionnaire, and the faculty were consistently rated an average of six on a seven-point scale.

A major incentive for Harvard faculty to teach evenings in the Extension School was the singular quality of the thousands of students who enrolled each year. Sometimes the Extension students began their studies at Harvard College and eventually graduated with an Extension degree. Such a student was Howard Abramson. He had graduated from Boston Latin School in 1936 and, like many of his classmates, he matriculated at Harvard College as a member of the Class of 1940. He planned on a medical career, but in his junior year he had to abandon his studies because of his father's serious illness, and he became the main source of financial support to his parents by selling sportswear. He served in World War II in Italy, earning a Bronze Star as well as other decorations, and he married and raised a family while developing his sportswear business locally and nationally. Eventually his wife and three children, who collectively had nine degrees among them, encouraged Abramson to take Harvard Extension School courses and complete his Harvard degree. In June 1990 he received his Bachelor of Liberal Arts (ALB) degree *cum laude* at the age of seventy, and he had the unique pleasure of marching in the academic procession in the morning with his fellow members of the Harvard Class of 1940, celebrating their fiftieth Harvard reunion. In the afternoon, attired in cap and gown, he joined his fellow members of University Extension Class of 1990 to receive his ALB degree at the diploma ceremony held at the Loeb Drama Center on Brattle Street. The dilemma of Howard Abramson on Commencement Day was resolved happily when he could be a part of both his Harvard classes separated in time by fifty years but combined successfully—and successively—on one memorable June day. His achievement was also recognized in the fall of 1990 when he received the Outstanding Continuing Education Student Award of the National University Continuing Education Association (NUCEA) for the New England region.[6]

Two years later another Harvard Extension School student, Deborah Sughrue, ALB '92, received the NUCEA award for having "demonstrated outstanding achievement and an unusual will to learn." While a student in high school, Sughrue experienced the deaths of her mother and father within two months of each other, and instead of thinking about college like her classmates, she assumed the dual roles of breadwinner and caregiver to her three younger siblings. She worked fifty to sixty hours a week to support her family financially, while also finding time to support them emotionally. She still managed to graduate from high school only one semester behind her classmates and began taking courses at the Harvard Extension School in the 1980s. When the family financial situation allowed her more time for her studies, she enrolled in courses on a more regular basis, and in the late 1980s and early '90s was named to the dean's list for academic excellence. In 1992 she was awarded the ALB degree, *cum laude*, and was elected a class marshal. While an Extension student she had married and had two children, and in the fall of 1992 she enrolled in Harvard Law School, a testament to her "unusual will to learn" as well as her "outstanding academic achievement."[7]

At a ceremonial banquet commemorating the 150th anniversary of the Harvard Alumni Association (HAA) on October 5, 1990, President Derek Bok made presentations to ten outstanding Harvard alumni, all of whom received the newly created Harvard Alumni Association Award (a Steuben glass base and a replica of the John Harvard statue with a sterling silver nameplate). Among the honorees was Edgar Grossman, Bachelor of Arts in Extension Studies '66, recognized for his role in founding the Harvard Extension Alumni Association (HEAA) in 1968 and serving as its first president. He served later as the HEAA representative to the parent organization, the HAA. Grossman would also become a major benefactor of University Extension over the years, notably endowing the Grossman Library and the Grossman Common Room.

In October 1991 a national senator from Medelin, Colombia, applied to the Certificate of Special Studies (CSS) in Administration and Management Program, and in response to the question of "Why are you interested in the CSS program?" he wrote: "I chose the CSS program because it offers many courses related to my goals. I hope to play a very important role in the political life of my country, to which the CSS Program will be useful." He started taking courses in the spring term of 1991, including courses in English as a second language, and he was awarded the CSS from the Harvard Extension School in the fall of 1993. The student's name was Alvaro Uribe, and in time he did "play a very important role in the political life of [his] country": he became president of Colombia, making him the first Harvard Extension School graduate to be elected president of a country.

Among the thousands of ALB graduates of the Harvard Extension School, Mary Fasano stands out because she received her degree, like Thomas Small, in the ninetieth year "of her age," thereby earning her the distinction of being the oldest undergraduate degree recipient in the history of Harvard University. She was born in Natick, Rhode Island, on May 12, 1908, to Italian immigrant parents who did not encourage her to pursue her studies, even though she was a promising student. At the age of fourteen she went to work in a cotton mill to help support the family. But, as she recalled, "I made a promise to myself that I would go back to school someday."

She married and raised five children while also working in the family business, Fasano Diner and Catering, in Braintree, Massachusetts. Although she tried to resume her education several times, the pressures of family and business inevitably frustrated her attempts. Only when she finally decided to retire, after nearly sixty years of work, and sold the diner while her children assumed responsibility for the catering business, did she resume her education. First, she earned her high school equivalency diploma from Braintree High School and then, in 1979, she enrolled in Spanish, her first course in the Harvard Extension School, at the age of seventy-one. She stayed on for eighteen years, earning honors grades in foreign languages, philosophy, mathematics, and literature in her late eighties, culminating in her ALB degree in 1997. She was the Commencement orator at the Extension undergraduate degree awarding ceremony. Her address was titled "The Power of Knowledge." Her grandchildren arranged for a limousine to transport her to Harvard Commencement, and her remarkable story was a feature on the local news stations as well as the "Today Show."[8]

In September 1995, the Harvard Extension School established a new graduate certificate, the Certificate in Publishing and Communications (CPC). Created by David Gewanter, director of the writing program, the program was designed to offer students academic, technical, and professional training for careers in the world of publishing and media production. Equivalent to one year of graduate studies, the program consisted of seven courses, including the two core courses, *Principles of Editing* and *Survey of Publishing*, and electives chosen from fields such as expository and professional writing, creative writing, journalism, technical writing, and media production. The program was capped by an invaluable 200-hour internship when students put the editing and writing skills they learned in class to practical use in publishing or editorial offices. "We've had nearly 100 inquiries about the program so far," reported Dr. Gewanter. "Most remarkable, though, was the diversity of backgrounds and skills of students coming here. Some want to learn new technology, others wanted to move to a new position in the publishing world, and still others had been writing for a while and wanted to enter the field." Soon the CPC Program was graduating students who entered the field of publishing in Boston and elsewhere.

In August 1996 the Harvard Extension School opened the Career and Academic Resource Center (CARC). It was operated by the staff of the undergraduate degree program under the direction of Suzanne Spreadbury, and was available to all registered Extension students. CARC maintained a reference library of graduate school directories, career handbooks, study abroad catalogs, Internet access for online job searches, computerized learning opportunities, and career assessment programs. Harvard Extension School course evaluations and syllabi were on file for review. CARC student services included a writing center, math center, career counseling, and academic workshops for adult learners. The usefulness of CARC was abundantly clear by the year 2000, when nearly 1,000 students availed themselves of its resources, especially the group and individual career counseling sessions as well as the academic and graduate school workshops. The writing center alone served more than 700 students.

Established in the fall of 1997, the instructional innovation fund of the Harvard Extension School provided financial support to faculty members who sought to introduce pedagogical innovations into their existing courses or were interested in developing new courses. As Dean Shinagel remarked when creating the fund: "Excellent teaching has always been a hallmark of the Harvard Extension School, and with this fund we have signaled our abiding commitment to this principle."

Among the first recipients were three faculty members teaching courses in the environmental management program at the Harvard Extension School: John Spengler, George Buckley, and Petros Koutrakis. For their three natural science courses, *Environmental Management I* and *II* as well as *Ocean Environments*, the faculty members were able to provide their more than 150 students videos-on-demand lectures, web slide show presentations, list servers, online teaching assistants, interactive Q&A testing, and visual field trips. According to one faculty member: "The expanded repertoire of active learning opportunities provided by these experiences is a most valuable addition to the courses."

Another recipient of the fund, Dr. Thomas Raymond, taught *Effective Written Communications* to students in the administration and management certificate program, many of whom were international students. He used the fund to collect and edit student-written case studies to address the needs of international students by focusing on international management communication issues. By using the assembled anthology of student-written cases, the professor and his staff examined communications problems from a cross-cultural perspective to train students in handling management issues resulting from imprecise writing styles. Students found this innovative approach especially helpful as they prepared themselves for entry into the global corporate world.

Other proposals were funded in psychology and government. The value of the instructional innovation fund became evident from the outset, as faculty and students appreciated the commitment of the Harvard Extension School to a shared partnership in promoting "active learning" as an integral part of adult education.

In the fall of 1998, the new Master of Liberal Arts (ALM) in Information Technology was established, resulting in a near doubling of enrollments in computer science courses, many of which were available online as distance courses. The new program was particularly attractive to international students, and the first person to earn the ALM in Information Technology in 2000 was Aamer Manzoor, a native of Pakistan with a remarkable background in the field. He already possessed an MBA and had founded a software development company and an Internet service provider before enrolling at the Harvard Extension School. Despite his sophistication, he soon found the curriculum highly relevant to his career objectives: "The program provided the opportunity to learn a broad range of IT-related technologies. And more surprisingly, I am a far better manager, one who is able to understand the needs and problems of the technical staff and as a result design more efficient and responsive systems, and manage my company more effectively."

At the end of the century, according to the annual report filed for the academic year 1999-2000, the Harvard Extension School maintained its strong enrollment with nearly 14,000 women and men accounting for almost 24,000 registrations among the 584 courses offered. By the end of the year a total of 226 undergraduate and graduate degrees were awarded as well as 303 graduate certificates, for a combined total of 529 graduates.

The international theme of the Harvard Extension School was evident among the seventy-nine graduates of the Master of Liberal Arts Program. Their places of birth included Canada, Chile, Germany, Japan, Jordan, Malaysia, Morocco, Saudi Arabia, El Salvador, and Thailand, and their prior academic training was done in Australia, the United Kingdom, Ireland, and Spain. Similarly, the 243 graduates of the Certificate of Special Studies in Administration and Management Program included 169 international students representing thirty-six countries, with Brazil, Mexico, Venezuela, Colombia, and Argentina accounting for the most graduates. Finally, the seven graduates of the Certificate in Public Health Program included four international students from Denmark, Korea, Germany, and Nigeria.

Predictably, the international theme was central to the mission of the Harvard Institute for English Language Programs (IEL), and during the year a record 1,369 students representing eighty-two countries participated, with forty-four native languages spoken, notably Spanish, Portuguese, Korean, German, and Chinese (Mandarin).

The success of the University's Tuition Assistance Plan was very much in evidence by the total of 1,548 Harvard staff members who enrolled and accounted for 2,281 course registrations. Whereas some staff enrolled for specific skills or general knowledge, many also availed themselves of degree and graduate certificate options. Of the graduate and undergraduate degrees conferred in the year, thirty-two were awarded to Harvard staff, and another seventeen employees earned graduate certificates with their TAP benefits.

The Harvard Extension School also addressed the needs of lower-paid Harvard staff who were recent immigrants to the United States and required basic English language skills that were organized by the director of IEL, Dr. Lilith Haynes. Nearly 250 Harvard affiliates were served by the IEL staff in assorted English classes both in Cambridge and in Boston at Harvard Medical School. Since English language proficiency was a necessity for employment and for career advancement, the Harvard Extension School was working with Harvard's central administration to establish the comprehensive Bridge Program to provide these workplace language skills to entry-level Harvard employees.

The Harvard Extension School also maintained its tradition of community outreach through the auspices of the Lowell Scholarships, whereby local high school students, teachers, and administrators received reduced tuition scholarships to take courses in the academic program. During the year 1999-2000, 150 students from sixty-seven schools registered in thirty-eight courses in the fall term and forty-four courses in the spring term. These students proved themselves able and motivated: 116 (80 percent) earned honors grades in their courses. Another thirty students from Cambridge Rindge and Latin School were awarded scholarships in cooperation with the school's Community-Based Learning Program.

As the Harvard Extension School rounded out ninety years of operation, the dean observed in his annual report that the scope and reach of the program had undergone a dramatic shift, from a small evening program designed to serve commuters from the local community to a greatly expanded academic program, with a distance education component, designed to "reach adult students regionally, nationally, internationally, and globally."

INDIAN COMPUTER ACADEMY

Top: Dean Govindarajulu's commencement address
at the 1993 graduation, Bangalore, India.
Bottom: Leila Almeida, Michael Shinagel, Paul Bamberg,
Prakash Ahuja, and Gope Gidwani in attendance
at the graduation exercises.

CHAPTER XII

A Passage to India

Creation of the Indian Computer Academy
in Bangalore, India (1989-94)

The prime mover behind the creation of a computer academy in Bangalore was a Boston businessman with strong ties to India, Gope Gidwani of the International Trade and Management Company, with offices in Dedham, Massachusetts, and Bombay, India. Gidwani was familiar with the reputation of the computer science courses at the Harvard Extension School, and in the spring of 1989 he approached Drs. Paul Bamberg and Henry Leitner, director and associate director of science instruction for continuing education, respectively, to discuss the possibility of a joint educational venture that he was willing to fund.[1]

Bamberg and Leitner had developed over the years a core curriculum in computer science at Harvard for courses in the Extension and Summer Schools leading to the Harvard Extension School graduate Certificate in Applied Sciences designed to train adult students to serve the needs of the local high technology industry in Greater Boston. Upon reflection, they considered it feasible to effect a technology transfer of the Harvard core curriculum to a proposed computer academy in India. They told Gidwani that they would propose establishing in India a private, not-for-profit postgraduate computer academy, using the Harvard Extension curriculum and training teachers to use that curriculum in India, for the benefit of Indian college graduates seeking employment in the emerging Indian software industry.

In the summer of 1989 Dean Shinagel dispatched Dr. Bamberg and his wife Cherry, accompanied by Mr. Gidwani, who financed the trip, to undertake an on-site survey of the situation in India and file a report upon their return. The party traveled to Delhi, Bombay, and Bangalore, meeting with key representatives from government, industry, and academia to assess the viability of introducing a Harvard-quality computer science curriculum in a suitable location in India. They returned from their twelve-day fact-finding trip and filed a detailed report on September 20, 1989, that indicated support of the concept of an Indian Computer Academy. The recommendations were "that Harvard conclude an agreement with the Indian Computer Academy to provide a curriculum for four courses, to train instructors for these courses, to write and grade all final examinations and a random sample of software projects, and to write an annual evaluation." The agreement also would stipulate that "the Academy would have full responsibility for finding classroom space, acquiring equipment, recruiting faculty, selecting students, and developing courses beyond the basic curriculum."

The Harvard team met on their last day in India with Prakash Ahuja and Gope Gidwani, the leaders of the Indian Computer Academy project, to resolve key issues of academic standards, facilities and equipment, staff, protection of the Harvard name, and future directions. The initial plans were grandiose, calling for "plans to open in Bombay and Bangalore in 1990, to expand to Delhi and Madras in 1991, then to Hyderabad and Pune in 1992." Upon more realistic reflection it was decided to locate the Indian Computer Academy in Bangalore because the city was evolving as the center of the burgeoning high-technology industry of India, very much like the Silicon Valley in California.

The prescience of choosing Bangalore as the proposed site for the planned computer academy was borne out several years later, when the August 1, 1993, edition of the *Washington Post* featured the headline "Indians, Foreigners Build Silicon Valley in Bangalore." In the article, Bangalore, a city of more than four million people, was described as "an island of relative affluence and social stability in this ancient land." Multinational high-tech firms, such as IBM, Texas Instruments, Digital, and Hewlett-Packard, had opened offices in Bangalore, attracted by its "temperate climate and low-wage but well-educated labor pool." Obviously such a mecca for computer-trained graduate students was an ideal place for Harvard's Division of Continuing Education to help establish the Indian Computer Academy.

Gidwani sought someone prominent in the Bangalore community who could assume the vital role of serving as the chief administrator of the computer academy. He settled on Mr. Prakash Ahuja, chairman of Mothercare India Limited, a company traded on the Bombay Stock Exchange that was doing well financially.

Harvard's Division of Continuing Education, on behalf of the Harvard Extension School, entered into a formal agreement with the newly incorporated Indian Computer Academy (ICA) in Bangalore in September 1990. A substantial grant from Citibank arranged by Peter Thorp, vice president of corporate university relations, enabled Bamberg and Leitner to revise all their teaching materials, based on their Harvard courses, for the core curriculum of the ICA. Also funding was made available for two ICA faculty members to attend the Harvard Summer School for training in the new curriculum.

The plan for the academy was to offer a core curriculum that was the equivalent of a year of full-time study at Harvard Extension and Summer Schools leading to the Certificate in Applied Sciences. The students at the ICA would be expected to devote at least twenty hours a week to programming on personal computers, to take the identical mastery tests as Harvard students, and to complete the same kind of software projects. A comprehensive six-hour examination, written by Bamberg and Leitner, would be administered at the ICA and graded at Harvard with the assistance of teaching fellows. Harvard Extension School would maintain the records of all students, their graded examinations, and their accumulated credits for certification. Students would be expected to perform at the same level of proficiency as Harvard Extension or Summer School students in their comprehensive examinations, and student software projects would be sent from the ICA to Harvard for grading by an examining committee. To ensure that the quality of instruction and learning were on a par with Harvard Extension School standards, representatives from Harvard, both teaching faculty and senior administrative staff, would conduct yearly visits to the ICA in Bangalore.

The plan for the ICA, beyond the core curriculum, was to have the courses and training of the graduate students be guided by the emerging needs of the local software industry. Soon the academy was developing advanced courses in software engineering and creating internship programs for its students. These ties to the local software industry proved an effective strategy in maintaining a curriculum that was responsive to local needs and prepared a new class of software professionals for India.

Harvard assumed responsibility for the selection and training of instructors, providing them with annual opportunities to attend courses at both the Harvard Extension and Summer Schools for updating on topics in the curriculum. To ensure a central role for Harvard's Division of Continuing Education in the ICA, it was agreed that Dean Shinagel would chair both the advisory board and the board of trustees. The main responsibility of the board of trustees was to ensure the efficient overall operation of the ICA, and the role of the advisory board was to ensure that the curriculum met the needs of the Indian computer industry and that students were placed in suitable internships as part of their program of studies.

As the signatory on behalf of the ICA in the capacity of trustee, Mr. Ahuja assumed responsibility for renting a suitable building for housing the academy and for overseeing the construction of the facility in terms of classrooms, offices, a library, and computer rooms. In October 1991 an academic dean was hired to administer the academic side of the operation, such as hiring faculty, admitting students, and maintaining academic standards in introducing the Harvard Extension School core curriculum in computer science. Fortunately, Dr. Regeti Govindarajulu, a professor of computer science at the Regional Engineering College in Warangal, was selected to assume this key role. Over the next two years he proved himself to be a dedicated, honest, and able administrator and teacher committed to upholding the academic integrity of the ICA

Although Harvard had assumed that the academy would be a not-for-profit project, at the outset the principals in Bangalore, led by Ahuja, treated it as a for-profit academic undertaking and solicited venture capitalists to become stakeholders. Accordingly, Ahuja of Mothercare as trustee of the ICA enlisted financial support from Sanjay Kulkarni, director of the Twentieth Century Venture Capital Corporation Ltd.; Gope Gidwani, principal of International Trade and Management Co.; and from himself as chairman of Mothercare India Ltd. to cover the start-up expenses of renting and outfitting the facility for the ICA in Bangalore.

In late March and early April 1991 Bamberg and Leitner traveled to Bangalore to interview prospective ICA teachers who would attend the Harvard Summer School and become proficient in the core curriculum. Construction of the facility was ongoing and supervised by Ahuja, who had assumed responsibility for the operation and maintenance of the ICA locally. The goal was to have the academic dean in place by the fall and to open the academy to students in January 1992. To preside over the inauguration of the ICA in January, Bamberg, accompanied by Gidwani, flew to Bangalore.

The maiden meeting of the ICA board of trustees on January 6, 1992, in Bangalore was chaired by Ahuja and included as directors Gidwani, Kulkarni, and Kannan, director of Mothercare. Clearly the board was controlled by the financial investors in the academy from the beginning, with the chairman explaining the status of the project in terms of the lease arrangement for the building and related matters of the infrastructure as well as the projected fees for full-time students (25,000 rupees) and the starting dates for the first and second batches of full-time students, March and August 1992. Bamberg, who was present at the meeting as an invited guest, recalled later that the discussion was mostly in financial terms, with little attention paid to academic matters.

The inauguration of the ICA in early January 1992 was hailed in the Indian press as a major event. *The Times of India* in Bombay on January 9 featured the headline "Harvard to Aid Software School." The *New Delhi Financial Express* on January 10 announced "Harvard-Assisted Computer Software Institute Set Up." Both articles cited the participation of Bamberg, at the inauguration of the Indian Computer Academy in Bangalore along with a number of distinguished guests, including P. Chidambaram, the Indian minister of commerce. As Bamberg later remarked, "The inaugural ceremony was held on an astrologically auspicious day and time in which I participated in an oil lamp lighting ritual." This academic technology transfer of computer courses from the banks of the Charles River in Cambridge to the banks of Sankey Lake in Bangalore marked the first time that the Harvard Extension School created a learning center outside of Boston in more than eighty years of continuous operation.

In late March 1992 Leitner and Shinagel flew to India to inspect the ICA and to attend the meeting of the board of trustees on March 26 in Bangalore. As chair of the board, Shinagel circulated the minutes of the last meeting held on January 11, 1992, chaired by Ahuja. The business of the board was routine, with favorable reports on student grades and financial status, and projections for the forthcoming year. All seemed to be going well.

In the summer of 1992 Professor Gerald Sacks, professor of mathematical logic at Harvard and the Massachusetts Institute of Technology, flew to Bangalore for several weeks to teach advanced courses on Windows programming. The academic work of the first and second batches of students on the comprehensive examinations graded at Harvard proved promising, and the consensus was that the Harvard curriculum was a success. But the positive results academically were offset by complaints emanating from the ICA academic dean that bills were not being paid promptly and that there were delays in faculty salaries. Students also wrote to complain that tuition deposits were not refunded and that the facilities often were inoperable. Harvard continuing education senior staff sent faxes to the ICA to ascertain why these complaints were coming in, but they were not successful in getting appropriate replies.

The next meeting of the board of trustees was scheduled for January 25, 1993, at Harvard. It was attended by trustees Ahuja, Gidwani, Peter Thorp (Citibank), and Gurchuran Das (Proctor and Gamble, India). Also present as invited guests were Bamberg, Leitner, and Sacks. By this time it was becoming increasingly evident that the ICA was facing serious financial and administrative problems, so much so that the board resolved that Citibank be authorized to appoint an independent auditor (A.F. Ferguson of Bangalore) to audit the ICA books for the fiscal year 1992-93, and, if necessary, for the preceding year as well. The auditor used for the ICA in 1991-92 by Ahuja was Dandekar and Company, who also audited Mothercare and therefore constituted a conflict of interest. Ahuja was asked to turn over all the financial records of the ICA to the new auditor.

When in the spring of 1993 Shoba Sethuram, the director of A.F. Ferguson in Bangalore, requested that Ahuja turn over the ICA financial books from the inception to March 1993, he at first questioned her authority and eventually admitted that his manager had left the books a mess and the computer system had crashed and destroyed the records. By summer Ahuja finally produced some partially reconstructed books for part of 1992 to Sethuram, but there were no supporting documents, and therefore the books could not be audited.

The board also resolved that, administratively, Mothercare and the ICA be separated, with the dean assuming responsibility for management of the academy until a business dean and an accountant were in place. Financially, Mothercare would approve temporary loans to cover a short-fall in the ICA 1992 budget, and Twentieth Century Venture Capital would postpone their loan repayment schedule.

Meanwhile the deteriorating situation at the Indian Computer Academy was documented dramatically by an eyewitness report filed by a Harvard Extension School faculty member. After a three-week teaching tour at the ICA in February and March 1993, David S. Platt, a Harvard Extension School instructor and the principal of Rolling Thunder Computing, wrote a detailed confidential report to Dean Shinagel describing his experiences teaching at the Academy in Bangalore. His findings were sobering. He described "the ICA's infrastructure as crumbling," from a "lack of modern computers" to poor lighting, broken desks and chairs, and even the absence of toilet paper in the bathrooms. His discussions with students, faculty, and industry representatives "about the course of study at the ICA ... were by and large positive." Students complained, however, that they came "primarily because of the Harvard name, but the actual product falls far short of the expectations raised by that name." Faculty morale was "low" because they were poorly treated and "they feel that the students are being cheated, and they don't like being agents of it." The advisory board "has met only once," and they are too busy to ensure academic standards or oversight. The library "is not operational in any sense of the word," containing few books, no periodicals, and no copies of software or videotapes as promised in the catalog. Although the catalog stated that "the Academy will offer scholarships to deserving candidates, nobody has received any form of scholarship aid." Platt discerned a palpable conflict between the ICA dean, Dr. Govindarajulu, who wanted to maintain academic standards and enhance the reputation of the academy, and Gidwani and Ahuja of the board of trustees, who wanted to lower standards in order to enroll more students and collect their tuition. Financial mismanagement had sent the ICA "on a downward spiral" because "the infrastructure, the day-to-day operations, the relations with industry [were] not good, and getting worse instead of better." Despite the potential of the ICA, the excellence of the dean academically, the high motivation of the students, and the quality of the Harvard course materials, Platt concluded that unless Harvard took drastic action to set things right financially and administratively, there was no future for the ICA and great potential "damage to Harvard's educational brand name."

By the end of March Ahuja wrote Dean Shinagel that "the process of delinking ICA from Mothercare is almost complete," that Mothercare added funds "to clear pressing needs," that Twentieth Century Venture Capital "agreed in principle to defer repayment of . . . loans," that the search for a business dean was in the process, and that the Citibank appointed auditors were scheduled to look at the ICA financial books.

A preliminary report from A.F. Ferguson on April 13 detailed assorted "proprietary lapses, apart from a number of systemic and control issues" with the ICA accounts. Additional documents were requested by Sethuram of Ferguson's from Ahuja, but they "don't expect it to change the picture at all." As a senior Citibank official commented on the audit of the ICA books: "It works like a Greek tragedy."

On July 2 a senior Citibank officer in Bombay wrote Dean Shinagel a disturbing summary of the findings of the A.F. Ferguson audit, noting that the audit was perforce incomplete because of difficulties in obtaining documents and supporting sources from ICA's managing trustees (Ahuja and Kannan), "particularly relating to the year 1991-92," but the results nonetheless were as follows:

1. "Statutory non-compliance."
2. "Irregularities in operation of the bank accounts, inadequate control, impropriety in handling cash receipts and payments."
3. "Improprieties in certain items of expenditure, unexplained differences in income recognition and non-provision of bank account transaction details."

4. "Lack of financial viability and consignment impact on the
   quality of facilities."

According to the Citibank evaluation of the audit, items two and three
were "of a fundamentally serious nature and may have spurred the current
crisis." Among the improprieties cited in the audit were the lack of supporting receipts to a number of payments, the use of ICA funds for non-
ICA expenses by Mothercare, the unexplained withdrawals from ICA
bank accounts, and the withdrawals of cash for unspecified use.

Despite Ahuja's letter of March stating that the board's resolutions
regarding Mothercare had all been complied with, Dean Shinagel received
a telephone call from Dean Govindarajulu on June 3 stating that
Mothercare still had not turned over control of ICA bank accounts to him
as agreed at the January meeting of the board, and that the faculty and
staff had not been paid their salaries for May, although contractors had
been paid with postdated checks. In the dean's words: "We view this as
unethical and unacceptable business practice." By late June Dean
Govindarajulu made public his decision not to remain at the academy
beyond his initial two-year contract. The remainder of the month of June
saw a deepening of the crisis, with letters and faxes coming to Harvard
from many of the principals involved. On June 25, Dean Govindarajulu
sent a handwritten note that stated succinctly: "I would like to bring to
your kind attention that we are in a deep financial crisis at the Academy."
And on July 7: "I am under great pressure from the vendors for payments."

On July 14 Gidwani sent a detailed report on the ICA crisis. He suggested that the operation of the ICA from the outset was problematic
because of "optimistic cash flow projections." He acknowledged that he
had initiated the idea and funded the initial phase. Ahuja had done some
background research prior to preparing his business plan for the ICA; he
provided seed money as a loan and became the operating trustee.
Unfortunately the business plan failed because capital expenditures
depleted the available funds and nothing was left for operating expenses.
The current problems facing the ICA were the lack of operating cash to
pay bills from vendors and salaries for faculty and staff as well as the
Ferguson audit and the missing financial documents on how funds were
spent and especially if they were spent properly. The solution proposed by

Gidwani was to locate a new sponsor, such as Pradeep Kar, chairman of Microland Ltd, Bangalore, who seemed willing to provide the necessary capital to keep the ICA solvent and operational.

On August 17 Gidwani sent a revised agenda for the Bombay meeting of the board of trustees scheduled for August 26:

   I.   Who are the directors?
   II.   Who has final authority for the ICA?
   III.   Financial audit
   IV.   Management audit
   V.   Future direction of the ICA?
   VI.   Recognition of departing Dean Govindarajulu

   I.   The current directors were:
Dean Shinagel (Harvard Division of Continuing Education)
Ahuja (Mothercare)
Kannan (Mothercare)
Gidwani (International Trade Management Company)
Kulkarni (Twentieth Century Venture Capital)
Rao or Sen (Citibank, India)

There was concern about a "weighted" board, so Twentieth Century Venture Capital, Citibank, and Harvard all wanted to appoint another director.

   II.   "ICA was started as a for profit corporation and then at the request of Harvard DCE, ICA was converted to a not for profit organization."

   III.   Dankokar was Ahuja's auditor for 1991-92 and 1992-93. He will make a presentation, but his report cannot be accepted for lack of supporting documentation. (He was also auditor for Mothercare.)

A.F. Ferguson was appointed as independent auditor by Citibank, as approved by the board of trustees at the January meeting, but it cannot complete its audit for lack of documentation.

The fateful meeting of the ICA board of trustees occurred on August 26, 1993, in Bombay. Dean Shinagel opened the meeting on a somber note by stating that the ICA "was going through a crisis, and some decision had to be made before my return to the US." The ICA issues related to academics, finances, facilities, and administration were presented as follows:

Academically, Shinagel pointed out "that Harvard DCE provided the academic course material, training, and help."

Financially, Shinagel noted that the ICA was experiencing enormous cash flow problems due to fewer students and fundraising that did not succeed.

Facilities were run down and the two-year lease would expire in December 1993. Student complaints were coming to Harvard about a breakdown in facilities, even the lack of toilet paper in bathrooms.

Administration was in transition, but it was not successful in maintaining the operation of the ICA, even though a business manager had recently been appointed.

It was decided that a new sponsor be sought, and several names of potential sponsors were presented for consideration.

Dean Govindarajulu in his farewell report said that the tuition was too high; there was no guarantee for student loans; there was a lack of industry support for internships; the computer lab needed an upgrade; the ICA needed a full-time librarian; the dean and faculty should decide on academic matters; the part-time program saw eight of fifteen faculty depart; and finally the board should address the grievances of the faculty.

The management audit by A.F. Ferguson was presented by Shoba Sethuram, who said she received inadequate support documents from Mothercare, and she pointed out the irregularities in bookkeeping by Mothercare.

It was resolved that an interim committee consisting of a Citibank nominee and a Twentieth Century Venture Capital Corporation nominee be formed to guide the operations of the ICA until a sponsor could be located, and that the interim committee "have all the powers of the Board of Directors."

At the follow-up board of trustees meeting on August 30 in Bangalore, Dr. Bamberg and Dean Shinagel briefed the board on the academic progress of the ICA students, noting that there was a perceptible decline in performance from the first to the third batch. The board discussed problems with the administration, and it was "unanimously agreed that Mr. Ahuja and Mr. Kannan will step down as trustees until the financial audit of the ICA is complete. This audit will include all records from the inception of the ICA. An interim committee of Citibank and TCVC representatives was constituted to oversee the administration and financial needs of the ICA; they agreed to take care of the financial needs of the ICA."

The board agreed to undertake a search for a new academic dean, a search for a new sponsor, and a search for a new audit firm for an internal audit of the ICA for its two years of operation. Finally, the board "unanimously agreed that the Board of Trustees and the Advisory Board be merged to constitute one 12-member Board."

On October 5, 1993, Dean Govindarajulu left the ICA to return to his former academic position, and Mr. N. Mahadevan assumed his place as acting academic dean until a search committee hired a new dean. Henry Leitner wrote Dean Mahadevan on October 18 of his disappointment in the grades of the third batch of students who scored "considerably below the level attained by students in the first two batches." Since he was copied on this letter, Professor Govindarajulu responded to Leitner, expressing his awareness of the poor performance of the third batch because they were admitted to the ICA with lower grades and without his approval. Because of cash flow problems, the administrators made admissions decisions on monetary rather than academic criteria. He added that "the state of affairs at ICA, the infrastructure and low morale, also contributed to the disappointing performance."

When the board of trustees met at the ICA on August 30, Dean Shinagel met in a private executive session with Ahuja and Sarangpani to inform them in confidence that Harvard's Division of Continuing Education would officially withdraw from the agreement signed in September 1990. In his letter to Ahuja dated September 7, he clearly outlined the situation from Harvard's perspective: the ICA had ninety (90) days since September 1, 1993 to clear up issues of financial mismanagement through another independent audit of Mothercare/ICA books for 1991-92 and 1992-93, to secure new sponsorship for the ICA, and to hire a new academic dean for the I.C.A." In summary, Shinagel reminded Ahuja that "if neither the ICA can resolve satisfactorily the outstanding issues nor a suitable sponsoring agent can be located by December 15, 1993, then Harvard University Division of Continuing Education will make public its termination of the Agreement with the ICA effective September 1, 1993 and fulfill its only remaining commitments to examining and grading the fourth and final batch of thirty (30) students currently enrolled in the I.C.A."

Although Shinagel had tendered the withdrawal notice to Ahuja and Sarangpani, he continued to work assiduously in finding a suitable new sponsor for the ICA. On September 7, he wrote to F.C. Kohli, director of the Tata Consultancy Services, to explore an association with Tata. Dr. Bamberg and Dean Shinagel had met with Tata officials in Bombay and Bangalore during a trip to India in late August and early September. Despite such overtures, no suitable sponsors for the ICA eventually were located, and it became time to go public with the decision of withdrawal from the ICA.

On December 1, 1993, Dean Shinagel wrote an official letter on behalf of the Harvard Division of Continuing Education to the Citibank officials in New York and Bombay who worked in support of the ICA and to the members of the board of trustees and the advisory board to announce the official withdrawal. Shinagel explained that he had waited ninety days to make public this decision in order to allow time to Ahuja and Sarangpani to resolve the financial and management crises, but since there was no resolution in sight, he had no recourse but to make the decision public to all interested parties.

Even though the Harvard Division of Continuing Education had withdrawn, it still felt a moral obligation to the ICA and its faculty and students. Accordingly, Dean Shinagel sent a check in the amount of $10,000 to Citibank India to "provide the necessary funds to keep the ICA operational until the fourth batch is through its training by the end of February." With this check the ICA account at Harvard was emptied of all funds, and any additional funding would have to come from other sources. Harvard promised to provide references for ICA faculty and staff as they sought new employment, and to ICA students who were interested and able, the opportunity to come to Harvard and complete the additional four courses for the graduate Certificate in Applied Sciences, an option that several students did pursue and complete successfully.

At the end of January 1994 Dean Mahadevan sent a distress fax from the ICA stating that "the present position of ICA is worse than it was in August. Our vendors have become belligerent since they have not been paid their dues for months. . . . I have had only assurances from Citibank and 20th Century Capital Corporation for the last 4 months but not a penny has been paid to us so that we can pay our vendors. The only recourse left to me now is to close ICA for sometime and reopen after the vendors have been paid."

A final meeting of the board of trustees was convened at Harvard on February 8, 1994, and it included reports on the current status of the ICA by Dean Mahadevan and Trustee Sarangpani as well as a decision on the future of the ICA. At this time there was no option, after a careful review of the relevant correspondence, reports, and financial information, but for Harvard to sever its ties with the ICA at the end of February.

On February 17, 1994, a public statement was issued on behalf of Harvard by Shinagel, Bamberg, and Leitner. It explained in detail the circumstances that made it necessary for Harvard to withdraw its affiliation with the ICA. Copies of the announcement went to Ahuja and Kannan of Mothercare, Professor Govindarajulu, Rao of Citibank India, and Sarangpani of Twentieth Century Venture Capital Corporation.[2]

A fax from Dean Mahadevan of the ICA was sent to Dean Shinagel two days after the public announcement expressing his distress at the news and his bleak "prospect of taking on the unenviable task of presiding over the funeral rites of I.C.A." That same day Ahuja wrote to underscore the point that the ICA was "a distinct legal entity . . . not with Mothercare India Limited." But on February 24 Gidwani, who read Ahuja's communication, wrote him to reiterate that Mothercare *was* the sponsor of the ICA: "The administrative and financial affairs of the ICA were mismanaged from the Mothercare office (you are the Mothercare CHAIRMAN)." On March 21 Dean Mahadevan maintained his elegiac mood in a message: "ICA has become an orphan whom no one wants to adopt." His final communication was on April 15, 1994: "Given the present circumstances and no inkling of the shape of things to come, I have but one option—to close the academy to prevent future shock. This I propose to do on 30th April 1994."

The final word on the ICA ironically came from Ahuja in a long letter addressed to "Dear Sir" and sent to Shinagel, with copies to Bhatia (Citibank), Sarangpani (TCVC), Gidwani, Bamberg, and Leitner. According to Ahuja, "the agreement was signed by you with the Indian Computer Academy and not with me or Mothercare." In actuality the agreement was signed by Ahuja as trustee of the ICA and from the outset the funds of the ICA and Mothercare were conflated, as the Ferguson audit made abundantly clear. The letter amounted to an attempt by Ahuja to dissociate himself from the ICA mismanagement mess and also to protect the brand name of Mothercare from the financial improprieties that were uncovered throughout 1993. As an attempted whitewash of his involvement, the letter was far from convincing, but it served as a fitting close to the academy because in the end it became, in the apt judgment of Dean Mahadevan, "an orphan."

The press in Bangalore on April 21, 1994, highlighted the key events of the Indian Computer Academy from its launch to its demise: "Two years after its launch, the Indian Computer Academy's partner pulls out, leaving the institute in a sorry state." A sidebar to the article summarized: "What really seems to be ailing ICA is the lack of a responsible and accountable person to handle funds."

The public announcement from Harvard's Division of Continuing Education (DCE) on February 17 provided the substance of the article, which stated that "DCE Dean Michael Shinagel cited financial and management problems at Bangalore as the reason for withdrawing the sponsorship." In its two years of operation, the ICA trained "approximately 150 students." The article concluded that "ICA's main assets remain the Harvard trained faculty and the experience gained over the past two years. However, the Harvard saga will end with the final batch of students passing out in March this year." The article had acknowledged that "Harvard DCE [imparted] its expertise in a pro bono manner," and that this marked the first time that it "was lending its name to any institution outside Cambridge." But this promising and well-intentioned project, despite the best efforts of dedicated teachers, administrators, and supporters, failed to succeed. All that could be done at the end was "to congratulate publicly Dean Regeti Govindarajulu as well as the entire ICA faculty and student body for their outstanding achievements in the face of very difficult circumstances."

To gain some valuable perspective on the failed Indian Computer Academy, Dean Shinagel consulted with John Kenneth Galbraith, Warburg Professor of Economics *Emeritus* at Harvard, and former Ambassador to India in the John F. Kennedy Administration, by sharing the short history of the enterprise with him. Professor Galbraith remarked that it was not surprising that the project failed because it was impossible to administer an academic program 8,000 miles from Harvard and to rely on the oversight and commitment of principals locally in India whose motives were more monetary than academic. The ICA did not have the necessary cash flow or the administrative and physical infrastructure to survive over the long term. When the academic quality was compromised, Harvard had no recourse but to withdraw its good name and its involvement with the project. It was a major disappointment to all the people from Harvard who worked on behalf of the ICA from its inception to its inevitable demise, but a hard lesson was learned about good intentions and academic adventures overseas without the proper safeguards in place.

As American academics, the Harvard Division of Continuing Education team failed to appreciate the motivation of businessmen who invest in start-up computer academies, particularly in India. As a recent study of universities in India explains, currently the emphasis is on "retailing knowledge" rather than on ensuring academic quality.[3] With hindsight, Dean Shinagel and his associates could have been more sensitive to the cultural differences between higher education in the United States and in India, to have projected more realistically the financial resources available, and to have been sure that the physical facilities were adequate for the needs of the faculty and students.

DISTANCE EDUCATION
AT HARVARD EXTENSION SCHOOL

Top: Antonio Aranda Eggermont, CAS '99, works
on the initial distance education videos in 1999.
Bottom: Leonard Evenchik discusses production of distance education
videos in the control booth at 1 Story Street, 2008.

CHAPTER XIII

University Extension Courses
Go Online

From Teleteaching to Distance Education
(1984 to the Present)

Harvard University Extension was not only a pioneer in the applications of radio and television for higher education instruction, it was also an early pioneer in interactive distance education.[1] In 1984 a grant from the Annenberg Foundation was awarded to Daniel Goroff, assistant professor of mathematics, and Deborah Hughes Hallett, senior preceptor in mathematics, to develop and teach online calculus courses for Harvard Extension School credit.

The Teleteaching Project, as it was designated, enabled distance learners to engage in a simulated Socratic interaction, whereby technology transformed the IBM-compatible personal computers of the students into electronic blackboards that were conjoined by using a single telephone line for each site. In this way an entire class could communicate while sharing prepared graphics using real-time typing, pointing, and annotation. Teleteaching, unlike other computer educational applications, did not eliminate the professor, but instead enhanced the professor's pedagogical role. To accomplish this expanded role, teleteaching required high quality courseware that included graphics and notes for class use. The grant from the Annenberg/CPB Division of the Corporation for Public Broadcasting was designed for this specific kind of development project. And the Cambridge Teleteaching Group, including Daniel Goroff and Deborah Hughes Hallett of the Harvard mathematics department, was selected as consultant to develop the courseware, while technical support was provided by AT&T Communications.

The outcome was that the Harvard Extension School introduced teleteaching equipment and courseware into its Calculus E-1a course, initially with an electronic blackboard for students in a regular classroom setting; and later technology enabled distance students to participate in class using their personal computers and telephones. To determine the effectiveness of the new technology, the Extension School calculus course taught by David Ellen, a teaching fellow, used the same syllabus, textbook, and class assignments as in previous years, including the same final examinations. An evaluation of the new courseware developed and implemented in the course was conducted by Research Communications Inc., a third party selected by the Teleteaching Project, whose advisory board included the president of Harvard, Derek Bok, who took a personal interest in the pedagogical potential of Socratic interaction in computer-assisted instruction at Harvard after he was invited to view a teleteaching demonstration during the summer of 1985.

By the fall of 1986 *The Technology Window*, a publication of Harvard's Office of Information Technology, published a feature article on this innovative initiative at Harvard begun in the spring of 1985:

> First taught as a math course to five students in Cambridge, New York, New Jersey, and Washington, the experiment linked personal computers with voice-data modems, enabling the students to hear and see everything transmitted from the instructor's and students' stations. The class could view and annotate a common screen of prepared graphics and ask questions about it. Material covered during the course included topics in elementary and applied mathematics as well as linear programming.

As the article outlined, the potential of teleteaching was to reach "the large market of non-traditional students for whom on-campus instruction is difficult or impossible." In addition to Harvard, other universities, especially in Israel and China, were beginning to consider the implementation of teleteaching as high quality software and graphics were being developed for use in such distance courses.

Eventually the *Boston Globe Sunday Magazine* on March 1, 1987, printed an illustrated article titled "Learning Math in the Space Age," which described in detail the successful pilot teleteaching course, *Introduction to the Calculus A,* taught in a Harvard Science Center classroom to sixty-one students and, simultaneously, to another twelve distance students in suburban homes in Newton, Danvers, and Brighton. As instructor of the course, Ellen reported that this pilot project answered the main question of whether we can teach with this technology successfully with a resounding yes. And Hughes Hallett observed that the technology promoted the Socratic method of teaching: "It leaves intact the human way of teaching we already have. The trouble with previous computer teaching is that students interacted with a computer instead of a teacher."[2]

The success of the Teleteaching Project promised great gains for the teaching of mathematics nationally, especially with a shortage of qualified teachers available. According to Hughes Hallett, the project "offers a way for college teachers to help high school teachers upgrade their skills and to help beginning math teachers with conferences and courses. Many teachers are hired to teach math although it is not their field.... Courses like this one could help them make the change." Another potential use of the calculus teleteaching course was to offer it in high schools for students seeking more advanced math courses. The New York State Department of Education already was funding such a project for high school seniors studying advanced placement calculus in remote upstate sites. The success of the original pilot project of the calculus teleteaching course paved the way for a follow-up grant of $535,000 from Annenberg with support services from AT&T.

By the spring of 1987 the success of the Teleteaching Project had elicited a letter of inquiry from Bang-Hua Shu, vice president of Jiangxi Normal University in the People's Republic of China, to President Bok, who forwarded the letter for reply to Goroff and Hughes Hallett, the principals of the teleteaching initiative. On May 5, 1987, they wrote Dr. Shu, explaining what teleteaching entailed technically and what it achieved pedagogically in providing courses to distance learners. They even expressed a willingness to cooperate on specific projects with Jiangxi Normal University using the teleteaching approach.

Although a joint venture with Jiangxi Normal University did not result from this overture, by April 1988 Harvard Extension School initiated an experimental program of interactive teleteaching with Beijing Normal University. Using a global telecommunications system—or bridge—whereby personal computers were linked to Cambridge by twenty students in Beijing, Henry Leitner, senior lecturer on computer science, taught a five-week course in artificial intelligence from a Harvard Square location. He worked closely with Professor Goroff and used the technology developed by the Teleteaching Project. In order to teach the course synchronously, he had to deliver the lectures from Harvard at eight o'clock in the evening so that the Chinese students were interacting with him in real time the next morning in Beijing. This Cambridge-to-Beijing international teleteaching experiment was another pioneering effort by the Harvard Extension School.

A visit to the University of Illinois in 1993 by Hughes Hallett, who by then was professor of the practice in the teaching of mathematics at Harvard, introduced her to a new software package named Mathematica, a product of Wolfram Research Inc., designed for numerical, symbolic, and graphical computations and visualization. Mathematica was being used effectively by the University of Illinois as a distance education model for rural high school students, who were learning calculus through courseware rather than traditional textbook teaching methods. Professor Hughes Hallett saw the potential for Mathematica in the Harvard Extension School and in the fall of 1995 she applied it in her distance course *Multivariable Calculus*. The grader and technical assistant for the course, Rebecca Rapoport, described how the course was run:

> We had an initial meeting with the registered students the week before the fall semester officially started. We explained to everyone that in order to do the work they would need access to a modem-equipped Macintosh computer capable of running Mathematica. By next semester we hope to support IBM-compatible personal computers as well.

All the students who planned to do the course away from the Harvard campus were given a copy of Apple Remote Access and Timbuktu software. Mastering the materials was straightforward and students used the Mathematica calculus courseware at their own pace, turning in completed assignments by the Internet or the Remote Access software connection to machines located in the "control center" for the course in Harvard's Science Center. Whereas Rapoport was responsible for the technical aspects of the distance calculus course, another assistant, Diko Mihov, served as advisor on course content and was reachable by e-mail and telephone. Timbuktu software enabled him to see on his Macintosh screen whatever the student had on his or her screen, thereby literally being able to look over the student's shoulder to provide assistance. His experiences with the *Multivariable Calculus* distance students were overwhelmingly positive:

> Mathematica visualization really helps in terms of a deep understanding of the material—a picture is clearly worth a thousand words in something like calculus. The calculation and graphing power of Mathematica enables one to work out and plot many more interesting examples than would be possible on the pages of a textbook.

Over the next several years Professor Hughes Hallett and her course assistants perfected the application of Mathematica to the teaching of calculus in the Harvard Extension School.

By the academic year 1997-98 nearly 100 distance learners had been enrolled in six different Harvard Extension School calculus courses using Mathematica courseware, which was developed with the support of the National Science Foundation, Addison-Wesley Publishing Company, Apple Computer Corporation, and Wolfram Research Inc. Most of the online participants in these Extension math courses were talented high school seniors from distant states like Alaska and Hawaii who were eager to study a calculus course at the beginning or undergraduate level but whose local high schools were not offering such courses for budgetary or staffing reasons. The Harvard Extension School provided Lowell Scholarships to these deserving students so that they could enroll at greatly reduced tuition rates. For the following year, 1998-99, the Harvard Extension School decided not to offer distance calculus courses and to limit itself to computer science courses because of the problems involved with supporting distance students' need to deal with software installation and modem or local-area network connections. The technically savvy computer science students were an easier cohort to serve for the Harvard Extension School teaching staff.

In the fall semester of 1997 the Harvard Extension School moved beyond Mathematica in its distance education program by introducing streaming video and audio in Leonard Evenchik's *Communication Protocols and Internet Architectures* courses, both to in-class and online students. Within thirty-six hours after the class met in Harvard's Science Center, students in Pennsylvania, Colorado, and California, as well as far off Sweden, were able to access the lecture on the web. The course lectures were recorded on digital tape before a class audience and the following day postproduction work created a file that got streamed to enrolled distant students on demand, including the instructor's transparencies and related audiovisual material. Using a standard web browser students could view the actual lecture in a small video window, hear the audio portion clearly, and watch the instructor's slides and other supporting information on the computer screen synchronized with the lecture. To enable distance students to interact with the instructor and his teaching assistants, other multimedia and Internet technologies were available for real-time conferences, homework assignments, class projects, and examinations, thereby creating in essence a "virtual classroom" for those noncommuters to Cambridge.

Access to course lecture videos through the Internet also proved popular with the in-class students, who used this feature as an added learning device to master the course material. No distinction was made between the in-class and the distance students in the course, as they all did the same problem sets and took the same examinations. Based on the success of this pilot computer science course, the Harvard Extension School decided to expand its online courses in the field the following year to include several state-of-the-art computer science courses. Dr. Henry Leitner hired one of his graduate students in Information Technology, Antonio Aranda Eggermont, to design and build an initial production and delivery system. This proved to be a complex undertaking that involved the integration of diverse hardware with various software platforms. Eggermont's determination and hard work, coupled with Leitner's encouragement and technical assistance from his colleagues, resulted in a system that would enable the Extension School to expand the number of courses available online.

For the annual report for 1999-2000, Dean Shinagel devoted a separate section to distance education, noting that "a coherent distance education strategy was employed throughout the year to guide the growth of this program successfully." The growth included the addition of courses in the humanities and the natural sciences to complement the computer science courses, resulting in the distance education initiative evolving from the experimental stage to an established academic program. Available on the Internet for the first time were Professor Gregory Nagy's *Introduction to Greek Literature: Concepts of the Hero in the Classical Period*, Professor John Spengler's *Environmental Management*, and Dr. Doug Bond's *Preventive Measures: The Politics of Disaster* as well as ten computer science courses, ranging from *Introduction to Personal Computers and the Internet* and *Introduction to Website Development* to *Advanced Topics in Data Networking Protocols and Network Architecture* and *Theory of Computation and Its Applications*.

To provide the necessary support for such an expanded set of distance courses, the newly hired director of distance and innovative education, Leonard Evenchik, worked individually with all the faculty to make their distance courses a success. The production and operations staff met their goal of making the course lectures and material available online within forty-eight hours of class meetings. The shift from student helpers to professional videographers resulted in significant enhancements to video and audio quality, as did the introduction of videoconferencing and also a new system of online course evaluations for the Harvard Extension School distance education program.

With a coherent distance education strategy now in place, Extension planned "to double the number of courses available via the Internet, while lowering production and support costs and improving scalability." Evenchik explained, "we hope to experiment with courses that combine video streaming, video conferencing, and other multimedia, as well as develop production and support tools to automate various processes." The expansion plans included the purchase and renovation of a nearby building to be used as a computer facility in support of the distance program.

Although the distance education courses were still at an early stage of development, preliminary data analyses indicated that the performance of online students compared favorably with in-class students, with roughly the same distribution of final grades and course completion rates. A timely grant from the Harvard Office of the Provost funded a comprehensive quantitative and qualitative evaluation of the Harvard Extension School distance education program to ensure its academic integrity and to measure its learning outcomes.

The study was undertaken in the spring of 2001 by Patricia Craig, executive director of the Harvard Center for European Studies, and Catalina Laserna, senior research analyst for the Division of Continuing Education, to address three fundamental questions: 1) Should the distance education program expand, and if so, how fast? 2) What motivates students to enroll in distance courses? 3) How does distance education change the traditional teaching and learning of in-class instruction?

The findings illustrated strong support by faculty and their distance students and recommended a strategy of continued growth, especially focus on "hybrid courses," whereby students had the option of attending class and reviewing the lectures over the Internet. This model proved particularly attractive because it served well three types of students: those commuters who could attend all the classes, those who combined class attendance with Internet viewing when they had to miss class, and those at a distance who only viewed the course online.

Other factors that emerged from the study supporting program expansion included offering more introductory-level courses and more technical courses for prospective distance students competent with computers. Since distance courses inevitably involved more work for faculty, it was necessary to develop a system of incentives to induce them to put their courses online, such as extra compensation and more support staff assistance. And since developing a course for distance involved independent learning curves, a two-year rollout was recommended for developing certain courses.

The motivation of students to enroll in a Harvard Extension School distance course was, predictably, the Harvard University image and reputation, which underscored the need for the program to live up to expectations of academic quality associated with the Harvard brand. The fact that the Harvard Extension courses were cost competitive, both locally and nationally, was also considered a significant factor motivating prospective students.

Lastly, teaching and learning in distance courses clearly were perceived as different, especially as faculty and students alike were experimenting on how best to create a sense of community in class and online with electronic communications. Distance students needed more supportive attention, particularly at the beginning, to ensure a good learning experience. Faculty also needed more support as they attempted innovations in their teaching styles when dealing with in-class and online students simultaneously. Teaching assistants required special training and support for their duties with websites, discussion groups, and bulletin boards because students demonstrated that they had different learning styles as they interacted with technologies associated with distance courses.

The initial findings and recommendations of the provost's grant study were on the whole encouraging and pedagogically useful. But from an institutional perspective, it was evident that the Harvard Extension School had to implement these findings as it did its long-range planning and decision making in this emerging field. Program evaluation and pedagogical innovation had to become an ongoing process of the Extension distance education program if it were to maintain its academic quality as it grew in scope and scale in the twenty-first century.

The distance education program expanded gradually in 2000-01 to a total of twenty-five courses that accounted for more than 2,200 student enrollments, of whom 10 to 15 percent were taking classes exclusively online because they lived far from Cambridge or had commitments that precluded class attendance. Computer science courses constituted the majority of the offerings (eighteen), with *Communication Protocols and Internet Architectures* as well as *Fundamentals of Website Development* showing enrollments of more than 200. But the seven courses in the humanities, social sciences, and natural sciences also proved popular, with *Greek Literature: Concepts of the Hero* enrolling 120; *Genomics and Computational Biology,* ninety-four; *Environmental Management I*, seventy-nine, and *II*, seventy-five; and *Philosophy: Introduction to Metaphysics*, seventy-two.

As the distance education production and delivery systems were becoming increasingly stable and sophisticated, the challenge was to attract more of Harvard's senior faculty to participate in the distance program. Over the years, a number of faculty who had expressed interest in teaching for the Extension School felt they could not afford the time to teach an additional course in the evening. As a member of the computer science department, Henry Leitner was feeling particularly frustrated by this situation, as the newly created Master of Liberal Arts in Information Technology Program was experiencing a dearth of involvement by his busy Harvard colleagues. In a brainstorming conversation with Catalina Laserna, a simple solution to this seemingly intractable problem appeared: If Harvard faculty members could not teach in the evening, could Extension instead adapt their daytime Harvard College course as an online-only option for Extension students? This novel idea raised a number of questions and concerns: Even if computer science faculty colleagues would agree in principle to having their courses made available to an open-enrollment audience, would the conservative Harvard administration balk? And if the academic deans could be convinced to allow Extension to conduct a limited experiment, would the heavy workload and other requirements of a daytime College course prove too much for an Extension School audience?

To help answer these uncertainties and provide an initial proof of the concept, Leitner approached H.T. Kung, the William Gates Professor of Computer Science and Electrical Engineering, a tenured and well-respected colleague who had demonstrated an interest in extending the reach of his teaching through the use of digital technologies. Simultaneously, Leitner was able to secure the explicit approval of the dean of the Division of Engineering and Applied Sciences, Professor Venkatesh Narayanamurti, as well as that of the dean of Harvard College, Professor Harry Lewis. Thus in the fall term of 2000, Professor Kung offered his *Computer Networks and Network Programming* course to more than 100 Harvard College undergraduates and eighteen Harvard Extension School distance students. Thirteen Extension students completed the course and the results were encouraging, as the overall scores on the final examination and the problem sets were essentially the same for the Extension students and the Harvard College students. As a test case, Professor Kung's Harvard College computer course proved useful and insightful in several critical ways. It demonstrated the crucial role of teaching assistants in adapting a course for open-enrollment and online students. It confirmed the Darwinian theory of self-selection and survival of the fittest for online students, as the better qualified students were motivated to enroll and succeed, whereas the less qualified and less motivated tended to drop out early in the course. It showed that faculty could teach simultaneously an in-class and online audience without cumbersome technology interfering in the teaching and learning processes. Finally, it made clear the logistical and administrative adaptations that the Harvard Extension School had to introduce, such as proctoring examinations at distant sites and providing access to library electronic resources, to ensure the success of its distance education program.

A similar experience was reported in the non-computer science distance courses in 2000-01. Professor George Church of the Harvard Medical School taught his *Genomics* evening distance course at the Harvard Extension School with the same lectures as his Harvard College course, actively encouraging a mingling of the day and evening students in both lecture and sections. The success of the two *Environmental Management* courses was owing in part to the pedagogical innovations provided, such as virtual field trips for the distance students. In fact, these two courses formed the foundation of the new graduate Certificate in Environmental Management (CEM) that the Harvard Extension School inaugurated in the fall of 2001 and that eventually could be earned entirely online. In addition to the CEM, the Harvard Extension School later developed a master's program in environmental management that attracted great interest both locally and nationally.

The success of the Harvard Extension School distance education program soon was reflected in the press. A technology writer for the *Boston Sunday Globe Magazine* on April 11, 1999, wrote a favorable feature story on the Harvard Extension School's evolving distance education program under the title "Plugging into the Electronic Campus."[3] An issue of *Newsweek* magazine (April 24, 2000) featured a distance student in St. Louis taking courses at the Harvard Extension School. And on April 4,

2001, the director of distance and innovative education was interviewed on the local PBS television show "Greater Boston" to highlight the expanding role of the Harvard Extension School distance courses. By adhering to a strategic plan of controlled growth, the Harvard Extension School developed a viable model of an Internet-based delivery system of high quality for continuing education courses. This prominence in the field resulted in the Harvard Extension School assuming a leadership role in advising other Harvard schools and departments on how to implement or improve their distance courses through technological and pedagogical innovations.

The strategy for the next few years involved both increasing the number of distance course offerings and improving their quality and sophistication, while also lowering production and support costs and improving scalability. There was also a commitment to experiment with courses that combined video streaming with other multimedia streams (such as digital recordings of all the action initiated by an instructor on his computer screen during class) as well as to develop production and support tools to automate various processes. In anticipation of these goals, the Harvard Extension School purchased and renovated 53 Church Street, a nearby building, to expand and refine the distance education offerings, a construction project that was successfully completed in January 2002.

In 2002-03, the Extension School sponsored thirty-six online courses, including six Harvard College courses. In addition, the rental and renovation of additional office and classroom space at One Story Street, across the street from the offices of the Harvard Extension School, moved the distance education production facilities and personnel, along with key academic computing individuals, to the second floor of this new facility. This 3,000-square-foot renovated space enabled the Harvard Extension School to create a much more professional environment for production as well as for research and development. The timely hiring of a senior software architect helped make the distance education software and hardware systems more efficient and adaptable.

As Extension School instructors became more familiar with digital media in presenting a course online, many of them proposed refinements and innovations. Their suggestions, coupled with an analysis of the literature on distance education, led to the proposal of a research and design effort that would focus on the construction of a discrete set of tools and associated pedagogical experiments. The fundamental premise in this proposal was that technological experimentation and innovation needed to be driven by a sound pedagogical perspective, and that this perspective in turn needed to be guided by research and innovation that others had accomplished, as well as the insights and pedagogical concerns of Extension faculty. To accomplish this goal, a formal proposal, "Student-Centered Enhancements for Learning at a Distance," was submitted to the office of the provost by Leonard Evenchik, Catalina Laserna, and Henry Leitner. The proposal was funded and supplemented with matching funds from the Harvard Extension School. With new facilities, office space, and funding in place, specific projects were proposed for development.

The overarching goals of the provost's grant were fourfold. One, to foster real-time and non-real-time collaboration and communication between students and between students and teaching staff, including the issues of how best to deal with the spontaneous ideas and contributions of distance students. Two, to integrate more easily material that was presented in live class meetings to a distance audience. Three, to utilize resources within Harvard (such as the University Information Systems' gateways for Internet-based video) and to transfer Extension's growing expertise to other departments and schools within the University. Four, to extend the formative evaluation efforts and automatically to feed relevant information back to instructors and teaching fellows so that they could enhance their pedagogy.

The research efforts of the Harvard Extension School team implementing the provost's grant resulted in the identification of ten potential enhancements for the distance learning experience. Among them were the following:

1. Many distance courses needed two-way synchronous section meetings, using either audio conferencing or videoconferencing (or a combination of the two). The distance program currently had the capability to run an occasional videoconference, but the logistics were far too complicated and time consuming to allow this to be done on a more widespread basis. The team proposed to assemble an integrated system that would allow the set up of a videoconference from any Harvard classroom almost as easily as

the set up of an overhead projector. The use of the University Information Systems gateway and bridging equipment allowed multiple parties located outside of Harvard to participate in live section meetings in real time.

2. Web-based statistics on the use of the online lectures were prepared for instructors during the term. Oftentimes instructors posed such questions as: Which lectures are being watched most often? Are the distance students "participating"? The web-based statistics provided online instructors with the answers.

3. There was no convenient way for students to submit and for teaching fellows and instructors to annotate homework assignments. While programming classes provided electronic submission of problem sets, handwritten work and other materials that could not easily be put into electronic form (e.g., a mathematical proof) were frequently sent by fax, an inefficient means for getting work into the right hands in a timely fashion. A facility that mimicked electronic drop boxes could be set up on a server, with automatic record keeping so that teaching staff could know exactly when work was turned in.

4. One of the primary complaints about slides that were synchronized to streaming video and audio was the distance student's inability to interrupt and ask questions. Even in lecture-format classes, where the opportunities to raise a question were severely constrained by class size, some students felt frustrated by the noninteractive nature of the presentation. The Harvard Extension School team proposed to augment each streaming lecture with a prominently presented "Help! I'm confused" button or icon, whenever a lecture was being viewed, as illustrated on the following page.

Upon clicking this button, the lecture would pause, and the student would be taken to a webpage in which he or she was asked, in a structured way, to provide information on what he or she had understood thus far and what was confusing. Students could then have the option of submitting their thoughts in an anonymous or self-identifiable manner. These submissions would be entered into a database, to be presented to instructional staff "in context," i.e., teachers would know precisely where during a class presentation the confusion occurred. Through database analysis and data mining algorithms, instructors would be able to obtain feedback regarding major sources of miscomprehension or misunderstanding. If the confusion

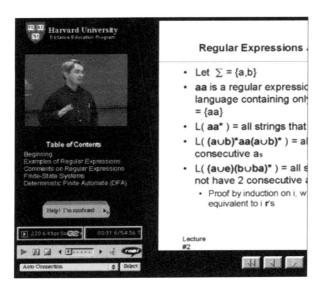

were an isolated event, of course, the student could simply be e-mailed a clarification; but if larger issues were uncovered, the lecture might need to be revised or additional material made available to the students.

These four enhancements, as well as others developed by the provost's grant team, were subjected to a design-experiments methodology to test their pedagogical effectiveness. The Harvard Extension School distance education program now had in place an ongoing system of pedagogical experimentation and evaluation with the following features:

Instructors as co-investigators. All experiments would address the educational goals pursued by the instructors, while examining the particular conditions that instructors considered necessary for success. As co-investigators, instructors would help formulate hypotheses, plan and carry out the intervention, make refinements in the plan as the experiment progressed, evaluate the effects of the different aspects of the experiment, and report the results to others.

Comparison of multiple interventions. To assess the relative effects of different tools and their associated pedagogies, the team would encourage instructors to try out multiple experiments. Where possible, they would like to establish systematic comparisons within and across courses. For example, in implementing the "Help! I'm confused" button, they might suggest that some students be required to rephrase what they understood up to the point of confusion, while others be allowed to express their confusion spontaneously.

Flexible design revision. When at an early stage in an experiment a particular design was not working or a tool did not appear to be effective, the team would try to analyze quickly why it was not working well, and take steps to fix whatever appeared to be the reason for the failure. They would collect information about failures, attempted repairs to the design, and whether at the end it succeeded or failed.

Objective evaluation of success or failure. Success or failure of a pedagogical experiment would not simply be evaluated in terms of how much students learned on some criterion or measure. Different kinds of evaluation were necessary for addressing questions such as the following: How sustainable was the design after the researchers left? How much did the design emphasize reasoning, creativity, and other modes of learning? How did the design affect the attitudes of students? To evaluate different variables, the team would use a variety of evaluation techniques, including standardized pre- and post-tests, survey and interview techniques, and systematic scoring of videos in the classrooms.

In 2003-04, the Extension School continued to grow its online course offerings, with 2,700 enrollments across forty-three distance education courses, and included the following Harvard College courses:

> MATH E-22, based upon Mathematics 122 *Abstract Algebra 1: Theory of Groups and Vector Spaces*, Professor Benedict Gross
> CSCI E-210, based upon Computer Science 222 *Algorithms at the End of the Wire*, Professor Michael Mitzenmacher
> GOVT E-1850, based upon Government 2724 *US-European Relations*, Professor Stanley Hoffmann and Dr. Louise Richardson

The positive experience with the Hoffmann and Richardson course—which was taken simultaneously by Harvard undergraduate and graduate students, Extension School students, and students at the *Institut d'Études Politiques de*

Paris—prompted the team to recruit other Harvard faculty whose courses would attract an international audience, and in doing so benefit the local students (whether enrolled at Harvard College, the Graduate School of Arts and Sciences, or the Extension School). What could be more enlightening than hearing directly from French students in a Harvard course that dealt with contemporary transatlantic political issues? It became apparent that this kind of development resonated with Harvard President Lawrence Summers' mandate on internationalizing the undergraduate experience at Harvard, while giving Extension School students access to both faculty and courses that had been previously out of reach. It could enhance the reputation of Harvard as an institution that does innovative teaching, not just world-class research, and it opened the possibility of influencing students and universities abroad. Moreover, this was an opportunity for Harvard undergraduate students to establish themselves in networks of peers and make contacts abroad through enrollment in distance education courses that reached peer institutions in other countries.

The willingness of the Harvard Extension School to invest significant sums of money to create the best classroom and production facilities resulted in a growing acceptance and even support of the distance education program by Harvard faculty and senior administrators, notably the president and provost. As the distance program grew in scope and diversity, so did its commitment to engage in research on key aspects of the online teaching and learning processes. Timely grants from the offices of the president and the provost helped to underwrite the costs of data collection and analysis that had a direct effect on course development and enhancement.

A notable innovation in the Harvard Extension School distance education program occurred in 2005-06 when the first courses were available as podcasts: David Malan's *Understanding Computers and the Internet* in the fall term and Harry Lewis's *Bits* in the spring. Initially available to Extension students enrolled in the courses and later to the public at large, the lectures could be downloaded, and the stored video and audio segments played on software like iTunes or a portal device like an iPod. Both computer courses were the first from Harvard in this format and both converted existing distance education technology to reach a worldwide audience. In fact, David Malan received e-mails of appreciation from around the world, and in the December 2006 issue of *Wired* magazine his podcast course was rated by the editors "the best podcast." They remarked that "If every undergrad watched this series IT help desks would be out of business."[4]

Careful short-term and long-term strategic planning studies informed the controlled growth of the Harvard Extension School distance education initiative over the years. By the academic year 2006-07 the total number of distance courses reached 100, including a growing percentage of Harvard College courses. Beginning with the historic first Harvard College computer course taught by Professor Kung in 2000-01, the percentage of Harvard College courses grew to better than one-in-four by the year 2007-08. Moreover, there had been evident a substantial growth in the number and percentage of Extension students who enrolled and participated solely online, from less than 4 percent in 2003-04 to more than 16 percent in 2007-08. As more Harvard College courses were introduced, the number of distance-only students was expected to continue to grow in future years.

As interim Harvard president, Derek Bok, who had been an abiding supporter of distance education, created a special innovation fund in the summer of 2006 to encourage and finance faculty interested in extending the reach of Harvard to distant constituencies and to promote critical evaluations of online teaching and learning outcomes. He awarded a major grant to Henry Leitner and Catalina Laserna for a detailed study evaluating the current distance education program and to consider creative ways of developing the Harvard Extension School and Harvard College "hybrid" course program in the future. The grant was applied to an examination of both theoretical and practical aspects of online education, particularly the pedagogical and the technical features.

The grant team decided to adopt a research approach that focused on detailed case studies of how Harvard College in-class courses were being adapted to online students by engaging in structured interviews with the key players: students, faculty, and course assistants. These case studies revealed how different types of courses could be transformed effectively from in-class to online modes, but as the grant team cautioned: "Despite commonalities among these courses, the case studies reveal a range of faculty interests, values, and concerns that need to be addressed." The awareness that differences among Harvard faculty were as important as commonalities among courses prompted the Harvard Extension School to adopt a policy that demonstrated a readiness to support the diverse interests of Harvard faculty.

Teaching fellows (TFs) played a pivotal role in adapting the way sections were carried out online, and therefore it was vital that TFs participate in the ordinary planning meetings for the Harvard College courses. When it came to the actual adaptation of section meetings, TFs were very much left to their own initiative and resourcefulness to create virtual learning communities. It was thus imperative that faculty select TFs who knew the course content well and who were interested in learning about online teaching tools and techniques; an interest in teaching nontraditional students was also helpful.

As courses turned into digital artifacts, faculty perceived different opportunities. While some worried about issues of intellectual property, others saw an opportunity to extend their reach to larger audiences. How an individual Harvard faculty member reacted to having their lectures online depended in part on their own intellectual production cycle, i.e., whether the course was associated with their current research and publishing.

A number of senior Harvard faculty had a keen interest in "targeted marketing" of their courses to specialized audiences. One distinguished professor was interested in his course reaching Latino school teachers across the country; another was interested in attracting senior software engineers who worked on complex algorithms; and another wanted to have his course marketed to museum professionals in certain geographical regions. There was great potential in such differentiated marketing.

Because the TFs were left on their own, it was crucial that the Extension School provide resources for helping them handle their pedagogical role. At the same time, the Extension School could collect and disseminate successful local innovations by asking experienced TFs to document their experimentation and be part of a TF network. The Office for the Study of Online Teaching and Learning was established by the Harvard Extension School as both a think tank and a training center, extending and transforming the traditional definitions and resources of brick-and-mortar higher education. The office would attend to the following:

- Sponsor workshops for faculty and their teaching fellows involved with online courses to discuss such topics as the use of web conferencing software to facilitate virtual online meetings, and office hours, and to foster collaboration between students who might be located thousands of miles apart.
- Provide mentorship opportunities, in which TFs who had discipline-specific success were paired up with TFs who were struggling with online teaching.
- Arrange individualized coaching sessions for both faculty and TFs.
- Develop and maintain an online support infrastructure. An evolving distance education portal website were launched as a "one stop shopping experience," answering both practical and pedagogical questions, and allowing experiences and best practices to be shared.
- Continue in-depth formative evaluation of the pedagogical dimensions of online courses. Such evaluation would help generate innovations for online teaching that could be incorporated into other courses, and these results would be shared with the broader Harvard community and beyond.

The Socratic style developed in the early online calculus courses at the Harvard Extension School was not compatible with asynchronous video. Nor was streaming video by itself suitable for seminars, writing courses, math courses, foreign language courses, and other courses taught in a more interactive style. To address these needs, Henry Leitner and Leonard Evenchik envisioned an infrastructure that could simultaneously support the participation of both in-class and online learners. In 2005, they applied to the office of the provost for seed innovation funding to jump-start building 6,000 square feet of immersive, collaborative learning environments in five classrooms plus a state-of-the-art control room.

These classrooms, which cost nearly $1 million, went online in June 2007 and greatly enhanced opportunities for pedagogical experimentation with online audiences by both instructors and their teaching fellows. Online students could view the live class meetings in real time (hearing and seeing the in-class students as well as the instructors), pose questions, and engage in discussions. In the spring of 2008, for example, Professor Robert Lue of Harvard's department of molecular and cellular biology and Professor Thomas Michel of the Harvard Medical School co-taught the first cross-faculty course available to Harvard College students using the new facilities. In *Cellular Metabolism and Human Disease*, students and faculty in two classrooms that were miles apart engaged in interactive teaching and learning activities, along with a substantial number of Extension School students who were dispersed across the United States and in several countries overseas.

In a relatively short span of time, the Harvard Extension School established a reputation for leadership, innovation, and academic excellence in distance education. From just one math course enrolling five students as part of a primitive online learning initiative in 1985, to the introduction in 1997 of state-of-the-art online streaming video and audio of the on-campus course *Communication Protocols and Internet Architectures*, to the offering of Dr. Tal Ben-Shahar's enormously popular *Positive Psychology*, enrolling a record 350 entirely online students in 2008, online courses accounted for one out of every six Extension School courses by 2007-08. In the spring term nearly 20 percent of all enrolled Extension students took their class completely online, and in fall 2008, the Harvard Extension School recorded its largest online enrollment with nearly 400 students from around the world registered for *Introduction to Finance.*

As online learning became a major aspect of higher education, both nationally and globally, the Harvard Extension School continued to provide both a range of online courses and a basic research and assessment program in this expanding field.

Top: President Derek Bok, Edgar Grossman, and Dean Shinagel
at the dedication of the Grossman Library in Sever Hall, 1982.
Bottom: Dean Shinagel, Shirley and Edgar Grossman,
and President Neil Rudenstine at the dedication
of the Grossman Common Room in 51 Brattle Street, 1991.

CHAPTER XIV

Harvard University Extension
in the Twenty-First Century

New Professional Degree Programs
(2000 to the Present)

The Harvard Extension School began the twenty-first century with a
noteworthy enrollment of 14,216 students, ranging in age from the early
teens to the late eighties. The educational background indicated that three-
quarters of the students had at least a bachelor's degree, including nearly 20
percent with a graduate degree. Numbered among the students were more
than 1,700 Harvard staff members enrolling under the auspices of the
University's Tuition Assistance Plan. Courses in the distance education program enrolled 1,743 students, with an estimated 10 to 15 percent taking classes exclusively online. The internationalization of the Harvard Extension
School student body was evident in the record 255 graduates of the
Certificate of Special Studies (CSS) in Administration and Management
Program, of whom 163 were international students representing thirty-nine
countries. At Commencement 224 degrees were awarded as well as 345 graduate certificates, for a combined total of 569 graduates.[1]

Whereas the traditional liberal arts fields had been the sole focus of the
ALM Program at the Harvard Extension School for more than two decades,
Dean Shinagel saw that it was time to supplement these disciplines with new
initiatives in professional studies: "Many segments of the labor market are
now demanding professional degrees of their employees; the ALM is under-
going a natural evolution as it adapts to changes in demography and to new
pressures of the labor market. I am confident that the new master's concentrations will advance the professional capacity of individual students, help to
generate new knowledge in a number of important domains, and also to contribute to the competitiveness of local industries and institutions."

199

In the spring term of 2000, the CSS Program witnessed a surge in enrollments in such courses as *Doing Business in the Internet Economy* and *Designing Effective Websites: A Marketing Perspective*, indicating a rapidly growing interest among Extension students, particularly from abroad, in e-commerce courses. The director of the program, Dean Raymond Comeau, noticed this trend and, after consulting with Internet professionals in the field, responded by developing a more comprehensive e-commerce curriculum with a new concentration in e-commerce management that featured courses in website creation and design, cyberlaw, global strategy, finance, business development, and marketing on the Internet. By introducing this new area of concentration, Dean Comeau sought to position his program to "embrace the Internet age."

As new professional graduate degree programs were introduced by the Harvard Extension School over the next several years, it was a natural development for the Certificate in Administration and Management (CSS) to become transformed into an ALM in Management, first as a Certificate in Management (CM) in 2005-06 and then as an ALM in Management the following year. The transition from graduate certificate to graduate degree was ably supervised by Dean Comeau prior to his retirement in 2008.

A comprehensive review of the management degree program, prompted by Comeau's pending retirement, resulted in the hiring of Margaret Andrews as the new associate dean. She had served for many years as executive director at the MIT Sloan School of Management, where she enhanced the school's reputation and national ranking by her innovative strategies in all phases of the operation. In the Harvard Extension School she devised a similar strategy for restructuring the management program with new concentrations while clearly distinguishing the ALM in Management curriculum and degree from comparable Harvard graduate programs at the Business, Education, and Government schools. Predictably, the ALM in Management soon established itself as the most popular professional degree program in the Harvard Extension School.

Another impetus for the Harvard Extension School to create more professional degree programs was the crisis in the Boston Public Schools created by a shortage of qualified mathematics teachers which prompted the Harvard Extension School to respond with a pilot program in 2001-02. The program was developed through collaboration between the department of mathematics at Harvard and the Boston Public Schools to train in-service middle and high school teachers and administrators who required certification to teach mathematics, as well as teachers seeking graduate credentials and professional development. Daniel Goroff, professor of the practice of mathematics at Harvard, provided the initiative for establishing the program at the Harvard Extension School. Begun with two courses initially, the program grew to six courses within a year to meet the mandated material by the Commonwealth of Massachusetts: "Subject Matter Knowledge Requirements for Teachers," including calculus.

To address the special needs of Boston mathematics teachers, the Harvard Extension School introduced a Mathematics for Teaching concentration in its existing Master of Liberal Arts (ALM) in Information Technology Program by adding modules devoted to pedagogy in basic courses and by increasing scholarship awards available to teachers. The success of this new mathematics concentration was evident in the fall of 2002, as eighty-six Boston public school teachers were awarded partial tuition scholarships from the Harvard Extension School, and they accounted for 117 course enrollments. According to Edward Joyce, senior program director in the Boston Public Schools, this number of students represented almost one-fifth of all the mathematics teachers in Boston's middle and high schools.

The dedication of the Harvard Extension School faculty associated with the mathematics program accounted in large part for its success as well. Citing the critical importance of this initiative, Professor Goroff observed that "the teachers and the students are great, and, in each case, we learn from each other about both mathematics and teaching." This shared commitment between teachers and students in the program was exemplified by Paul J. Sally, professor of mathematics at the University of Chicago, who commuted to Cambridge on weekends in the fall term of 2002 to teach *Theory and Practice of Teaching Geometry*. In 2000 Professor Sally had received the American Mathematical Society's Award for Distinguished Public Service in recognition of his work to improve the teaching of mathematics in the United States. As one of his Extension

students wrote of Professor Sally's course: "I learned more about geometry, and, as a result, so will the eighth grade students in my town. We are
implementing a new unit that features many of the hands-on activities
from the Extension School course." As another mathematics teacher from
Boston wrote in summary: "My colleagues and I are grateful to the
Extension School for the opportunity to develop professionally and learn
mathematical insights that we can put into practice in our classrooms."

By the academic year 2004-05 the ALM in Mathematics for Teaching
was established as a distinct graduate degree program at the Harvard
Extension School. It consisted of ten courses: five required courses, four
electives, and a mater's thesis project that involved producing a documented and detailed investigation of some aspect related to the teaching of
mathematics. In its first few years of operation, the program awarded
eleven master's degrees, and nearly fifty students were active degree candidates. According to the current director, Dr. Andrew Engelward, "The
success of the program resulted from a confluence of several factors: an
urgent need for relevant mathematics courses available to Boston area
math teachers; a core of faculty members from the Harvard mathematics
department committed to teaching math teachers from public and private
schools in Greater Boston; and dedicated support, both programmatic and
financial, from the Harvard Extension School towards the important goal
of improving significantly the current state of math education locally."[2]

As credentialing became a key factor for achieving a competitive
advantage in a tight job market, the Harvard Extension School in the fall
of 2004 responded to this growing need by introducing, in addition to the
ALM in Mathematics for Teaching, three other ALM degrees: in
biotechnology, environmental management, and museum studies to complement the ALM in Information Technology that was initiated six years
earlier. These five professional graduate programs were designed for students seeking practical skills and applied knowledge in specific fields, and
as such they served as an alternate route from the traditional liberal arts
fields of the ALM Program, which offered academic training in fields
such as government, history, psychology, literature, and biology.

The ALM in Information Technology, directed by Dean Henry
Leitner, had evolved over the years in response to the marketplace, and it

added a new concentration in information management systems for students interested in learning both the theory and practice of interactions between technology and management, particularly the transformative effects on businesses and globalization by developments in computing, database management, web technologies, and data communications.

The ALM in Biotechnology was assembled with the informed advice of an advisory board comprising representatives of the Massachusetts Biotechnology Council, whose members included senior officials of the leading biotechnology firms in the Greater Boston area, such as Genzyme and Millennium. The director and associate director of the program, Dr. William Fixsen and Dr. Amanda Benson, worked closely with members of the advisory board to draft a two-track degree program: one in biology for those with experience in biotechnology that led to a thesis demonstrating original research, another in project management for those with terminal degrees who needed business skills to supervise research and development projects. To give students an informed understanding of what was expected of project managers in the industry, the Massachusetts Biotechnology Council sponsored a special course, *Biotechnology Project Management,* at its Cambridge headquarters for the Harvard Extension School degree program. Given the great growth in the biotechnology industry in Boston and the supporting role of the Massachusetts Biotechnology Council, Dr. Benson anticipated a surge of interest in the new Extension graduate degree: "We see multinational companies such as Pfizer, Merck, and Novartis setting up research and development organizations in and around the Cambridge-Boston area, so we're hopeful that a growing number of local biotech companies will be able to sponsor our students." As the only biotechnology master's degree in the Boston area that could be earned in the evening and part time, the Harvard Extension School was well positioned to meet an educational need.[3]

The new ALM in Environmental Management was directed by John D. Spengler, Akira Yamaguchi Professor of Environmental Health and Human Habitation at the Harvard School of Public Health, and it was a natural outgrowth from the graduate Certificate in Environmental Management that had been operating successfully for a number of years and was designed to provide students with relevant knowledge of environmental issues on the local, national, and global level. The new master's program gave students a choice of two tracks: ecology management and sustainability. All students were required to complete the new proseminar, *Graduate Research Methods and Scholarly Writing in Environmental Management,* and conclude their studies with a thesis on environmental management practices or educational programs dealing with aquatic systems, pollution, solid and toxic waste, and wetlands. The scope of the new program was designed to be global in reach because many of the courses were presented online. According to Professor Spengler, "The power of the Internet to reach so many more students throughout the world is important for our global environment. To date, we estimate that through the Extension School we have helped 4,000 people gain a better appreciation of their environment. But our goal is to increase this a thousandfold. We need an environmentally literate populace willing to make a difference in their own lives through their jobs, families, neighborhoods, and practices."[4]

The ALM in Museum Studies, like the ALM in Environmental Management, evolved from a graduate certificate program because a master's degree was the required credential for a career in the field. The director of the new program was David Gordon Mitten, James Loeb Professor of Classical Art and Archaeology at Harvard as well as curator of ancient art at Harvard's Sackler Museum. Professor Mitten and Linda Newberry, the program's assistant director, worked closely with an advisory board of museum professionals from Harvard University and the Greater Boston region to ensure that the curriculum was current and comprehensive. The advisory board members represented Harvard's Sackler Museum and Peabody Museum as well as Boston's Museum of Science, Museum of Fine Arts, and Museum of Afro-American History, among others. In addition to museum studies elective courses such as *Collections and Curation* and *Information Technology for Museums,* candidates were required to complete *Introduction to Museum Studies,* the proseminar *Graduate Research Methods and Scholarly Writing in Museum Studies,* an internship, and a concluding thesis on some basic aspect of museum culture: administration, preservation, exhibits, digitized collections, or historic homes.

In the spring of 2002, Extension students interested in careers in journalism found that the Certificate in Publishing and Communications

(CPC) Program had responded to their demand by introducing a new concentration in journalism consisting of eight graduate-level courses and representing a full year of graduate study. A core course for the concentration was *Principles of Journalism*, co-taught by two experienced Harvard University editors. For the capstone experience to the program, candidates had to complete a 200-hour unpaid internship at a newspaper or magazine office.

The popularity of the journalism concentration eventually led to the creation of the Master of Liberal Arts in Journalism degree in the fall of 2005. The first journalism degree offered at Harvard University, the ALM in Journalism provided training and experience for students interested in pursuing careers in print journalism. John Lenger, editor in chief and assistant director of Harvard's Office of News and Public Affairs, sat on the program's advisory board and taught *Basic Journalism* and *Feature Writing*. According to Lenger, "Our ... journalism program will shape tomorrow's journalists by teaching them the profession's principles and skills and then helping them to apply what they've learned in real-world settings." The required core courses gave students a solid foundation in news and feature writing, and in the ethics of the profession. Journalism electives helped students build specialized skills in various types of journalistic writing, such as travel writing and investigative reporting. General electives in government, health, science, technology, business, and the arts allowed students to develop a field of expertise relevant to their career interests.

Upon completion of several courses, candidates put their skills to the test by completing their internships at newspaper or magazine offices. In many cases, students' work had been rewarded by appearing in print in local newspapers. To complete the program, students could pursue either a capstone project of a series of several short articles on a specific topic or a thesis encompassing an in-depth investigative report and an analysis of the research involved. The program celebrated its first graduate, Jin-ah Kim, in June of 2008. An international student from Korea, Kim focused her studies on business journalism and published an article on women in business in the *Bay State Banner* newspaper.

In January 2002 President George W. Bush had signed into law the "No Child Left Behind Act" that was designed to improve the education of children in the United States at a time when the test results of students in reading, science, and mathematics had fallen to alarming levels. As early as the academic year 2000-01 the Harvard Extension School had created the new graduate Certificate in Technologies of Education (CTE) that was designed, like the US Department of Education Act, to find ways to enhance the teaching and learning process with technology. According to the CTE director, Dr. Catalina Laserna, the new program "addressed a critical concern by giving teachers and school administrators a vision of how to incorporate technology into teaching and learning in a way that goes beyond what has been done with traditional media, such as books and chalkboards." In order to assist teachers and professionals in the field of education to adopt technology as an innovative teaching tool, Laserna taught the core course *Technologies of Education*.[5]

School teachers interested in qualifying as instructional technology specialists needed to meet guidelines established by the Massachusetts state certification authority of the Department of Education, and the new CTE Program introduced a special concentration for these students. By providing professional development options to teachers in instructional technology, the CTE Program hoped to train experts who would have an influential role in policy decisions in schools by investing in the best technologies to promote effective teaching and learning at all levels. The requirement of an internship was a centerpiece for this instructional technology concentration because it enabled students to receive supervised instruction from a technology specialist in elementary and secondary school settings.

As part of its community outreach, the CTE Program established strategic partnerships with six local public and private schools to promote the use of technology. Reports from interns at these schools indicated the many successful adaptations of technology and the resourcefulness of the students in applying in practice what they learned in theory. As one student wrote: "Having access to the courses in the CTE Program enables me to deepen my understanding of the educational opportunities that these cyber-learning environments offer our students and faculty. The program has also given me a lot more confidence in my current teaching, as well as valuable new skills, information, and ... essential theory, such as 'teaching for understanding.' More importantly, the CTE affords me valuable reflection on my current practice.... The scholarship support shows that Harvard University really cares about the needs of local teachers and schools."

A year after its inception, the CTE had its first graduate, Stephanie Burton, a school teacher from Switzerland, who commented that "after more than ten years of teaching, I was looking for an opportunity to reflect upon my experience and the educational applications of technology, [and] the CTE was an ideal fit." By the academic year 2005-06, the CTE had been upgraded to an ALM in Educational Technologies.[6]

Although the professional degree programs date from the early years of the twenty-first century, the original ALM Program in liberal arts dated from the founding year of 1979, first under the directorship of Dean L. Dodge Fernald until his retirement in 2001, and then under the dynamic direction of Dean Sue Weaver Schopf to the present. In its long history, the ALM Program had enrolled a total of 3,406 candidates, but only 1,831 had earned the degree at the end of 2008, a graduate rate of roughly 50 percent or the national average of graduate program completions. Over the years the five most popular fields of concentration have been government, biology, psychology, history, and English, accounting for nearly three-quarters of the graduates. An estimated 10 percent of the ALM graduates have gone on for doctoral degrees, sixteen at Harvard.

As a prominent feature of the Harvard Extension School's community outreach, the Lowell Scholarships program maintained its estimable record of providing partial-tuition scholarships for University Extension courses to local high school students, teachers, and administrators. In 2000 Lowell Scholarships were awarded to 150 students from sixty-seven high schools; 116 Lowell scholars received honor grades in their courses (an 80 percent rate). The Harvard Extension School also made available thirty scholarships to students from Cambridge Rindge and Latin School as part of an ongoing relationship with that school's Community-Based Learning Program. Over the years many able and motivated high school students successfully completed college-level courses at the Harvard Extension School in preparation for their college careers, including matriculation in Harvard College.

The international reach and reputation of the Harvard Extension School was most evident from the graduate student enrollments. In the year 2000 the original ALM Program celebrated its twentieth anniversary with a graduating class of seventy-nine students whose countries of origin included Canada, Chile, Germany, Japan, Jordan, Malaysia, Morocco, Saudi Arabia, El Salvador, and Thailand. Similarly, among the 243 graduates of the CSS Program, 169 or more than two-thirds came from thirty-six countries, with Brazil, Mexico, Venezuela, Colombia, and Argentina sending the most international students. Even the Certificate in Public Health (CPH) Program, which graduated only seven students in 2000, included students from Denmark, Korea, Germany, and Nigeria.

Nowhere was the international composition of the student body more pronounced than in the Harvard Institute for English Language Programs (IEL) for 2000, as nearly 1,400 students, representing eighty-two countries enrolled, and they spoke forty-four native languages, with Spanish, Portuguese, Korean, German, and Chinese among the most popular. IEL also extended its reach to Harvard staff needing English language training and registered 243 employees from the Boston and Cambridge campuses. This was a prelude to plans by Harvard University to mount a comprehensive bridge program to address the workplace language needs of Harvard workers for whom English language proficiency was essential to career advancement and job success.

After years of frustration in attempting to establish a chapter of *Phi Beta Kappa* at Harvard for outstanding graduates of the Harvard Extension School, Dean Shinagel in the academic year 2002-03 worked successfully with the national honor society for nontraditional students, *Alpha Sigma Lambda*, to establish a *Phi Beta* chapter at the Harvard Extension School. At Commencement the first thirteen inductees, representing the top 10 percent of the ALB graduating class, were honored at a special ceremony held at the Harvard Faculty Club. Founded in 1945, *Alpha Sigma Lambda* had a network of nearly 300 chapters across the United States that recognized the outstanding academic achievement of adult nontraditional students. By having joined the society, the Harvard Extension School followed the lead of other local institutions, such as Boston University, Northeastern University, Emerson College, and the University of Massachusetts-Boston, in affording their top students national recognition for their academic excellence.[7]

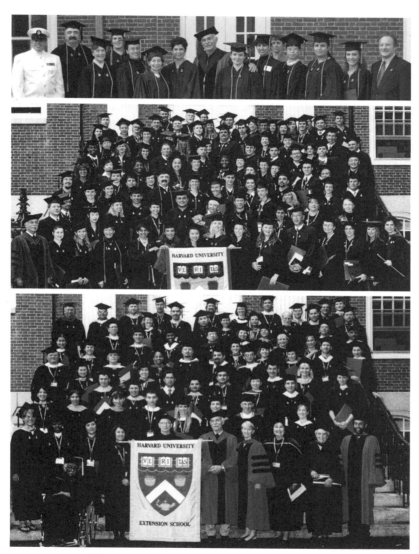

COMMENCEMENT, JUNE 2003

Inaugural induction of top Extension School students into the *Phi Beta* chapter of the *Alpha Sigma Lambda* honor society, Harvard Faculty Club; and, below, the undergraduate and graduate degree recipients.

A gratifying trend at the Harvard Extension School early in the twenty-first century was the significant growth of enrolled students under the age of eighteen. According to the Extension School registrar, Susan McGee: "In 2001, approximately 106 students were under eighteen. Just last year it was 208, doubling in four years." Most of these high school age students attended local schools, but a growing number were home schooled. To provide some supervision for the home-schooled student contingent, the Harvard Extension School appointed Dr. Paul Bamberg, senior lecturer in mathematics and an autodidact who taught courses in physics, mathematics, and computer science, as advisor to this cohort. In his advanced geometry course he observed: "I had a half-dozen Extension School students combined with Harvard undergraduates in my class. The top two students happened to be Extension School students, and the top student was home schooled." In evaluating the many home-schooled students he had taught and supervised, Bamberg reported that they were "more inclined to speak up, more careful with all the detail on their homework." In response to the widespread stereotyping of home-schooled students, he responded candidly: "I've heard them—that home-schooled students are antisocial, a liability to high schools, [but] I haven't met any of those types yet."

The *Harvard University Gazette* on January 20, 2000, ran a feature article titled "Young Scholars Find Challenges, Acceptance at Extension School" to highlight the experiences of two middle-school-aged students, aged eleven and thirteen, who were home schooled and in the fall enrolled for courses at the Harvard Extension School. David, the older boy, was taking *College Algebra, Spanish*, and *Shakespeare: The Early Plays* four evenings a week; and Amos, the younger boy, was only taking *College Algebra*, which met two nights a week. The Harvard instructor of the algebra class, Andrew Engelward, said: "It's been a privilege having them in class.... they do bring things to class that other people certainly can't. They try experimenting with things through a much more intuitive approach. They are both doing great. They've got a lot of insight, and both work hard." The boys had no idea about their career choices, but they were clear about their choice of Extension courses for the spring term: David would enroll in Spanish, precalculus, computer science, and expository writing, while Amos would take precalculus and Latin. When asked why they chose Harvard, they smiled and said, "It's the best!"[8]

Home schooled since she was two years old, when her mother read to her regularly, Aidin Carey took courses at the Harvard Extension School, and by June 2003 had earned enough credits for the Associate in Arts degree. She was not sure how the combination of home schooling and Harvard Extension School would be regarded by college admissions officers, but in the spring she received the welcome news that she was accepted to Harvard College and would matriculate in the fall. According to Sean Boyce, the Harvard undergraduate admissions officer and liaison for nontraditional schooling, Harvard College accepts home schoolers at the same rate as traditional students because "it is treated as another form of education." But it helped to combine home schooling with formal education in a community college or an evening program like the Harvard Extension School where academic transcripts and course catalogues provide corroborating evidence of academic achievement.[9]

The Cambridge triplets Ellora, Claire, and Julia Berthet, age seventeen, who were home schooled since the eighth grade, represented another interesting aspect of the Harvard Extension School experience as a complement to home schooling. They found that their age was not an issue in their Extension classes. What mattered was their strong motivation to learn, especially their shared passion for the study of history. The combination of home schooling and Harvard Extension School served them well, as they went on to college at Harvard, Swarthmore, and Wellesley.[10]

Another noteworthy example of a home-schooling success story at the Harvard Extension School was the case of Amit Chatterjee, the son of academics, who began his undergraduate education at Extension at the age of twelve and soon was pursuing his studies in earnest, earning the Bachelor of Liberal Arts degree in 2002 at the age of eighteen, thereby becoming the youngest undergraduate degree recipient in the history of the Harvard Extension School. He also was instrumental in the creation of the Harvard Extension Student Association (HESA) in 2002.[11]

Whereas the growth of home schoolers and students under eighteen years of age was a relatively recent phenomenon in the Harvard Extension

School, the presence of seniors at the other end of the age spectrum had always been a feature of the evening program. Unlike Harvard College where the age cohort rarely reached beyond the traditional teens to early twenties, the Harvard Extension School regularly saw an age range of sixty years or more between the youngest and the oldest students. The case of Santo Joseph Aurelio was both representative and unusual among graduates of the Harvard Extension School. Born in 1932 the tenth and last child of Italian immigrants in Boston's West End, Aurelio had to postpone college to help support his parents, and he trained at the Stenotype Institute of Boston to prepare for a career as a court reporter, notably at the Massachusetts Superior Court for thirty years. After his four children finished college, he enrolled at the Harvard Extension School and graduated with the Bachelor of Liberal Arts degree, *cum laude*, in 1983 at the age of fifty-one. He went on for his ALM in 1985, and in 1989 completed the doctoral program in education at Boston University, all the while working full time as a court stenographer. He retired from the court in 1990 and devoted himself to teaching and community service. In 1993 he met with Dean Shinagel to establish the Santo Joseph Aurelio Prize at the Harvard Extension School "for a graduate older than 50 who has exemplified excellence in his or her academic career and his or her personal life." Dr. Aurelio remarked: "My greatest satisfaction in life is my Harvard education," and the prize that bears his name is awarded annually at Commencement to an outstanding graduate who exemplifies Dr. Aurelio's motivation and academic distinction. In 2001 the Harvard Extension Alumni Association elected him president, and he has remained active in the affairs of both the Harvard Extension Alumni Association and the Harvard Alumni Association.[12]

Over the years many inspirational seniors had earned their Extension degrees at advanced ages, such as Sarabelle Madoff Annenberg who received an ALB *cum laude* in 1997 at the age of eighty-one (thirty-nine years after registering for her first Harvard Extension course) or Elizabeth V. McNeil, who received an ALB in 2006 at the age of eighty-two, making her the oldest graduate that year and resulting in profiles in the *Boston Globe* and the *Harvard University Gazette*, and featured on a WCVB-TV newscast. When asked what she would do after graduation, she replied that she would take more courses: "I'm not going to stop just because I have a degree."[13]

At Commencement in June 2007 Rosemary Dowling, age seventy-nine, of Dorchester, and her daughter Rosemary McCarthy, age fifty-five, of Duxbury, both received ALB degrees, thereby becoming a part of history as the first mother and daughter to graduate from the Harvard Extension School with the same degree in the same year, a newsworthy item that the local press highlighted.

According to the dean's annual report for 2007-08, the Harvard Extension School maintained significant student enrollments and record course registrations: nearly 14,000 students and more than 25,000 registrations. Given the introduction of new graduate programs, notably the professional ALM degrees, there was a steady increase in graduate credit enrollment in evidence as 42 percent of the total registrations fell in this category—almost the same figure as undergraduate credit enrollments. The educational background of the students also reflected a greater sophistication, as three-quarters had at least a bachelor's degree, almost a quarter had a master's degree, and one-twentieth had a doctorate.

The internationalization of the student body was clear from the continued growth of foreign nationals enrolling in the academic program. During the year a total of more than 2,500 international students enrolled, accounting for almost one-fifth of all registrations. These students represented 123 countries, with Brazil (447), the Republic of Korea (220), India (213), Germany (150), Canada (147), the People's Republic of China (133), and Mexico (131) sending the largest contingents. More than 200 were candidates for Harvard Extension School degrees or graduate certificates, with nearly one-third enrolled in the Institute for English Language Programs noncredit courses, 30 percent in graduate management courses, and nearly one-quarter in distance education courses.

Harvard staff continued to avail themselves of Harvard's Tuition Assistance Plan (TAP) by enrolling in Harvard Extension School courses in record numbers. Nearly 2,000 Harvard staff members enrolled, mostly for graduate credit, accounting for more than 3,500 course registrations. The thirty-nine Harvard staff who graduated during the year by using their TAP benefits showed a distribution pattern across the spectrum of degree and certificate options, with the traditional ALB and ALM Programs attracting the most, followed closely by the management and information technology programs.

The Harvard Extension School distance education program also continued to grow, with a total of 7,700 course registrations in distance education courses, and approximately 4,000 registrations were from students who never came to campus for lectures. Students enrolled in a total of 108 distance courses sponsored by Extension during the year, including twenty-nine Harvard College courses taught by senior Harvard faculty. The distance education component of the Harvard Extension School promoted both graduate enrollments and the internationalization of the student body.

When the Harvard Extension Alumni Association (HEAA) was founded in 1968, a total of only 452 Extension degrees had been awarded since the Harvard Extension School was created in 1910. On the occasion of the fortieth anniversary of the HEAA in 2008, the dean commemorated the event by observing at the annual Extension alumni banquet that the Harvard Extension School had conferred 481 degrees and graduate certificates during the year, significantly more than the 452 graduates recorded in the first fifty-eight years of the Harvard Extension School by the time the HEAA was established.

An analysis of the 481 graduates in 2008 revealed that the seven AA and 111 ALB recipients as well as the ninety-one traditional ALM awardees in the liberal arts were very much in line with the graduation patterns of recent years. What was noteworthy was the major growth of graduates (220) in the professional ALM Programs, notably management (105), information technology (fifty-seven), biotechnology (nineteen), environmental management (sixteen), museum studies (fourteen), educational technologies (four), math for teachers (four), and journalism (one). Obviously the addition of these professional degree options resulted in the recent growth of graduates, a trend that was certain to continue. Whereas the total number of Extension degrees awarded when Dr. Phelps retired in 1975 was less than 1,000, the introduction of graduate programs, both at the degree and certificate levels, resulted in a grand total of 12,464 graduates since the creation of the Harvard Extension School in 1910.

Over the years the Harvard Extension School had attempted to establish joint programs with other Harvard schools, such as the joint graduate certificate program with the Harvard School of Public Health. Other attempts at collaboration, such as the graduate certificate and later ALM in Educational Technologies, with the Harvard Graduate School of Education did not succeed and the Harvard Extension School developed the program itself. In 2008 the Harvard Extension School joined with the Harvard Divinity School in sponsoring a joint graduate citation in religious studies and education, designed for prospective or in-service teachers. Although the potential enrollment in this program might be modest, it was seen by both schools as a worthy undertaking in promoting their mission.

As John Lowell grew older, he designated his son William A. Lowell administrator of the Lowell Institute. Like his predecessors, William Lowell was born in Boston and attended Harvard College, graduating with an AB degree *cum laude* in 1977. He matriculated at Boston College Law School, graduating with a juris doctrate *magna cum laude* in 1980. He was admitted to the practice of law in 1980, specializing in wealth management, trusts, and estates at Choate, Hall, and Stewart in Boston. Among his many community services are trustee of WGBH, Perkins School for the Blind, and the Museum of Science. He is also a member of the corporations at Northeastern University, Wheelock College, and the Boston Biomedical Research Institute.

Like his father, William Lowell had a cordial relationship with Dean Shinagel and was supportive of the goals of the Harvard Extension School, especially its outreach efforts to the Greater Boston secondary school community of students and teachers interested in taking courses at Extension. The Lowell Scholarships met this goal very effectively.

William Lowell significantly furthered the educational aim of John Lowell, Jr. by the manifold array of cultural programs the Lowell Institute sponsored annually for the benefit of the citizenry of Boston. In addition to the Lowell Lecture each year co-sponsored by the Harvard Extension School, the Lowell Institute supported lecture series at the National Heritage Museum, the Paul Revere Memorial Association, the Old South Meeting House, the Peabody Essex Museum, the Bostonian Society, the Museum of Science, the USS *Constitution* Museum, the John F. Kennedy

Library, the Cambridge Forum, the Ford Hall Forum, the Museum of Fine Arts, Boston College Lowell Lectures, and the Boston Public Library. The Lowell Institute Cooperative Broadcasting Council, through its WGBH Educational Foundation, which controlled the public radio and TV broadcast operations of WGBH-FM and channels 2 and 44, promoted the education and entertainment of the public through its assorted programs.

The Lowell Institute also supported programs at the Lowell Institute School at Northeastern University, Wheelock College, Simmons College, Suffolk University, and the Harvard Extension School. In addition it sponsored films, exhibits, and concerts at the Boston Symphony Orchestra, the Museum of Fine Arts, the Citi Performing Arts Center, and the Boston Children's Museum. Surely the shade of John Lowell, Jr. would have rejoiced to see how his vision of the Lowell Institute had been realized so creatively and comprehensively by the trustees to this day.

John Lowell, Trustee of the Lowell Institute, 1978–,
with painting of Ralph Lowell; and William Lowell (inset),
Administrator of the Lowell Institute, 2001–;
surrounded chronologically by the founder and previous
Lowell trustees and Extension directors and deans.

CHAPTER XV

Conclusion

A Century of Service

As the Harvard Extension School moved into its centennial year, it could cast a backward glance over the years and appreciate what a remarkable role it had played in the history of the University in the twentieth century. This role may have been neglected by the chroniclers of the University because Extension was nontraditional and the teaching and learning took place at night or, as in the case of the PACE Program or the Indian Computer Academy, far from Harvard Yard. But as this history has attempted to demonstrate, the Harvard Extension School was a pioneer in many ways in the field of continuing higher education and it had served for a century as a vital resource to the community, both outside the University and, in more recent years with the Tuition Assistance Plan, inside as well. Throughout its storied existence, it had maintained a reputation for academic excellence in its outstanding faculty, mostly drawn from Harvard; its classic curriculum, based largely on the Harvard course program; and its mature, motivated, and able student body of men and women of all ages, from the early teens to the early nineties. This combination rendered University Extension at Harvard *sui generis* for a century.

The histories of Harvard in the twentieth century properly highlight the role of the faculty in transforming the University into the premier research institution in the world, with a record number of Nobel laureates, among other noteworthy national and international awardees, in all the Harvard schools. But it would be a disservice to the dedication of distinguished members of the Harvard faculty over the years to neglect to mention their contributions to the success of the Harvard Extension School. Every dean and director of University Extension was able to induce outstanding members of the faculty to present their courses at night. They taught because they valued the opportunity to reach a diverse and motivated student population, not because the pay was a major inducement, as it was always modest at best. Their numbers were never large, but they were dedicated and, as Dr. Phelps liked to announce, they constituted a dream faculty for the evening program at Harvard.

Just as John Lowell, Jr. in 1835 left half his estate for the establishment of the Lowell Institute to promote the educational opportunities for the women and men of New England, so A. Lawrence Lowell in 1910 created the Commission on Extension Courses in Boston and University Extension at Harvard to make available to the community the educational resources of the University. The *pro bono publico* spirit and vision of both Lowells was the same. The importance of the "two bushels of wheat" as a fixed cost for the evening courses was symbolic; it ensured that the programs were dedicated to reaching the largest audiences without imposing a financial burden on those seeking an education. Unlike other extension or continuing education programs that were designed to make as much money as possible at the expense of the public, the Harvard Extension courses were always priced as low as possible so that the early programs broke even or that in later years the cost of the courses was among the lowest in the Boston area. As A. Lawrence Lowell wisely wrote in *What a University President Has Learned* in 1938: "Anyone who sees in his own occupation merely a means of earning money degrades it; but he that sees in it a service to mankind ennobles both his labor and himself."[1] Happily, all the directors and deans of University Extension at Harvard for the past century have seen their service as ennobling.

By the end of its century of service the Harvard Extension School had made available to an estimated half-a-million women and men the opportunity to study in its academic programs. From the outset the Harvard Extension School featured open enrollment and required no tests for admission and no residency as a condition of enrollment. The public was free to enroll and study what they wished for credit or noncredit, for personal enrichment or career advancement. The first half-century saw the academic program constrained by a limit of thirty courses or less because of its reliance on funding from the Lowell Institute, and the number of degrees awarded remained relatively small. But as University Extension managed to increase the number of courses offered through the resourcefulness of Dr. Phelps when he assumed control, the number of degrees granted increased sharply. The growth in the academic course program and the commensurate growth in the number of degree and certificate graduates accelerated, with the advent of graduate liberal arts and professional degrees under Dean Shinagel's tenure. Each year now the Harvard Extension School awards more degrees than were awarded collectively in the first fifty years.

But the high academic standards of the Harvard Extension School were never compromised for earning a degree. Even though many more degrees are awarded now, it is important to bear in mind that the nearly 12,500 graduates to date represent but a minute percentage of the estimated 500,000 students who have taken classes in the Harvard Extension School. As the dean reminds the Extension graduating class at Commencement each June, when it comes to earning a degree, now as before, "many are called, but few are chosen."

The creation of the Tuition Assistance Plan by the University in 1976-77 proved an immediate success as Harvard staff members availed themselves in growing numbers of the educational opportunities it provided. But since staff release time during the day presented obvious problems, the great majority of staff chose the evening courses at the Harvard Extension School for their studies. The registrar's office of the Harvard Extension School compiled a comprehensive record of Harvard staff who actually earned degrees and graduate certificates by using their benefits during the thirty-year period of 1978-2008. The results were impressive as more than 700 staff members were awarded degrees and certificates: notably 328 Associate in Arts and Bachelor of Liberal Arts degrees, 105 Master of Liberal Arts degrees, and 166 graduate certificates in management. This record was all the more noteworthy when one included the many thousands of Harvard staff members who took courses for personal satisfaction and professional enhancement during this period in the Harvard Extension School, even though they chose not to pursue a formal degree or graduate certificate program.

Since its inception in 1979-80, the Health Careers Program by the end of the Harvard Extension School's centennial year in 2009 had sponsored nearly one thousand adult students for admission to medical school, and more than 845 had received offers of admission for a remarkable acceptance rate of 85 percent over a thirty-year period. This record of success was all the more impressive when considering that the national acceptance rate to medical school during this period was an average of only 35 percent. Under the dedicated direction of Gloria White-Hammond (1979-81), Sylvia Field (1982-91), and William Fixsen (1992-present), the Health Careers Program had established a national reputation for preparing adults for admission to medical school, attracting students from many parts of the country to Harvard at night.

As early as 1949 University Extension, in conjunction with the Lowell Institute Cooperative Broadcasting Council, helped pioneer educational radio courses with college professors in the United States. This initiative was a result of a suggestion from President Conant of Harvard to Ralph Lowell as trustee of the Lowell Institute to establish the Lowell Institute Cooperative Broadcasting Council in order to present educational programs on the radio. And beginning on December 5, 1949, people in New England could tune in on their FM radios to listen to lectures by eminent professors on psychology, history, and economics. This experiment proved successful, and by the early 1950s WGBH-FM radio courses in the humanities, social sciences, and natural sciences were sponsored by the Commission on Extension Courses. The contributions of the Harvard Extension School to this historic achievement were owing to the efforts of the director, Reginald H. Phelps.

The advent of television predictably inspired Ralph Lowell and the Lowell Institute Cooperative Broadcasting Council to capitalize on the educational potential of this new medium, an interest that Dr. Phelps fully shared for the field of adult education. By the late 1950s the radio courses on WGBH-FM were replaced by television courses from the studio at WGBH-TV, first in anthropology in 1956-57, followed by geology and modern drama in the fall and spring of the next year. These pioneering courses marked the successful adaptation of television to adult education in New England, and by 1959 Dr. Phelps could announce that WGBH-TV would telecast for Extension credit courses by two distinguished Harvard history professors, Robert G. Albion and Crane Brinton, fall and spring terms.

The success of the radio and television courses attracted the attention of the US Navy, and from 1960-61 Dr. Phelps, on behalf of the Commission on Extension Courses and with the support of WGBH-TV, embarked on an ambitious and innovative program of creating kinescopes of television courses, first for the Polaris submarine fleet and then for the surface fleet as well. Between 1960 and 1972 a two-year curriculum of forty televised courses in mathematics, chemistry, physics, English composition, engineering, metallurgy, and foreign languages was assembled by the Commission for the US Navy, first under the title of "Polaris University" and later as PACE (Program for Afloat College Education). When the program ended it had recorded nearly 6,000 registrations by Navy personnel for 443 presentations of the forty televised courses prepared by the Commission and WGBH-TV, making it the most comprehensive educational television undertaking of the 1960s.

The social upheaval of the late 1960s in the United States in general and in Greater Boston in particular again called into service the resources of University Extension by Harvard to help improve relations with the community, particularly Roxbury and Cambridge. Although the Harvard Extension School historically was a traditional liberal arts program, the exigencies of the time forced it to adopt nontraditional programs, under such rubrics as urban studies, Roxbury program, and Jamaica Plain project to highlight the communities it attempted to serve. As the PACE Program ended in 1972, Harvard Extension School shifted its resources to meeting community needs with such programs as Training Teachers of Teachers, Cambridge Model Cities Program, and the Cambridge Economic Opportunity Committee. Dr. Phelps responded during this period of urban crisis with a proactive approach to community needs and community involvement on behalf of University Extension.

Not all of the undertakings of University Extension in the past century proved successful, however, as the case of the Indian Computer Academy in Bangalore amply demonstrated. Harvard Extension School had developed in the 1980s a core curriculum in computer science courses for the graduate Certificate in Applied Sciences designed for candidates interested and able to work in the Greater Boston high technology industry. When interested parties from India expressed their willingness to finance a technology transfer of the Harvard Extension School curriculum to a computer academy in Bangalore, an agreement was reached between Harvard and the Indian Computer Academy in Bangalore to offer the Harvard Extension School computer science curriculum as a two-year program, but as events unfolded over a period of six years, the project succeeded curricularly but failed in all other respects so that the Harvard Extension School had to withdraw when financial and management problems became insurmountable and the Harvard name had to be protected from an operation whose quality and integrity had become compromised.

The failure of the Indian Computer Academy project was offset by the successes of the University Extension essay into distance education from the mid-1980s on. Once again the Harvard Extension School was a pioneer in interactive distance education, first with the Teleteaching Project for online Socratic interaction in calculus courses, and later with the introduction of Mathematica, which was a mainstay of online mathematics courses until 1997, when streaming video and audio were adapted effectively for computer science courses online, and eventually more than 120 courses in all fields were sponsored by the Harvard Extension School. Today the distance education program has become established as a national leader in the quality of its courses and the relevance of its research into what is important in this medium for teachers and students to be successful.

The introduction of graduate degrees dating from 1979-80 enabled the Harvard Extension School to expand its availability to students interested in pursuing a degree, since nearly three-quarters of the enrollees in Extension by this time already had an undergraduate degree. Predictably, enrollments in the master's degree program soared, as did the numbers of graduates. This growth in graduate studies was accelerated since 2000 by the expansion of professional studies programs, first as graduate certificates and eventually as ALM degree programs in such professional fields as biotechnology, environmental management, information technology, museum studies, educational technologies, journalism, mathematics for teaching, and management.

Over the century the composition of the students in the Harvard Extension School had evolved from an exclusively local clientele at the time of the creation of the Commission on Extension Courses in 1910 to an increasingly national and international student body with the introduction of graduate certificate and degree programs dating from the 1980s and, more significantly, the development of the distance education course program since 2000. Whereas in the first half century and more the Harvard Extension School was geared, through the vision of A. Lawrence Lowell and Ralph Lowell as trustees of the Lowell Institute, to realizing the aims of the founder, John Lowell, Jr., in serving the citizens of Boston, in the past three decades the scope had been extended to a global scale, while also continuing to be readily accessible to the local community of Boston and environs.

The Lowell Institute has been the beneficiary of a dedicated and innovative line of trustees who valued the prescience and vision of the founder as they discharged their duties over the years. They understood that they had to interpret the will of John Lowell, Jr. from time to time to make his bequest to the citizens of Boston current and effective. Today's extensive program of benefactions by the Lowell Institute is a testament to the creativity and commitment of the trustees. Similarly, today's University Extension is vastly different from the academic program first assembled by Dean Ropes on behalf of President Lowell and the Commission on Extension in 1910. This is as it should be, for both educational institutions have remained vital and viable as they adapted to changing times.

The last word of this history properly belongs to the creator of University Extension, President Lowell, whose critical role in establishing and promoting the evening academic program at Harvard and, through the Commission on Extension Courses, in Greater Boston, has regrettably been overlooked by his biographers and the chroniclers of the University in the twentieth century. He, however, was never in doubt about the significance of University Extension. As he wrote to Arthur Whittem, the director, in 1938, five years after he left the presidency of Harvard but still was active as trustee of the Lowell Institute: " . . . the Extension Courses . . . have given a service to the public . . . which seems to me of the utmost importance." If Lowell were surveying the century of service provided by his evening academic program at Harvard, he doubtless would have invoked his favorite biblical benediction: "Well done, good and faithful servant."

Appendix A

Lowell Lecturers and Their Topics (1980-2008)

McGeorge Bundy, former Harvard dean and professor, national security advisor, and president of the Ford Foundation, "Americans in the Un-American World: How Not to Think About Foreign Policy in the 1980s" (1980)

Alfred E. Kahn, former chairman of the Civil Aeronautics Board and the Council on Wage and Price Stability, "Are We Going to Have to Live with Inflation throughout the 1980s?" (1981)

Edwin Newman, veteran news correspondent for NBC, "Preserving a Civil Tongue" (1982)

Gloria Steinem, editor of *Ms.* magazine, "Feminism and Democracy" (1983)

Carl Sagan, astronomer, "Dust Storms on Mars and Nuclear War on Earth: A Tale of Two Planets" (1984)

Art Buchwald, satirist and syndicated columnist, "Washington Politics" (1985)

Amiri Baraka (LeRoi Jones), poet, playwright, activist, "Contemporary Black Writers and the Afro-American Tradition" (1986)

Frances FitzGerald, Pulitzer Prize-winning journalist and National Book Award recipient, "Religions and Utopian Communities in the U.S.: Social Change and the Creation of Culture" (1987)

Doris Kearns Goodwin, award-winning author, "The Issue of Character in Presidential Politics" (1988)

Jean Mayer, president of Tufts University and nutrition expert, "National and International Food and Policy Issues" (1989)

Mortimer Adler, noted philosopher, author, editor, and professor, "The Great Books, the Great Ideas, and a Lifetime of Learning" (1990)

Ken Burns, documentary filmmaker, "The Role of the Documentary Film in the Study of History" (1991)

Gore Vidal, man of letters, "America First? America Last? America at Last?" (1992)

Ellen Goodman, Pulitzer Prize-winning journalist and *Boston Globe* columnist, "Value Judgments" (1994)

Harold Bloom, Sterling Professor of Humanities at Yale, "Shakespeare and the Canonical Sublime" (1995)

Robert Reich, secretary of labor in the Clinton Administration, "The Role of Education and the Future of the American Labor Force in a Global Market" (1996)

John Shattuck, assistant secretary of state for democracy, human rights, and labor in the Clinton Administration, "Conflict Resolution in the Post-Cold War World" (1997)

James Carroll, author and *Boston Globe* columnist, "Sacred Hatred: Religious and Political Lessons of the Holocaust" (1998)

Jill Ker Conway, author and former president of Smith College, "Studying Women's Lives" (1999)

Mark Plotkin, Extension School alumnus and executive director of the Amazon Conservation Team in Washington, D.C., "Witchdoctors and Biotechnology" (2000)

Thomas H. O'Connor, professor of history at Boston College and "dean" of historians of Boston, "Highlights of Boston: A Historical Perspective" (2001)

Christopher Lydon, broadcast journalist, "A Culture Trying to Happen" (2002)

Sissela Bok, ethicist and author, "Pursuits of Happiness" (2003)

Robert Brustein, drama critic, author, and founder of the American Repertory Theatre, "The Drama as a Secular Faith" (2004)

James Freedman, former president of the University of Iowa and Dartmouth College, "Prospects for Higher Education" (2005)

Margaret Marshall, chief justice of the Supreme Judicial Court of Massachusetts, "Our Judiciary: Why It Belongs to All of Us" (2006)

Sol Gittleman, former provost and University Professor at Tufts University, "Has Liberal Education a Future in the Twenty-First Century?" (2007)

Robert Coles, Pulitzer Prize-winning author for *Children of Crisis*, "Personal Reflections on a Career Studying Children Living Through Conflict" (2008)

Robert Kuttner, economist, journalist, and author, "Obama's Economic Challenge and the Prospects of Success." (2009)

Appendix B

Text of Public Statement regarding
Harvard University's Division of Continuing
Education's Cessation of Affiliation with
the Indian Computer Academy, Bangalore, India

February 17, 1994

To the Students, Faculty and Staff of the Indian Computer Academy:

At a special meeting of members of the Board of Trustees and the Advisory Board of the Indian Computer Academy (ICA) held at Harvard University (Cambridge, Massachusetts) on February 8, 1994, it was unanimously decided that, given the serious financial and management problems of the ICA, Harvard University's Division of Continuing Education (DCE) had to withdraw its sponsorship because academic quality could not be maintained under the existing circumstances.

The members at the meeting addressed the concerns of both ICA students and faculty. It was resolved that the fourth batch of students (and those students from the third batch who needed to retake part or all of the comprehensive examination) would be given the opportunity to sit the examinations scheduled for the 14th and 16th of February in Bangalore. These examinations will be graded by Harvard DCE faculty, as in the past, and the results of the examinations will be sent to Dean Mahadevan at the ICA by the end of February.

Students who pass this examination will be issued a special certificate of completion from Harvard DCE with the appropriate authorizing signatures to indicate their academic achievement, exclusive of the internship component. We are mindful of our obligation to the students who have enrolled at the ICA, and, consistent with Harvard standards of academic attainment, we will provide the certification that students require. We will work closely with Dean Mahadevan to ensure the complete fulfillment of these obligations.

The members of the Board of Trustees and the Advisory Board were no less committed to discharging their responsibilities to the ICA faculty. Mr. Ravi Bhatia of Citibank, who attended the Harvard meeting on February 8, will work closely with Dean Mahadevan to ensure that salary payments are met. We at Harvard DCE are ready to provide, upon request, individual letters of reference for the teaching that has been done over the past two years.

Harvard DCE also wants to underscore the point that the teaching materials are the property of Harvard University, and should not be used for commercial purposes after Harvard's official withdrawal, which becomes effective at the end of February 1994. However, Harvard DCE is more than willing to have the ICA faculty members use the skills they learned at the Harvard Summer School as enhancement in their future job prospects and careers. We sincerely hope that the training and teaching experiences have made the ICA faculty members more marketable in the growing software industries of Bangalore. We thank the faculty for their dedicated teaching efforts with the four batches.

We enclose a copy of a news release that will appear in local newspapers and computer publications to announce Harvard's withdrawal of sponsorship. This press release is for the information of the students, faculty and staff. Kindly note at the close of the press release our tribute to all of you for your effective teaching and learning under increasingly difficult circumstances. While we regret the need to withdraw Harvard DCE sponsorship from the ICA, we share with you—the students, the faculty, and the staff—a sense of achievement in what has been accomplished, as more than 150 deserving students have received instruction in a core curriculum for computer science. Again, we will work closely with Dean Mahadevan to ensure that the Academy's closing is handled thoughtfully and effectively.

Harvard DCE initially contracted with Mothercare, Inc., solely for the purpose of providing the educational materials for the curriculum (as well as training teachers, writing and evaluating comprehensive examinations). We have done that. And now that we have withdrawn our sponsorship, it falls to Mothercare in Bangalore to discharge the remaining administrative and financial duties connected with the ICA We have every confidence that Mr. Ahuja, Mr. Kannan, and the other Mothercare representatives will honor their commitments to the ICA in its final phase.

In closing, we thank everyone involved in this significant venture for the kindness you extended us during our visits to India, and we wish you the best for your future success.

On behalf of Harvard University's Division of Continuing Education,

Dr. Paul Bamberg	Dr. Henry Leitner	Dr. Michael Shinagel
Director of	Assoc. Director of	Dean
Science Instruction	Science Instruction	

Introduction

1. Samuel Eliot Morison, *Three Centuries of Harvard*, 1630-1936 (Cambridge, MA: Harvard University Press, 1946). Henry Aaron Yeomans, *Abbott Lawrence Lowell*, 1856-1943 (Cambridge, MA: Harvard Unversity Press, 1948). "Abbott Lawrence Lowell" [Memorial Minute], March 2, 1943 (Cambridge).
2. Michael Shinagel, "Seamus Heaney's 'Villanelle for an Anniversary,'" in *Seamus Heaney, A Celebration*, ed. Stratis Haviaras (A Harvard Review Monograph, 1996), pp. 73-74.

Chapter I

1. Ferris Greenslet, *The Lowells and Their Seven Worlds* (Cambridge, MA: Riverside Press, 1946), pp. 196f.
2. Edward Weeks, *The Lowells and Their Institute* (Boston: Little, Brown and Company, An Atlantic Monthly Press Book, 1966), pp. 3-35. Copy of a letter to J.A. Lowell from John Lowell, Jr., dated August 1, 1835, from Thebes that includes his will. Courtesy of the Lowell Institute Archives at the Boston Athenaeum.
3. Edward Everett, *A Memoir of Mr. John Lowell, Jr.* (Boston: Charles C. Little and James Brown, 1840), p. 3.

Chapter II

1. Harriette Knight Smith, *The History of the Lowell Institute* (Boston: Lawson, Wolffe and Company, 1898), p. 13.
2. Smith, pp. 21-25.
3. Smith, pp. ix-x: For "A List of Lecturers and the Subjects of their Lectures in the Lowell Institute, 1839-1898," see pp. 49-125. Also see Ferris Greenslet, *The Lowells and Their Seven Worlds*, pp. 233-35.
4. Edward Weeks, *The Lowells and Their Institute* (Boston: Little, Brown and Company. An Atlantic Press Book, 1966), pp. 36-78 on John Amory Lowell and pp. 79-100 on Augustus Lowell.

Chapter III

1. Weeks, *The Lowells and Their Institute*, pp. 101-144 on the career of A. Lawrence Lowell.
2. A. Lawrence Lowell's annual reports as trustee of the Lowell Institute are on file in the Lowell Institute Archives at the Boston Anthenaeum. The author is grateful to John Lowell, current trustee of the Lowell Institute, for permission to have access to the archive while researching this history.
3. For newspaper and other clippings related to University Extension at Harvard, see HUE 25.110 in Harvard University Archives.
4. J. Donald Hall, *Copey of Harvard* (Cambridge, Mass.: The Riverside Press, 1960), pp. 150-151, 226-243.
5. Harvard University Archives (HUA). *Reports of the President and the Treasurer of Harvard College*, 1908/1909. HU 30.10. For all annual reports of the President of Harvard University: Harvard/Radcliffe Annual Reports, 1826-1995. Harvard/Radcliffe Online Historical Reference Shelf.
6. (HUA) *Reports of the President and the Treasurer of Harvard College*, 1909/1910. HU 30.10.
7. The correspondence of President Lowell dealing with University Extension at Harvard is available in the Harvard University Archives under UAI 5.160 (Series 1909-1914), "University Extension," folder 1461 and (Series 1914-1917), folder 817. See also Michael Shinagel, "Pro Bono Publico," *Harvard Magazine* (May-June 1980), pp. 37-41, and "*Pro Bono Publico*: President A. Lawrence Lowell and the Early History of University Extension at Harvard," *Harvard University Commission on Extension Courses 70th Year* booklet, (Harvard University Printing Office, 1980), pp. 1-12.
8. (HUA) Papers of Abbot Lawrence Lowell. General Correspondence, series 1914-1917, in folder 110. UAI 5.160.

Chapter IV

1. *Dictionary of American Biography*, Vol. XVI (New York: Charles Scribner's Sons, 1943), pp. 151-152. "Minute on the Life and Services of Professor James Hardy Ropes," *Harvard University Gazette* (April, 1933).
2. UAI 5.160 (Series 1909-1914), "University Extension," folder 1461.
3. HUE 25.510.77. James Hardy Ropes, "The Possibilities of University Extension in Boston" [Reprinted from *The Harvard Graduates' Magazine* (June 1910), No. LXXII], pp. 608-13.
4. Harvard University Class of 1889 Twenty-Fifth Class Report for J.H. Ropes, BA HUD 289.25, Harvard University Archives.
5. UAI 5.160 (1909-1914), "University Extension," folder 1461.

6. From a copy of a letter in the files from Dean Ropes to Florence Leadbetter dated April 8, 1910 explaining the Associate in Arts designation rather than the AB
7. Letter from Lowell to Ropes dated September 30, 1914 in (HUA) Papers of Abbott Lawrence Lowell, folder 110. UAI 5.160.
8. Harvard University Class of 1889 Fiftieth Class Report for J.H. Ropes, BA HUD 289.50, Harvard University Archives.

Chapter V

1. *Harvard University Gazette* (March 14, 1959).
2. Harvard University Class of 1902 Twenty-Fifth Class Report for A.F. Whittem, BA, AM., PhD HUD 302.2, Harvard University Archives.
3. On the occasion of the fiftieth anniversary of the founding of the National University Extension Association, a commemorative volume titled *Expanding Horizons ... Continuing Education* (Washington, D.C.: North Washington Press, 1965) was published that included brief histories of the charter member continuing education programs. On behalf of Harvard University and the Commission on Extension Courses, Reginald H. Phelps, director, opened his remarks: "In the Harvard tercentenary year 1936, Dean Arthur Whittem, then Director of University Extension, addressed the National University Extension Association on 'A Century of University Extension at Harvard.' He conceded that the title was a trifle exaggerated, explaining that the 'century' referred to the year when John Lowell of Boston died, leaving a will which established a trust through which was created one of the most remarkable education institutions of the country, the Lowell Institute." (p. 50).
4. For archival material related to A.F. Whittem and G.W. Adams, see the Papers of James Bryant Conant (1932-1955), UAI 5.168, Harvard University Archives.
5. *Harvard University Gazette* (March 14, 1959).
6. UAV 378.15, Box 12, Folder 1.
7. Report of the President of Harvard College and Reports of Departments for 1948/1949. HU 30.10, Harvard University Archives.

Chapter VI

1. Harvard University Class of 1930 Fiftieth Class Report for R.H. Phelps, B.A., A.M., PhD HUD 330.50, Harvard University Archives.
2. Reginald H. Pehlps, "Three Score and Ten," *Harvard University Commission on Extension Courses* 70th *Year* (Harvard University Printing Office, 1980), pp. 6, 20.

3. Harvard University Class of 1912 Fiftieth Class Report for R. Lowell, BA HUD 312.50, Harvard University Archives.

Chapter VII
1. For archival material related to University Extension and Submarines, Polaris/PACE: Commission on Extension Courses, see HUE 25.56xx, Harvard University Archives.
2. For archival material related to Dr. Phelps and Dean of FAS Bundy, see Records of the Office of the Dean of the Faculty of Arts and Sciences, UA III 5.55.26, Harvard University Archives.
3. R.H. Phelps, "A College Program for the Polaris Fleet." HUE 25.562.72, Harvard University Archives.
4. Commission on Extension Courses. PACE Program, 1966-67. Pamphlet by Phelps outlining courses and faculty. Box 86, HUE 25.567.68, Harvard University Archives.
5. Interview of R.H. Phelps conducted by John F. Adams of the Harvard Extension School staff on May 8, 1984. The author is grateful to Mr. Adams for sharing his detailed notes of the interview, especially as they related to Phelps's recollections of the PACE and Roxbury programs.

Chapter VIII
1. *The University and the City: The Wilson Report* was the product of a University committee appointed by President Pusey and chaired by Professor Wilson in a "time of social and political restlessness ... [to] determine an appropriate interrelationship of university and city." The full text of the report appeared in the *Harvard Alumni Bulletin* (February 3, 1969), pp. 16-40. For the discussion of "Extension and Summer School Programs," see pp. 35-36.
2. Detailed notes of the interview of Dr. Phelps by John F. Adams on May 8, 1984 helped to clarify the role of the Roxbury programs, of Charles Whitlock, advisor to the president, and Peter Elbow, the writing workshop instructor.
3. Quote from Phelps interview by John Adams (May 8, 1984).

Chapter IX
1. Frank Pemberton, "Education After Dark," *Harvard Today* (Autumn 1963), pp. 6-10.
2. Reginald H. Phelps, "Three Score and Ten," *Harvard University Commission on Extension Courses* 70th *Year* (June 1980), p. 25.
3. Phelps, "Three Score and Ten," p. 24.

Chapter X

1. "Professors Emeriti Enhance CSS Program." *Harvard Extension School Newsletter*, vol. V, no.1 (Fall 1984), p .2.
2. "Certificate in Advanced Study in Applied Sciences," *Harvard Extension School Newsletter*, vol. III, no.1 (Fall 1982), p. 3.
3. K. Patricia Cross, *Adults as Learners: Increasing Participation and Facilitating Learning* (Jossey Bass Higher and Adult Education Series, 1992), pp. 2-3.
4. Michael Shinagel, "Why Every College Now Needs Two Missions," *Planning for Higher Education*, vol. 19 (Fall 1990), see "Viewpoint."
5. Mason Hammond, "The Genesis and Symbolic Significance of the Extension School's Coat of Arms," *Harvard Library Bulletin*, XXXIV, 3 (Summer 1986), pp. 254-55.
6. "First City of Cambridge CSS Scholarships Awarded," *Harvard Extension School Newsletter*, vol. V, no.2 (Spring 1985), p. 2.
7. "Harvard Extension School: 75 Years of Community and Classroom," a special supplement of the *Harvard University Gazette* (26 April 1985). Robert Coles, "Learning After Hours," *Harvard Magazine* (May-June, 1985), p. 56B.

Chapter XI

1. "Certificate in Public Health Begins Its First Year," *Harvard Extension School Newsletter*, vol. VII, no. 1 (Fall 1986), p. 3.
2. "Harvard Faculty Emeriti Teach in Extension," *Harvard Extension School Newsletter*, vol. VI, no. 2 (Spring 1986), p. 4.
3. "Extension School Scholarships for Special Cantebrigians," *Harvard Extension School Newsletter*, vol. VII, no. 1 (Fall 1986), p. 2.
4. Joseph R. Paolino, Jr., "A Time of Choices," *Harvard Extension Alumni Bulletin*, vol. 23 (Sept. 1989), p. 11.
5. "Graduate Honored Among Ten Outstanding Young Women in America," *Harvard Extension School Newsletter*, vol. VIII, no. 2 (Spring 1988), p. 3.
6. "Howard Abramson Honored," *Harvard Extension School Newsletter*, vol. XI (Fall 1990), p. 2.
7. "Harvard Extension School Graduate Receives Regional Achievement Award," *Harvard Extension School Newsletter*, vol. XIII (Fall 1992), p. 1.
8. Mary Fasano, "The Power of Knowledge," *Harvard Extension School Alumni Bulletin*, vol. 31 (Fall 1997), p. 12.

Chapter XII

1. The author is grateful to his colleagues, Henry Leitner and Paul Bamberg, for their assistance in providing primary sources on the Indian Computer

Academy project from their personal files. All the material cited in this chapter is based on original documents in the files of the Harvard Extension School. Eventually these files will be sent to the Harvard University Archives for processing.

2. See Appendix B for the complete text of Harvard's Division of Continuing Education's decision to cease its affiliation with the Indian Computer Academy project.

3. "Beyond Retailing Knowledge: Prospect of Research-Oriented Universities in India," in Philip G. Altbach and Jorge Balan (eds.), *World Class Worldwide: Transforming Universities in Asia and Latin America* (Baltimore: The Johns Hopkins University Press, 2007), pp. 70-94.

Chapter XIII

1. The author gratefully acknowledges the assistance of Henry Leitner, Leonard Evenchik, and Daniel Goroff in providing first-hand information on the evolution of interactive distance education at the Harvard Extension School. Catalina Laserna outlined the results of her research from the provost's grant in detail in this chapter.

2. Elizabeth New Weld, "Learning Math in the Space Age," *Boston Sunday Globe*, (1 March 1987), p. 45.

3. Hiawatha Bray, "Plugging into the Electronic Campus," *Boston Sunday Globe Magazine*, (11 April 1999), p. 20.

4. *Wired* magazine (December 2006), "Podcast Lectures 101" by Jeff Howe, citing Harvard Computer Science E-1 by David J. Malan as "the best podcast we found," p. 64. See also *Harvard Crimson* article (November 30, 2006), "Ext. School Podcast Tops List."

Chapter XIV

1. Harvard University. Reports of University Extension, 1999/2000. Unprocessed.

2. "Learning How to Teach Mathematics," *Harvard Extension School Lamplighter* (Spring 2003), p. 5.

3. Henry Leitner, "Gaining a Competitive Edge," *Harvard Extension School Alumni Bulletin*, vol. 38 (Fall 2004), p. 18.

4. Ibid., p. 19.

5. "Extension School Unveils Two New Graduate Programs," *Harvard Extension School Alumni Bulletin*, vol. 39 (Fall 2006), p. 4.

6. "CTE Program Inspired by the 'No Child Left Behind' Act," *Harvard Extension School Lamplighter* (Spring 2004), p. 2.

7. Suzanne Spreadbury, "ALB Graduates Inducted into National Honor Society," *Harvard Extension School Alumni Bulletin*, vol. 37, no. 1 (Fall 2003), p. 14.

8. Louise Miller, "Young Scholars Find Challenges, Acceptance at Extension School," *Harvard University Gazette* (20 January 2000), pp. 1, 8.

9. Laura Pappano, "Family Pupils are Homing in on College," *Boston Globe* (30 March 2003), p. A23.

10. Ursala Pawlowski, "All the World's a Classroom," *Harvard Extension Alumni Bulletin*, vol. 39 (Fall 2005), p. 19.

11. Suzanne Spreadbury, "From 18 to 82: The Extension School Celebrates Age Diversity," *Harvard Extension Alumni Bulletin*, vol. 36 (Fall. 2002), p. 8.

12. "Why do Harvard Extension School Alumni Establish Endowment Funds?" *Harvard Extension School Alumni Update*, vol. VII (Feb. 1993), p. 1.

13. Ruth Walker, "I'm not going to stop just because I have a degree," *Harvard University Gazette* (8 June 2006), p.29. Caroline Louis Cole, "At 82, she takes a degree," *Boston Globe* (8 June 2006), p. T1.

Chapter XV

1. A. Lawrence Lowell, *What a University President Has Learned* (New York: The Macmillian Company, 1938), p. 41.

INDEX OF NAMES

 Michael Shinagel has served Harvard as a senior administrator and teacher for forty years, currently as dean of continuing education and university extension and as a senior lecturer on English. He was master of Quincy House from 1986 to 2001. He has been active both in his scholarly field of English literature and in his professional field of continuing higher education. He is the author and editor of books on Daniel Defoe and Jonathan Swift as well as many articles and reviews. He is also a frequent contributor to professional periodicals on continuing higher education. For many years he has been editor of the *Continuing Higher Education Review* (the official journal of the University Continuing Education Association) and publisher of the *Harvard Review*. In 2004 he received the Julius M. Nolte Award of the University Continuing Education Association for outstanding leadership and achievement in continuing higher education, and a Special Recognition Award of the Association for Continuing Higher Education for exemplary service to the field of continuing higher education.